THE RELIGIOUS CRITIC
IN AMERICAN CULTURE

THE RELIGIOUS CRITIC
IN AMERICAN CULTURE

William Dean

STATE UNIVERSITY OF NEW YORK PRESS

Published by
State University of New York Press, Albany

For information, address State University of New York
Press, State University Plaza, Albany, N.Y., 12246

Production by Diane Ganeles
Marketing by Theresa Abad Swierzowski

Library of Congress Cataloging-in-Publication Data

Dean, William D.
    The religious critic in American culture / William Dean.
        p. cm.
    Includes bibliographical references and index.
    ISBN 0-7914-2113-9 (alk. paper). -- ISBN 0-7914-2114-7 (pbk. :
alk. paper)
    1. Religious thought--United States--20th century. 2. United
States--Civilization--20th century. 3. Religion and culture--United
States--History--20th century. 4. United States--Religion--1945-
5. United States--Religion--1901-1945. 6. United States-
-Intellectual life--20th century. 7. United States--History-
-Philosophy. 8. United States--Moral conditions. I. Title.
BL2525.D43 1994
200'.973--dc20   93-42683
                                                           CIP

10 9 8 7 6 5 4 3 2 1

For Patricia

CONTENTS

PREFACE

This book is a response to a specific question in American society, one that in the course of the twentieth century has loomed larger and larger: Why is the spiritual character of American public life so seldom critically analyzed? Why, when intellectuals get around to discussing the American identity (a rare occasion in any case), do they concentrate on the social and aesthetic identity exclusively, as though the public simply had no religious identity, no views on what is ultimately important for themselves or for the life of the nation? Why is the critical religious thinker deep within most people, the thinker preoccupied with questions of ultimate importance, so lame in its efforts to affect the public thinker within those same people? Beneath these questions lies sleeping the much larger question: What happens to a society whose implicit religious values are left to grow or decay in the darkness of inattention?

I argue that some public intellectuals should focus on the religious identity of the nation. They would be one among at least two other types of public intellectuals: "culture critics," who focus on aesthetic and artistic culture, and "social critics," who focus on political and material culture. I am urging that some intellectuals become "religious critics," who focus on the nation's "spiritual culture."

By "religious" I refer not only, not even primarily, to activities that occur within churches, synagogues, or mosques. As John Dewey once did, I refer to a person's or a people's "sense of the whole," a sense that binds together and gives relevance to the parts of a person's internal and external worlds. Equally, the sacred refers, not to a supernatural being, but to a historical activity, to whatever is ultimately important within "the whole" as it is understood from a particular culture. Accordingly, "the

ix

religious" is not opposed to "the public." Rather, the religious runs through the public and gives it a kind of coherence, so that without the religious the public is jeopardized.

In pursuit of the religious critic, I traverse some of America's dense historical and cultural terrain. How I do this may appear arbitrary. Not only do I skirt, rather than directly enter, the aesthetic and artistic terrain of the culture critic and the political and material terrain of the social critic, but my discourse is not, strictly speaking, either theological or philosophical. While the writing that follows is sometimes scholarly, it is not disciplinary, if to be disciplinary means to live within the prevailing standards and criteria of a specific academic discipline. Nevertheless, I have reasons for working with the history of American philosophy and theology, with the myths and symbols of American Studies and American history, with contemporary religious thought, and with ideas from contemporary science and the new field of philanthropic studies. Thus, while my selection of areas of inquiry may occasionally appear merely idiosyncratic, it is meant to be anything but idiosyncratic.

I have attempted to make these pages intelligible to the reader who happens not to be a professional religious thinker, philosopher, or historian—a minimal requirement, it would seem, for a book so strenuously protesting the inaccessibility of intellectuals. At the same time, I have attempted to catch the strands of current academic debate and to respond to needs for constructive theory. If this particular combination is not successful, I know others have accomplished it, and I would prefer to fail having tried it.

I intend to offer a pragmatic hypothesis about American public life and the role of religious critics in that life. I propose, but do not undertake, an American religious criticism that would again be specific and important, as specific and important as American social criticism and American culture criticism sometimes still is. Exactly how and where American religious criticism now should be conducted or one day will be conducted is not yet clear to me.

This book was written on two campuses but was suspended, unexpectedly, from a web of nonacademic connections. If there was a center to that web, it was our temporary home in In-

dianapolis, once a hotel that hosted the national radio perfor-
mances of the Indianapolis Symphony Orchestra and a campaign-
ing Senator John Kennedy, now an apartment house occupied by
middle class blacks and whites and standing in the midst of urban
poverty. There, over the course of eighteen months, I knew
kindnesses that made me doubt claims about an America irre-
vocably fragmented and led me to question the experience of
those who made those claims.

The months in Indianapolis, during which most of this book
was researched and written, were supported in large part by a
generous grant from the Indiana University Center on Philanthropy (itself generously funded by a grant from the Lilly En-
dowment). Robert Payton, then Director of the Center, contributed not only to my understanding of American philanthropy
but to my freedom to think in new ways. At Indiana University-
Purdue University in Indianapolis I received significant support
from Dwight Burlingame and solid, patient, and memorable help
from members of the Department of Religious Studies: Jan
Shipps, without whom the Indianapolis phase of this research
would have gone unrealized, as well as Conrad Cherry, Rowland
Sherrill, William Jackson, James Smurl, Tessa Bartholmeusz, and
Theodore Mullen. I thank David and Mary Frisby for their ex-
cellent index and David for his cheerful assistance during my
months in Indianapolis.

I have been supported also by a sabbatical from Gustavus
Adolphus College. Like the sea, this college changes; unlike the
sea, it grows warmer and saltier. It continues to provide the
interdisciplinary conversation now found almost exclusively at
small liberal arts colleges, which grow more precious as their
share in American higher education diminishes.

I received crucial support from numerous others: from Wes-
ley Robbins and, especially, from Sheila Davaney, for the kind of
persistent and intelligent criticism anyone should envy; from
Donald Crosby, Jerome Stone, Michael Moody, Hollis Johnson,
Ed Stephenson, Andrea Dean, Richard Fuller, and Martin Krei-
ger, who have read and usefully criticized parts of this manuscript; from the challenging example of Nancy Frankenberry;
from Creighton Peden, for his sage leadership of the Highlands
Institute for American Religious Thought, which has given me an
intellectual home for so much of my recent work; and from Colin

Dean, who issued prophetic criticisms of this book. Cassandra Loeffler, Jennifer Dean, and Jean Pallo provided important secretarial and managerial support. Delwin Brown's *The Boundaries of Our Habitations: Tradition and Theological Construction,* read in manuscript during my work on this book, demonstrated to me liberalism's mistake in neglecting tradition. I continue to witness in amazement the uncharted and unchartable ruminations of Richard Elvee and to profit from his encouragement. I am enlightened by Roy Phillips, who explores chambers of the heart seldom entered by intellectuals.

Patricia Dean has practiced on this book an editorial analysis unmatched for its rigor and accuracy. Her words outrun me; but she continues to find my own stray words, unbranded and grazing in canyons of prose, and to chase them home.

Finally, I thank the people of SUNY Press, without whom American religious and philosophic thought would not have become what it has become over the past dozen years, which is much better. I thank especially Lois Patton, Diane Ganeles, Theresa Swierzowski, and Jacqueline Price.

Chapter 1 is based on "Religion and American Public Philosophy," *Religion and American Culture: A Journal of Interpretation* (winter 1991). Chapter 4 is based on "Humanistic Historicism and Naturalistic Historicism," *Theology at the End of Modernity,* ed. Sheila Davaney (Trinity Press International, 1992). Chapter 3 has one distant ancestor, "Empirical Theology: A Revisable Tradition," *Process Studies* (summer 1990). Chapter 5 has two very distant ancestors, "From Piecemeal Supernaturalism to Piecemeal Jamesism," *The American Journal of Theology and Philosophy* (January 1994) and "Empiricism and God," *Empirical Theology: A Handbook,* ed. Randolph Crump Miller (Religious Education Press, 1992). This book was a gleam in the eye of my programmatic essay, "A Present Prospect for American Religious Thought," *Journal of the American Academy of Religion* (winter 1992).

Grateful acknowledgement is given to New Directions Publishing Corporation for permission to quote from the following copyrighted works of William Carlos Williams: *Collected Poems: Volume 1, 1909–1939* (copyright 1938 by New Directions Publishing Corporation; copyright © 1982, 1986 by William Eric Williams and Paul H. Williams); *Paterson* (copyright © 1946, 1948, 1949, 1958 by William Carlos Williams).

INTRODUCTION

And a pervasive spiritual impoverishment grows. The collapse of meaning in life—the eclipse of hope and absence of love of self and others, the breakdown of family and neighborhood bonds—leads to the social deracination and cultural denudement of urban dwellers, especially children. We have created rootless, dangling people with little link to the supportive networks—family, friends, school—that sustain some sense of purpose in life. . . .

The result is lives of what we might call "random nows," of fortuitous and fleeting moments preoccupied with "getting over"—with acquiring pleasure, property, and power by any means necessary.

Cornel West, *Race Matters*[1]

[T]he image of a society guided largely by cornucopian aspirations devoid of deeper human values tends to undermine the global appeal of the American social model, especially as the symbol of freedom.

Zbigniew Brzezinski, *Out of Control*[2]

As I was completing this project, two books that could have occasioned the discussion that follows functioned instead as corroborations.

One book was written by an amiable American democratic· socialist of African descent, then Professor of Religion and Director of the Afro-American Studies Program at Princeton University; the other, by an austere, anticommunist of the American establishment, now a counselor at the Center for Strategic and International Studies and a professor at The Johns Hopkins University, and once Jimmy Carter's National Security Advisor. Each concluded that the social issue he addressed was rooted in an American spiritual emptiness. While this emptiness is felt by separate persons, its true home is the American public itself. In *Race Matters,* Cornel West attributed problems over race to despair and nihilism and to a preoccupation with easy, self-indulgent gratification as they infect not the black community alone, not the white community alone, not even the two in interaction, but the nation as a whole. In *Out of Control,* Zbigniew Brzezinski attributed the forthcoming collapse of America's world leadership, not to politics, economics, or the rise of rivals, but to the growing spiritual illness of the whole American culture.

While I will discuss these conditions, my specific intention is to ask why more intellectuals in America have not risen to address this crisis and what new framework of thought might enable them to do so. Why are so few intellectuals doing what West and Brzezinski do in these books? What might be done to alter that condition?

Intellectuals, I argue, have avoided these public responsibilities partly because most of them now work in those societies called universities. Faculties (and students) have become not only academic but simply blinded by their own academic methods. They are not only not significantly connected with the public world, they move and breathe within the university as one moves and breathes within a tribe surrounded by an empty wilderness. They are academic to a fault.

In assessing this condition and in seeking a framework for its resolution, I narrow my analysis, asking not about public intellectuals in general, but about those public intellectuals I call "religious critics"—as opposed to those public intellectuals who are social critics and culture critics. That is, among public intellectuals there are at least three types: (1) social critics, who study social phenomena, particularly the political and material culture; (2) culture critics, who study qualitative meanings, particularly the aesthetic and artistic culture; and (3) religious critics, who study ultimate meanings, particularly the spiritual culture. And I treat only religious critics—such people as the authors of *Race Matters* and *Out of Control.*

The spiritual culture discussed by religious critics is constituted by the myths, rituals, narratives, traditions, and theories that inform and mold a society's deepest purposes. Religious critics ask how these felt purposes shape not only the society's spiritual culture but its entire identity. Further, religious critics, if they are constructive as well as analytic, help to reinterpret those resources and purposes in order to make them more effective.

Just as social critics are often social thinkers (often historians, political scientists, and economists) who become public thinkers, and culture critics are often cultural thinkers (often scholars of literature or art) who become public thinkers, religious critics are often religious thinkers (often religious studies scholars or theologians) who become public thinkers. It is likely, however, that the best public intellectuals, particularly the best religious critics, rise not from these expected disciplines but from other disciplines or from no academic discipline at all.

I do not argue that America has no religious critics but that the ranks of the religious critics are thinned from two sides.[3] From the religious side, openly religious thinkers tend not to function either as intellectuals or as public thinkers. Not only are fundamentalist, charismatic, and new age religious thinkers drifting away from intellectual worlds but so are their counterparts in mainline denominations. That is, while religious thinkers may be thoughtful, many ignore dominant intellectual institutions in America, like universities, university presses, and journals, as well as their fashions, such as their poststructuralist/postmodernist attacks on theory. Nor do religious thinkers in America tend to function as public thinkers. That is, religious thinkers even in academic worlds seldom attempt to establish the public roots and branches of their thought. If American religious thinkers—or any American thinkers, for that matter—have a theory of America, it is usually only implicit.

From the other side, duplicating this self-imposed truncation, the few surviving public intellectuals tend not to think religiously. Of course, many public intellectuals reject religious thought because, as Garry Wills and Steven L. Carter have noted, they are suspicious of conservative religious attitudes[4] (just as they are suspicious of popular patriotic attitudes). Those suspicions are often legitimate, and those suspicious intellectuals are often important critics of religious critics. But public intellectuals seldom criticize their own suspicions. Further, they make them normative and impose them on all religious theory, refusing to take seriously even the critical definitions of religion generated by their colleagues in the university. "The prevailing orthodoxy among intellectuals in the West," says Bzrezinski, "is that religion is a waning, irrational, and dysfunctional aberration."[5]

I. The Absence of Religious Thought

I use the word "religious" in the broadest sense. I use it, not to refer specifically to organized religion's denominational forms and supernaturalistic meanings, but to a people's sense of the whole of the world and of themselves in that world. I refer to an evaluation of the world so encompassing and so basic that out of it all other evaluations directly or indirectly grow. I refer to a commitment so basic that, when all other commitments are challenged and peeled back, they come down to this commitment, which is so elementary and so elemental that it stands on nothing deeper. This commitment is itself a response to something that functions like a sacred reality, whether or not it is called sacred. The sacred, so interpreted, is what is ultimately important within the whole. John Dewey, Reinhold Niebuhr, or Paul Tillich were religious in this way and argued as religious critics when they affirmed that only a sense of the whole could ground an adequate religious criticism.

Religious criticism also works out of some sustainable public myth, which provides a standpoint for a sense of the whole. But, typically, academic intellectuals abandon public myths—apparently thinking those myths have sunk irrecoverably into intellectual disrepute—and then, as Thomas Bender has argued, fill the void with an academic discipline.[6] It is not necessary to follow this path to the bitter end, however. Even though Dewey, Niebuhr, Tillich, Jane Addams, and Walter Lippmann each lived in a culture drunk on public myths and welcomed the breakdown of those myths, each avoided devolution into disciplinary specialization and found and developed religious myths they could support. They were able to offer to American society a mythic standpoint for a sense of the whole, an interpretive framework within which to understand American spiritual culture and, finally, America itself. I write in defense of their potential successors, those framemakers who might succeed Dewey, Niebuhr, Tillich, Addams, and Lippmann in our time.

They need defense. When Russell Jacoby argues that a particular "transmission belt of culture—the ineffable manner by which an older generation passes along not simply its knowledge but its dreams and hopes—is threatened,"[7] he is pointing, among other things, to the loss of what I am calling religious criticism. Possible consequences of that loss are not hard to find. Without the interpretive frameworks provided by religious critics, the society tends to become fragmented. In the 1920s it seemed obvious to Dewey that "within the flickering inconsequential acts of separate selves dwells a sense of the whole which claims and dignifies them." In the 1930s he went on to say, "The sense of an extensive and underlying whole is the context of every experience and it is the essence of sanity. For the mad, the insane, thing to us is that which is torn from the common context and that which stands alone and isolated . . . "[8] In the 1990s, Daniel Bell, can review the "utopianism and universalism, the direction of history" set down by Enlightenment thinkers. He can argue that "those larger visions have receded" and been replaced by nihilism, melioristic liberalism, and conservative defensiveness, "all of which are oriented to present issues." Recalling the Enlightenment visions, he can conclude: "[T]here are no unified sets of beliefs to take their place, only the splintering of cultures and political fragmentation. And that is the transition to the 21st century."[9]

If Jacoby is right in believing that the last of a breed of public intellectuals is passing, this may be attributed, in part, to a diminishing capacity to entertain what Dewey calls "a sense of the whole" and Bell calls "those larger visions." And this diminishing capacity can be partially attributed to the severing of the bond between public life and religion—a bond once obvious in America but now rarely understood or even remembered. American historians have long agreed that religion has been a principal, perhaps the primary, determinant of America's culture (consider, for example, religion's role in the formation of American attitudes toward nature, America's belief in its manifest destiny or its capitalism). But today, political scientists and journalists, to take two examples, tend to regard all religious involvement in public issues with suspicion.

Although religion is now often trapped in obscure corners of the American mind and American history, this has not always been the case. Max Weber speaks of the socially important prophet whose religion works from "a unified view of the world derived from a consciously integrated and meaningful attitude toward life." This religion asks: "if the world as a whole and life in particular were to have a meaning, what might it be, and how would the world have to look in order to correspond to it?"[10] Historically, Western religious thought has been associated with a sense of the whole, and typically, Weber maintains, intellectuals helped to form a religious sense of the whole.[11]

But, as I will argue, if intellectuals are to accomplish this, they would do well to move beyond seclusion in universities,[12] academic disciplines,[13] ideologies,[14] or professional mindsets.[15]

II. The Absence of Public Thought

For a variety of reasons, academic intellectuals tend to become ivory scholars and to avoid public theories of the meaning of American public life or of the nation. The simplest reason for this avoidance is the wish to be uncontaminated by any enterprise remotely connected with the ugly past of chauvinism, parochialism, xenophobia, and nativism. Often they are uncomfortable with the very term "America."[16] When they substitute "The United States" for "America," as they often do, they make an understandable gesture, avoiding the presumption and offense of using America to refer to one nation rather than to the two continents of the Americas. Nevertheless, "The United States" designates only the state, while "America" catches up the nation—the cultural river that incontestably runs earlier, deeper, and wider than political currents. Thus, to shun "America" is to blind oneself partially to the fuller meaning of a nation's public life, particularly its spiritual culture—its heritages, passions, and hopes, fully expressible only in myth, metaphor, or symbol as they provide a standpoint for a sense of the whole.

But for academic intellectuals these fuller meanings are not very palatable in our poststructural (or postmodern) era,[17] where a thorough pluralism, relativism, and historicism have undermined not only the universal structures on which to place the human subject or reason, or natural fact, but also any sense of a nation and its common culture. Typically, poststructuralists shun public thought, not only spurning a common culture, but doubting claims to its very existence. But again, this avoidance is costly. For example, a justifiable respect for relativity, plurality, and historicity has begun, ironically, to reconstitute just those social hierarchies most intellectuals despise. The conviction that people are irreconcilably diverse, that there is no web of relations and meanings that binds them together, begins to convince those with power that they have no obligation to the poor or the uneducated. This justifies abandoning the public itself, let alone any sense of the whole; it lubricates despair about social change and undermines the very idea of a vision broad enough to encompass emerging differences. Robert Reich has found such attitudes among those people most inclined to poststructural ideas, the self-serving and narcissistic symbolic analysts of America, who are psychologically seceding from America.[18]

It is not surprising, then, that academic intellectuals adopt what Michael Walzer finds to be the style of "endless refinement, esoteric jargon, romantic posturing, and fierce intramural polemic."[19] Discerning the same behaviors, Robert Westbrook closes his *John Dewey and American Democracy* with this valedictory sentiment: "Very little of the sort of public philosophy that Dewey advocated and exemplified is being done these days, and we have no public intellectuals who can match him—or, indeed, his adversaries Randolph Bourne, Walter Lippmann, Lewis Mumford, and Reinhold Niebuhr."[20]

III. Myths and Conventions

Divorcing themselves from public myths, intellectuals married their disciplines. With no national myth to lure them, they could be chaste in public.

The most important official myth of America, the myth of exceptionalism, once claimed that this nation lived within history but was guided from beyond history. America, the original version of the myth went, had received a promise that made her God's New Israel, an exception among nations. This promise gave her a sacred purpose—one that first emanated from the God of the Puritans and then from the secular gods of Democracy or Capitalism or Liberty. Today, none of these exceptionalist myths is supported by any religious intellectual I know—with the possible exception of a few neoconservatives at extreme moments.

Nevertheless, as William McNeill has said, Americans, like any people, need some "metahistorical synthesis,"[21] some large public vision or myth of history. The question is how to replace the unsustainable exceptionalist myth of America with a myth that can both make historical sense and survive poststructuralist criticism. Is it possible, in short, to understand how a national myth can abandon universal structures of thought and still frame a common culture? Is it possible to acknowledge that mythic words like "ultimacy," "sacred," or "God" refer to nothing given or universal and still claim that the sacred is not just a subjective construct but refers to an historical reality? Can the plurality, relativity, and historicity of everything be accepted without abandoning the meaning of the whole? Can the mythical grounding of a nation co-exist with the best of current historicism (the notion that nothing lies deeper than history because everything is born of historical interpretation and arises and perishes in particular times and locations)? Or will this reliance on a national myth lure intellectuals into an uncritical, fascist absolutization of a single historical story? Will the reliance on history eliminate, not only the supernatural and the supra-historical, but any appropriate sense of religious mystery whatsoever?

The heart of this book is a constructive proposal designed to answer those difficult questions. The proposal is based on the idea of social conventions. I will argue that a national myth is a convention and that the sacred is a convention, and that seeing them as conventions preserves their reality without violating poststructural pluralism, relativism, and historicism. A convention is the result of a critical social process: people imaginatively construct ideas; if these ideas are able to withstand social criticism, they enter a common historical stream; eventually these ideas free themselves from their inventors, take on independent historical power and, in unforeseeable ways, impact the very society that created them. These imaginative constructions become, in short, social conventions with real life and power. How else explain the social power of the more-than-political justice and love first advocated by Jesus of Nazareth and his prophetic predecessors and successors? How else explain that process Garry Wills calls "inventing America,"[22] whereby America literally began in the private minds of individuals and then became a world force? The American Constitution and its amendments, for example, are imaginative, late-eighteenth-century constructs that became conventions. Originating in the minds of constitutional framers, they were daily augmented in the courtroom and became an uncannily active force in history. Witnesss, for example, the unforeseen power and meaning of the first and the fourteenth amendments. The myth of America, I will argue, is real as a convention is real. Equally, I will argue that the sacred is a convention about what is ultimately important in the world, even as it is seen from the standpoint of a national myth.

Further, I argue that this theory of conventions can equip religious critics to do their very practical work. Knowing that America is a nation built on conventions, religious critics should be involved in convention-criticism and convention-making. Religious critics should be not only principal caretakers and critics of their culture's old spiritual conventions but principal devisers of their culture's new spiritual conventions. Acknowledging that they work not with universal truths but with conventions, they would contribute to building the spiritual culture of the nation without side-stepping the new strictures of poststructuralism.

Admittedly, those religious critics who work in universities will find such convention-making virtually impossible if they continue to treat the university, with its ideology of professionalism, as their psychological home. They are more likely to see their public involvement understood and supported if—for the time being, at least—they ally themselves, not occupationally, but psychologically with voluntary organizations outside the university, in the third, nongovernmental, not-for-profit sector. Or stated positively, involvement in the third sector may give religious critics a place where they can interact with American anti-intellectuals, with a whole people who, in Daniel Boorstin's terms, prefer the "ways of the many" to the "accomplishments of the few," and with American practicalism, where "the reasons men give for their actions are much less important than the actions themselves."[23]

IV. A Sense of the Whole

If there is a key to my own interpretation of the religious critic, it is that the religious critic should look to a society's "sense of the whole." This places at least one condition on the religious critic, a condition that will guide the discussion that follows: that whatever is sacred to a society cannot be confined to a part of a society's history and culture—for, if it is, it will not pertain to the society's operative sense of the whole. This is axiomatic to Dewey's, Niebuhr's, Tillich's, or, I would argue, to any sustainable understanding of the spiritual culture of a society. It is this, rather than some sense of the transcendent, that the spiritual culture should be about, for that which transcends a history transcends it precisely because, in some ways, it is not related to some aspects of that history. In this strange way, then, the antithesis of religious criticism is to attach ultimate meaning to fragments, to anything historically unrelated to everything else. It follows—as William James, Alfred North Whitehead, and other American thinkers, knew—that it is a mistake to isolate science from the humanities, mind from body, spirit from matter. Again, language of the sacred is introduced only because, as John Dewey argued, without that language history as a whole is unevaluated.[24] Myths of America are introduced only because, as William McNeill argued, without them a society's separate energies thrash in isolation.[25]

This interpretation of the task of the religious critic explains, perhaps, the odd shape of this book, which connects studies of historical practice and theories of historical reality. A friendly critic has encouraged me to break this book into two amplified books: Parts I and IV of this book to be a book on practice and the religious critic; Parts II and III to be a book on theory and religious criticism. But I have chosen to continue with the classical American pragmatists, who for over a hundred years have upheld another view: that theory unrelated to physical practice is meaningless, that practice unexamined for implicit theory is ignorant.

There is a tension between practice and theory, and I hope this book's signature will be its effort, not to resolve that tension, but to make it productive. I do not offer a sufficient idea of the practice of religious criticism; nor do I begin to offer a sufficient myth of America; nor do I even seek to offer an independently sustainable theory of conventions or of the sacred convention. Rather, I argue that religious critics might relate these ideas in order practically to develop a more sustainable sense of the whole in the American context.

PART I

ABANDONING AMERICAN CULTURE

CHAPTER 1

THE RELIGIOUS CRITIC
AND THE END OF AN ERA

> But in a larger sense we cannot dedicate, we cannot consecrate, we cannot hallow this ground. The brave men, living and dead, who struggled here, have consecrated it far above our poor power to add or detract. The world will little note nor long remember what we say here, but it can never forget what they did here.
>
> Abraham Lincoln, Gettysburg Address

> The crowd departed with a new thing in its ideological luggage, that new constitution Lincoln had substituted for the one they brought there with them. They walked off, from those curving graves on the hillside, under a changed sky, into a different America. Lincoln had revolutionized the Revolution, giving people a new past to live with that would change their future indefinitely.
>
> Garry Wills, *Lincoln at Gettysburg*[1]

Lincoln was inclined toward Transcendentalism and its belief that what happens in history is real and important because it copies something eternal and universal lying outside history. And yet on that dark day on which he dedicated a cemetery for men who might have died in vain, Lincoln asserted that this American ground was consecrated, not by the Eternal beyond history, but by "the brave men" in history. Moreover, contrary to his expectations, Lincoln's own words did add something; they were not only remembered but hallowed the ground at least as effectively as did the physical deeds of warriors.

While today most intellectuals, including those who might be religious critics (those public intellectuals who analyze and reconstruct the spiritual culture), have dropped Lincoln's Transcendentalism, they still readily agree that "the world will little note nor long remember what we say." Believing that their words are of little public consequence and that they are not compelled, as Lincoln was, to address the public, they devote their energies to their isolated professions and abandon the public audience that Lincoln addressed. The consequence is that today's public culture, unlike Lincoln's, sails without the kind of intellectual rudder Lincoln so effectively offered.

Like Lincoln, America's religious critics once were animated by the belief that Americans were God's chosen people or the special instrument of some sacred force, and thereby an exception, religiously or morally superior to the other nations. This original Puritan myth of God's New Israel was sometimes replaced by equivalent myths, making America the birthplace of democracy, the home of freedom, the nerve center for capitalism. America became a nation on an errand not only into the wilderness of a continent but into the wilderness of the entire world. "Exceptionalism"[2]—the belief that Americans, among all the world's peoples, were an exception—had offered to Americans a unity of purpose. Religious critics could ground themselves in the belief that beneath the variety of American meanings there was one core meaning: that America had received an extraordinary blessing, one that set her apart from other nations.

But over the generations, that unified influence became implausible and was replaced by the recognition that America was shaped by a variety of disparate influences and was one among a variety of nations. Exceptionalism had given to America a spiritual character. With the death of exceptionalism, an era vanished and with it vanished the confidence that had once inspired American thinkers. The pluralism that replaced exceptionalism may have reached its apotheosis in today's multiculturalism. Thus, a grand, monistic confidence was replaced by a disappointing pluralism and a consequent pessimism that have been damaging to American spiritual culture and disabling to those who might be religious critics. Robert Bellah, in the course of many books, has demonstrated that the loss of such a myth can contribute to the loss of an American public philosophy.[3]

In one sense, exceptionalism carried the seeds of its own undoing, for the very success of exceptionalism made America unusually vulnerable to pluralism. When exceptionalism made America a chosen people, it said the sacred operated directly in American history. In effect, it drew the sacred out of a world safely apart from history and placed it directly into the workings of American history; this was true even of the secular forms of American exceptionalism. Unexpectedly, this exposed the sacred to the very forces of history from which previously it had been protected. Thus, when the unitary meaning of America was shattered into a plurality of forces, the sacred itself was shattered.

If this chain of events (from exceptionalism, to pluralism, to the death of exceptionalism's God) is correct, then it is also correct that, to restore American spiritual culture, Americans must learn how to respond deliberately and constructively to these circumstances. They must accept that, despite the blandishments of optimistic national leaders, they can neither regain a plausible exceptionalism nor shed a plurality of national ingredients. The demise of exceptionalism and the onset of pluralism, however, do not preclude the recovery of a viable religious sense of the whole, of a viable spiritual culture, or of the office of religious critic.

In this chapter I discuss the demise of exceptionalism, as well as the cure for exceptionalism as it was offered by religious critics, such as Reinhold Niebuhr. I argue that, while these religious critics rightly attacked the pride endemic to an exceptionalist nation, they wrongly concluded that what Americans most need is contrition. I argue that America, as it struggled to live after the fall of the myth of exceptionalism, was afflicted by pessimism. And I suggest that the last thing America—or, at least, American intellectuals—may need is more contrition.

I do not argue that American pessimism is caused exclusively by the failure of the myths of exceptionalism, nor do I argue that some new myth of America will neatly restore the spiritual culture that grew up around the myth of exceptionalism. The problems of American spiritual culture are various and complex beyond current analysis or, at least, my current analysis. I offer only one approach of possible use to a religious critic.

I. Why America Lost its Sense of the Whole

In *The End of American History*, David W. Noble argues that in the 1940s there occurred what we now understand to be a revolution among American historians. Using Thomas Kuhn's theory of revolution, Noble argues that the historians' longstanding paradigm for understanding America was abandoned. Young American historians had risen to attack Charles Beard's claim that American democratic industrialism had set her apart from corrupt European capitalism. In effect, by attacking Beard, they attacked America's own 300-year metaphysics of exceptionalism, which had set America apart from all nations as God's elect people or, in later years, as a nation exceptional for its spiritual, moral, political, or economic destiny. The earliest exceptionalist interpretations were fortified by the great American historians. George Bancroft and Frederick Jackson Turner, for example, had argued that, in its simple and pure freeholder-agrarian economics and democratic politics, America had set itself apart from complex and corrupt Europe with its capitalistic and implicitly feudal politics. Charles Beard was merely one more variation on the theme; so the young historians' frontal attack on Beard was, in effect, an attack on the grand American illusion that had explained America's superiority.[4]

Earlier, in *Historians Against History*, Noble had argued that the exceptionalist myth had had at least three phases: the Puritan rhetoric of the sixteenth and seventeenth centuries, the Enlightenment rhetoric of the eighteenth and early-nineteenth centuries, and the Romantic rhetoric from 1830 to the mid-twentieth century.[5] In this progression from Puritan to Enlightenment to Romantic periods, Noble followed a standard narrative of American intellectual history.[6] The Puritans had seen America as the land of God's elect, a New Israel destined to fulfill God's promise. The Enlightenment interpretation of Franklin and Jefferson looked to the writings of John Locke and the French *philosophes* to argue that America's mission was to return to the state of nature discerned by reason. The aim of returning America to a purer condition functioned much like, and often was explicitly associated with, the Puritan mission of fulfilling God's promise. The Romantic interpretation—evident in the Jacksonian era, the poetry of Whitman, and the writings of the leading American Renaissance thinkers (Emerson, Thoreau, Hawthorne, Melville)—was based on the common person's intuition of an ideal or elemental life and on the belief that that life was uniquely American. All three phases of exceptionalism used some version of the Puritan's three-part jeremiad, proceeding from promise, to declension (declining the promise), to a prophecy according to which the original promise would be fulfilled. First, America had received the promise to be God's or Reason's or Intuition's exceptional people; second, America had violated the terms of the promise and fallen into declension; and, third, America would accomplish what was prophesied for it and become an ideal people.

Sacvan Bercovitch, in his *American Jeremiad,* argues that the jeremiad represents "an ideological consensus" that has characterized American culture.[7] His argument concentrates on two points: (1) the jeremiad outlived the Puritans, becoming simply "the myth of America," and (2) the tone of the jeremiad is optimistic. In this analysis, Bercovitch counters the American intellectual historian Perry Miller. First, he rejects Miller's claim that the Puritan outlook, in spite of being naturalistic and rationalistic in non-Calvinist ways, was so tied to a Calvinistic, transcendent, and inscrutable God that when that particular notion of God died so did the Puritan interpretation. Bercovitch argues that, in fact, the Puritan influence on political philosophy lasted well into the twentieth century, revealing itself in such figures as Martin Luther King, Jr. Second, Bercovitch rejects Perry Miller's emphasis on the Puritans' preoccupation with failure (the failure of the errand into the wilderness); Bercovitch claims, in fact, that the Puritans saw their critique as only a step in the eventual fulfillment of a promise. Ultimately, the jeremiad is not pessimistic, but optimistic. "The essence of the [Puritan] sermon," Bercovitch states, "is its unshakable optimism. In explicit opposition to the traditional mode, it inverts the doctrine of vengeance into a promise of ultimate success."[8] Absorbing the optimism of the jeremiad, American history came to be read as sacred history and as a redemption story.

However, this grand jeremaic metaphysics of America was disconfirmed by historical realities, frustrating the historians who used the jeremiad myth or its later variations. Actual history simply would not fulfill the prophecy of ideal history. The demise of the jeremiad was first definitively argued in the 1940s, but it was not until the 1950s, 1960s, and 1970s that the demise of the jeremiad was seen to be, in fact, the failure of the dominant American myth. In this, historians Richard Hofstadter, William Appleman Williams, Sacvan Bercovitch, Gene Wise, and J. G. A. Pocock were important, but it was Reinhold Niebuhr, a religious thinker, who led the way. All of these thinkers described the depth and pervasiveness of the accepted distinction between an undefiled America, informed by high ideals (biblical truth, natural law, the ideal spirit) and able to fulfill its prophecy, and a Europe devoid of a unique promise. It was this categorical distinction between America and Europe that gave resonance to the American Puritans' claim that they had left behind medieval Europe and her decadent ways, as the Israelites had left behind Egypt. On this model American optimism was built. When the rebel historians of the 1940s attacked this paradigm, they not only ended American history, so understood, but made the most fundamental American optimism illegitimate.

David Noble demonstrates that Niebuhr, Hofstadter, and Williams replaced exceptionalist categories with new categories: divine providence and natural law were replaced with experience; unitary national and international systems with a variety of systems; and deduction from a myth with pragmatic testing. The conclusion of the revisionist history is that Americans should see themselves as not unlike, and certainly as not superior to, Europeans or the rest of the world and that they should abandon the jeremaic metaphysics of optimism. America is a plurality of peoples and is a nation among a plurality of nations. Its best hope is to acknowledge its former pretensions and to muddle through. In short, America should be contrite and practical.

This American pluralism did not spring up suddenly in mid-twentieth century; it had been implicit throughout American history. Noble notes that "For Hofstadter, the United States in 1800 provided a political model of a pluralistic democracy to the world because its leaders had chosen not to live by the European ideology of the republican tradition, which declared the possibility of harmony with the universal, but by the encounter with the dynamic flow of particulars, which was their American experience."[9]

The pluralism of America is deeply rooted. The European immigrants occupied a land they understood to be without an established native tradition. They lived without a common bloodline, without a geography developed through centuries of habitation, and without the institutions that grow up amid such continuities. Nor did Americans succeed in directly transferring to their new land the traditions that unified their mother countries. To put it in Henry James's extravagant language:

> one might enumerate the items of high civilization, as it exists in other countries, which are absent from the texture of American life, until it should become a wonder to know what was left. No State, in the European sense of the word, and indeed barely a specific national name. No sovereign, no court, no personal loyalty, no aristocracy, no church, no clergy, no army, no diplomatic service, no country gentlemen, no palaces, no castles, no manors, nor old country houses, nor parsonages, nor thatched cottages, nor ivied ruins; no cathedrals, nor abbeys, nor little Norman churches; no great universities nor public schools—no Oxford, nor Eton, nor Harrow; no literature, no novels, no museums, no pictures, no political society, no sporting class—no Epsom nor Ascot! . . . The natural remark, in the almost lurid light of such an indictment, would be that if these things are left out, everything is left out.[10]

Americans compensated for the absence of institutions and traditions by repeated efforts to define and to distinguish themselves. As though drunk with a mixture of ethnic, religious, and cultural ingredients, they staggered on, from decade to decade, in search of the historic and cultural lamppost that would show them the way to go home, that would illuminate some clear route from their true past, into their proper future.[11]

Pluralism in America is partially attributable to specific features of the immigrant population. The immigrants originated from a wide variety of cultures. Further, with the exception of the African Americans, the immigrants were atypical before arriving. They were a minority in their mother country, forced to acknowledge their strangeness, odd in their willingness to leave the ancestral land to struggle for a new life in a distant land. Further still, the Americans were unusually egalitarian, less structured by social status than were the Europeans. The sources of American equality and its horizontal pluralities are numerous. Alexis de Tocqueville points to two when he asserts that "the happy and the powerful do not go into exile, and there are no surer guarantees of equality among men than poverty and misfortune" and that "the soil of America was opposed to a territorial aristocracy," for it was so hard to clear and its produce was so meager that it "was not sufficient to enrich at the same time both an owner and a farmer."[12] Factors such as these combined to keep America moving in a pluralistic direction.

While many Americans, despite such pluralism, were able to sustain in the twentieth century a unifying monism based on the exceptionalist myth, that monism was largely destroyed for them by a plurality of another sort. This was not a quantitative pluralism, where singularity of type and tradition is overwhelmed by the variety of immigrants and their diverse traditions. Rather, it was a qualitative pluralism, where an unambiguously good destiny is overwhelmed by irremediable evils always present beneath whatever is good about America. This qualitative pluralism was brought home most vividly in international and domestic politics. Two world wars, the cold war, and, particularly, the Vietnam War presented a variety of experiences that shook the belief that Americans were a protected and virtuous people, invulnerable to compromising entanglements. How, Conrad Cherry asks, can America in a pluralistic international world see itself as a persuasive "light to the nations" or as a "chosen people" without risking imperialism on one hand and isolationalism on the other hand?[13] On the domestic side, many Americans recognized that the nation's treatment of African Americans and women was not the behavior appropriate to a blessed and righteous people.

Admittedly, a kind of exceptionalist monism still lives on, but it is certainly not robust. Even Ronald Reagan, its most vociferous recent champion, acknowledged its sickness even while propping it up. In admitting to a biographer that his primary mission as president was to "restore America's self-confidence," he tacitly conceded that resoration was necessary, that Jimmy Carter's July 1979 speech on the malaise of America had had its truth.[14] Reagan's failure to overcome that malaise might be measured in people's unwillingness to vote: by 1988, at the end of Reagan's eight years, the United States had the lowest rate of voter participation of any democracy in the world.[15]

America's pluralism, always there covertly, now works overtly. Sometimes it seems that the very identity of America is to deny any identity at all, that the sameness of the American people lies in the regularity with which they want to be mavericks, that the togetherness of the American people lies in the ease with which the foreign is felt as native to the American national body. America is a traditional society in one respect: it is the planet's oldest uninterrupted democracy. But democracy, as it is conceived in the United States, is the institutionalization of plurality, of the separate rights and powers of individuals, groups, and branches of government. This institutionalized plurality is protected officially (even if often unsuccessfully) against the domination of the society by any single ethnic, racial, gender, religious, cultural, or sexual-preference group or ideology.

Why should plurality be so peculiarly devastating for America? The answer can be traced to exceptionalism: America was made unusually vulnerable to plurality when its sacred and extrahistorical depths were brought into the surface of its lived history. The American myth declared that the foundation of America's spiritual culture was immediate, at hand, living in its very historical events. America's day-to-day history was sacred history; this was the keystone to exceptionalist thinking from the beginning. Despite the Puritan scenario that seemed to make this world a place of sojourn, a mere preparation for the other world, Puritan theology was primarily a theology of divine providence operating in this world. This theology did not represent a religion of private salvation but a divine mission acted out on the plane of social history to regenerate social history. In this respect, the Puritan religion was a nationalistic religion. The new Americans would not merely act out their religion somewhere within the boundaries of history; they themselves would become the chosen people, their land would become the promised land, and their story would be the story of the New Israel. They would see Europe as Egypt and their America as the promised land. They would be a chosen people, and their history would be a religious history. In the words of Giles Gunn, what might have been merely the "religion *in* America" became the "religion *of* America."[16] This commitment to sacred history was, at the same time, a commitment to a sacred empiricism, an empiricism that saw ultimate meanings not in ideal essences but in overt events. But because the sacred had been located in history, the eventual pluralization of history went all the way down. This sacred history and this sacred way of knowing meant that, when plurality was recognized in history, it was an unmitigated plurality, unrelieved by some unifying reality beyond history. The God that would unify America was so caught in the surface of America's history that that God was shattered when that history's unity was broken.

By comparison, the Continental European could gain relief from historical plurality through reflection on extrahistorical realities known through rational ideals, mystical experiences, totalitarian ideology, or institutional religion. Even its late-twentieth-century philosophies of deconstruction and hermeneutics tended to become, more than anything else, purely formal methodologies, making the ahistorical ideal of interpretive play more real than anything in particular, local histories. That is, Continental poststructuralism escaped the full impact of historical plurality and the challenge of acting in that history, by reifying a uniform and always-consistent method of interpretation.[17]

Today America seems, therefore, to be an uncongenial home for a myth of meaning or for a distinctly spiritual culture. Having brought the sacred into history and then having fragmented the sacred, America had no remaining grounds for a myth of meaning or a spiritual culture. How then can Americans understand, let alone produce, religious critics who would work out of a common spiritual culture?

II. The Religious Roots of American Pessimism

When Walter Lippmann made "public philosophy" famous in 1954, he put on that phrase just the construction that America was abandoning. He argued that a growing pluralism must be replaced by a recrudescent public philosophy which represents "a universal order on which all reasonable men were agreed," an order that is not "discovered or invented," but that is "known" and can be "revived and renewed" in current society. Such a sense of the whole can be traced at least to Alexander the Great, who chose to treat the Persians not as barbarians but as fellow citizens living with the Greeks under one common order; it was continued under the aegis of Roman law until 1800, when modern pluralism began to assume real importance. Lippmann was convinced that such a transcultural sense of the whole is a "necessary assumption," without which liberty, free institutions, even the right of private property are, "unworkable."[18]

Ironically, it is because Americans first accepted, and then saw shattered, another kind of monism (the unification offered by the exceptionalist myth) that they cannot now accept Lippmann's classical monism. But the question remains, can some other, specifically American, identity be found after the waning of exceptionalism? Is the old optimism associated with the myth of exceptionalism to be replaced simply by a newly dominant pessimism associated with a myth of America as a meaningless plurality of voices—a veritable myth of cacophony?

Admittedly, in the eyes of most students of American history and culture, it is a mistake even to suggest that an American pessimism exists, let alone to claim that it is distinctively American. Religious scholars in revolt against the old Protestant liberalism—virtually all Protestant religious scholars for the last fifty years—find the distinct trait and sin of the American character in its typical optimism. Among these scholars are not only neo-orthodox religious thinkers such as Reinhold Niebuhr, but even post-neo-orthodox thinkers such as Langdon Gilkey.[19] And as we have seen, historians of American culture like Bercovitch and Noble center their critiques of American exceptionalism and progressivism on the naive optimism they find still to be endemic to the American character.

Ironically, the scholars' attack on optimism may contribute to a pessimism that is more virulent than the optimism they disparage. While I agree with efforts to undermine exceptionalism and its accompanying optimism, I question whether the new revolutionaries have examined the full implications of their own efforts, particularly their attitudinal impact. Bercovitch and Noble may have established that for three hundred years Americans were, in one sense, optimistic. They may have shown that Americans thought they wore a metaphysical mantle entitling them to a supreme place in world history and that, as a result, the glorious prophecies about America would be fulfilled. They may have established that that optimism is historically unwarranted—or at least unfashionable for late-twentieth-century American historians—and is therefore to be rejected. But have they surveyed the wreckage left when the exceptionalist paradigm and its optimistic spirit are abandoned?

When Americans identified the sacred with their secular history, they blocked their escape from secular history.[20] Their European cousins could see their secular histories as fraught with ambiguity and as clearly in declension from the ideal world; but then, such realism was not particularly costly because, when secular history seemed most inhospitable, this more or less log-ocentric and idealistic people could repair to the ideal world. But when Americans affirmed that the sacred was embodied in their own actual history, they blocked their escape to an ideal refuge beyond this history. Admittedly, Americans were officially opti-mistic about their historical possibilities. But, after all, history was all they had, and it is dangerous to be less than optimistic about the only thing one has. By comparison, historical pessi-mism was cheap for the European, who tended to have a meta-physical home beyond history. But when the twentieth century drove Americans to acknowledge that they had been deluded in their optimistic belief that their prophecies would be fulfilled, that acknowledgement led to a different sort of pessimism. Just as they, like other exceptionalist nations, had been unusual in identifying their own history with the sacred, now they were unusual in experiencing a historical failure that was at the same time a failure of the sacred.

Within this story lies the significance of American pluralism for determining American attitudes. When Americans sought to identify their history with the sacred, they affirmed that a divine providence unified, made one and whole, their history. But, as America's lack of a traditional culture, its history of immigration, and its recent international and domestic problems suggested, historical monism never had been quite right for America. All along there had been a pluralism tugging at the sleeve of Amer-ican religious chauvinism. This historical pluralism, together with its implication that God is broken in the swirl of historical par-ticulars, may have bred an incipient pessimism even in such re-puted optimists as Ralph Waldo Emerson, William James, and John Dewey.[21] In any case, by mid-twentieth century, the lessons of history frontally attacked America's chauvinistic monism. A newly manifest secular pluralism opened America, not simply to the implicit pessimism of the American Romantics, but to the explicit pessimism of the postexceptionalist culture.

Because the pluralism was qualitative as well as quantitative, the problem was aggravated. Because a God beyond history was not treated as knowable and usable by the nation (so that the activity of the sacred must be sensed in history or not at all), and because American history is morally ambiguous, the implication was either that the sacred must be abandoned or declared morally ambiguous. With a qualitative plurality, one where evil is as prominent as good, there is little empirical basis for the conclusion that American history is guided by anything consistently good. In a nation that has abandoned extrahistorical moorings and then begun to recognize itself as morally ambiguous, is there any basis for a spiritual culture, let alone for religious critics?

To illustrate: for many Americans, the Vietnam War was a shock not merely because the United States was stalemated by a third-world guerrilla army or because the world would not make way for American manifest destiny or because the world was unmanageably complex. More importantly, Vietnam was a shock because America appeared to be more a menace than a force for good. Admittedly, many people were able to fit that war into an exceptionalist interpretation, seeing it as a noble effort blocked by those who failed to appreciate its nobility. Nevertheless, for many people, Vietnam undermined claims to America's underlying goodness and fostered a sense of the moral ambiguity of America.

If, from an American perspective, the sacred is to be found either in history or not at all, then the simple conclusion is that America's God was either morally ambiguous or dead. Because there is no theologically orthodox way to see the ambiguity of the sacred, many Americans are pushed toward the denial of the sacred or to an unusual view of the sacred and, in either case, toward an aggravated pessimism. Neither Bercovitch nor Noble seems to recognize that this pessimism, whether theological or nontheological, appears for many to be the only answer.

Bercovitch's and Noble's "abandon optimism" prescription rests on theological reasoning that is, itself, problematic. Such reasoning can be found in the writings of Reinhold Niebuhr, whom Noble treats as the great prophet for the historians' paradigmatic shift of the 1940s and 1950s. It rejected the two-worlds notion (a corrupt Europe and an innocent America), the virtuous American republic notion, the jeremiad motif that expressed these notions, and the grand categories behind these notions. These rejections ended American historical interpretation as it had been known. In naming a theologian the leader of the historian's revolution, Noble cites Thomas Kuhn's contention that "the person who provides leadership for the radical restructuring of the set of hypotheses on which a scientific community has been operating is often an outsider to that particular field."[22] Niebuhr's attack on the exodus myth and its pretensions to innocence and virtue was implicit in his 1932 *Moral Man and Immoral Society* and was stated most completely in his 1951 *The Irony of American History.*[23] Niebuhr had hoped that his instruction would affect how America acts: if Americans see the irony of their own history, if they become conscious of the contradiction between their historic pretensions and the lessons of recent history, at least they will be more capable of acting so as to avoid the foreign policy disasters that otherwise await America.

Like most historians and political scientists who have used Niebuhr's insights, Noble omits any theological underpinning for his own Niebuhrian interpretation of history—even though theological underpinnings function as the *sine qua non* for Niebuhr's view of history. Niebuhr's religious anchorage is especially clear in his category of irony, which he compares to the categories of pathos and tragedy. The pathetic view sees the self as a victim of circumstances; the tragic view responds to historical ambiguity by merely accepting the self's complicity in historical evil. The ironic view not only makes the self conscious of its pretensions, but it gives the self a measure of control—blocking the excuses of both the pathetic victim of circumstances and the tragic collaborator with an inexorable evil. But here the linchpin is inserted: irony is possible only for one able to transcend his or her historical situation. Only from such a transcendent position can one have enough distance to see the good intentions beneath bad pretensions, to be contrite about the worst extremes caused by those pretensions, and to be able, thereby, to revise one's attitudes. Further, such transcendence is achieved only "on the basis of the belief that the whole drama of human history is under the scrutiny of a divine judge who laughs at human pretensions without being hostile to human aspirations."[24] The point is that "consciousness of an ironic situation tends to dissolve it," but—and this must be added—this consciousness can be acquired only through faith in a particular God.[25] Consequently, for Niebuhr, the insights derived from religious faith not only do not contradict the facts of our historical civilization, but "are, in fact, prerequisites for saving it."[26]

The unrecognized irony of Niebuhr's *The Irony of American History* is that its attack on American presumption (that America is informed by God or some higher good), is made possible by Niebuhr's own parallel presumption (that he is informed by God). The book's attack on American national optimism (that America contains the sacred in its history) arises from Niebuhr's personal optimism (that he has contact with the sacred beyond history). It is possible that Niebuhr's failure to acknowledge the irony in his own condemnation of irony made him all the more unsympathetic with the irony of America. Having hidden his own presumptions, it was easier for him to be harsh with those who have their versions of the same failings.

This criticism is not to say that Niebuhr is wrong when he claims that the exceptionalist myth makes America optimistic to a fault. Nor are Bercovitch and Noble wrong when they claim that America is inordinately optimistic. Nor do I object to the irony of Niebuhr's optimism: that his critique of American optimism is fueled by his own hidden optimism. Nor, realistically, do I object even to Niebuhr's failure to acknowledge his own optimism. After all, what self-respecting opponent of national optimism can confess his or her own private optimism?

However, I do regret Niebuhr's failure to anticipate the effect of his attack on American pretensions. Niebuhr, as well as other Americans, needed some kind of personal optimism. Could he not have anticipated, then, the pessimism that would follow when he and others convinced Americans to abandon just the optimism he, himself, seemed so much to need?

On the whole, I contend, American intellectuals have abandoned their optimism, have acknowledged that their predecessors were wrong to find an unambiguously sacred reality operating in their history, and are quick to recognize that Americans are not a blessed people and never were. This acknowledgement appears to have undermined the exceptionalist spiritual culture out of which their predecessors had worked and to have bred a pessimism in just those intellectuals who might once have been religious critics.[27] The question remains: How can American intellectuals negotiate with that pessimism in order to regain a sense of the whole?

If they are to negotiate successfully, then it may be a mistake to focus on their sin (Niebuhr) or on their moral ambiguity (Bercovitch and Noble). If the exceptionalist myth is believed and still instills optimism, then perhaps contrition is needed. However, if the problem is not excessive optimism but excessive pessimism, a heavy dose of contrition may aggravate rather than cure their condition. Analogously, Valerie Saiving notes that it is dangerous for male theologians who see pride as "man's" principal problem to tell women to become self-sacrificial. For, says Saiving, women typically suffer, not from excess ego, but from a profound loss of ego, not from the stereotypical masculine sin of pride, but from the sin of passivity or acquiescence, of yielding to circumstance.[28] Consequently, self-assertion may be the proper Christian virtue for women, and self-sacrifice may be the masculine medicine that poisons women.

That is to say, if the illness is misdiagnosed, the prescription can be wrong. For American intellectuals captured by pessimism, the best answer may not be the one that rails against American pretensions but the one that finds—even amid pluralism, relativism, and historicism—new practical grounds on which to speak positively about American responsibilities. American intellectuals, particularly American religious critics, if they are to be publicly effective, need a vision out of which they might acquire the confidence, once again, to address the public.

CHAPTER 2

_____

THE RISE OF THE
PROFESSIONAL INTELLECTUAL

Well, they want to *feel* earnest, . . . but it seems as if
they took it out in theories mostly. Their radical views
are a kind of amusement; they've got to have some
amusement, and they might have coarser tastes than
that. You see they're very luxurious, and these progressive ideas are about their biggest luxury. They
make them feel moral and yet don't damage their position.

Henry James, 1881[1]

The exceptionalist myth, despite its unwarranted optimism,
had kept alive a spiritual culture. When it prevailed, religious
critics had a sense of their whole national history. They had a
story on which to hang their deepest theories about the meaning
of their society and their bodily and emotional feelings for the
texture and purpose of social events.[2] The exceptionalist myth
had made it possible for religious critics to refer to the meaning
of America and to call for social change. When this myth and its
aura evaporated, they left behind a pessimism that disabled potential religious critics.

In their place nothing came to fill the void in American
spiritual culture to which the religious critic might repair. Rather,
academic professionalism came to occupy the mind of the American intellectual as an American myth had once occupied it. The
intellectuals became professionals, professional intellectuals. The
academic career gave structure and meaning to the intellectuals,
even if it made no claims to fill the newly voided spiritual culture.

19

In effect, a public philosophy was replaced by a merely private philosophy. When American intellectuals lost their sense of participating in an American promise, they retreated into the university, became academic intellectuals, and largely abandoned public responsibility. They thought of themselves, not as those who might enlighten the citizenry of a unique democracy, but as physicists, philosophers, religious studies scholars, literary critics. Their talk was not now public talk but talk within an academic discipline and among academic intellectuals.

Admittedly, for a few decades, professionalism offered its own promise, one not altogether unconnected with the public, even if it did not speak to the public spiritual culture. Because the new professional intellectuals were highly competent specialists, authoritative in a specific area, they could be experts, equipped to speak and be heard publicly. This professional promise depended, in large part, on the professional agreement that work within a discipline is authoritative, that it says something solid and objective about the world, and that, for this reason, it could be endorsed as publicly plausible.[3] However, just as the promise of exceptionalism had been undermined by history in the third quarter of the twentieth century, it began to appear in the last quarter of the century that the promise of professionalism would be itself undermined by history. Poststructural (commonly, "postmodern") analysis argued that there was no historical evidence for objective structures of nature or human nature that could ground professional knowledge. Again, historical analysis was the destructive agent; careful historical analysis emphasized the arbitrariness of professional expertise. Most of what once gave meaning to expert knowledge and authority to the experts began to appear local, accidental, morally ambiguous. And professional ideology began to crumble from within. Academic collegiality, rooted in a shared vision, began to be supplanted by factionalism.

While not all professional intellectuals accepted the validity of poststructuralism's new pluralism, relativism, and pragmatism, virtually all acknowledged that these methods had brought crisis in the ranks. Poststructuralists argued that local perspectives had replaced universal or general laws, that the relativity of ideas had replaced absolute ideas, that contingent explanations had replaced necessary explanations, that a pragmatic focus on con-

sequences had replaced an epistemological focus on rational origins. While the poststructuralists may not have been the larger
faction or have had the better arguments, in one important respect they won the argument, for they shifted academic discourse
from the quest for objective knowledge to the examination of the
historical circumstances of knowledge, from inquiry into what is
real to inquiry into what is fashionable. Opponents of poststructuralism had to abandon what they saw as the proper professional harvest of general truths and concentrate on defending
their methods and, thereby, unintentionally collaborate with
those they opposed. The new preoccupation with deconstructionism, neopragmatism, hermeneutics, and the new historicism
affected the university's curricular decisions and hiring policies.
What constitutes a discipline? What constitutes a discipline's
canon? Must one be African American to teach African American
Studies or female to teach Women's Studies? A tendency toward
consensus among intellectuals was replaced by a tendency toward
dissensus—eroding, in turn, much of the authority and public
plausibility of the intelligentsia.

Hardly noted in all this was the fact that the most interesting
intellectual debates moved farther and farther from a consideration of what might be true and good and spiritually valid for the
society at large. It was as though an emphasis on the historicity
of everything had brought what no one desired, an ahistorical
preoccupation with formal method. "The method becomes an
end in itself," complained Russell Jacoby.[4] Although professionalism never claimed to provide a platform for public philosophy,
it soon became clear that the professionals' expert knowledge
would no longer elicit even public confidence.

Wrestling with these problems in *The Last Intellectuals,* Jacoby argues that today's public intellectuals are aging, and there
is no younger group poised to replace them. Among people born
since 1940, there is no sizeable cohort of public intellectuals, let
alone what I am calling religious critics. "With few reservations,
by the end of the 1950s, American intellectuals decamped from
the cities to the campuses, from the cafés to the cafeterias."[5] Or
they moved from the small magazines (like *The Dial, The Masses,
Partisan Review*)[6] to the learned journals, or from the Bohemias
(like Greenwich Village) to suburbia, or from an elegant public
prose to an esoteric language for a few colleagues. In short, the

new intellectuals are no longer interested in attracting a public audience. They have become professional and look to a professional audience. The important consequence, says Jacoby, is the public loss: "The larger culture rests on a decreasing number of aging intellectuals with no successors. Younger intellectuals are occupied and preoccupied by the demands of university careers. As professional life thrives, public culture grows poorer and older."[7]

Of course, this is not the entire story. By itself, this account neglects those poststructuralist thinkers who claim that their relativism should be no obstacle to the public intellectual. I will discuss these later in this chapter and then turn to the more profound social or emotional reasons for the death of the public intellectual. First, however, I examine the professionalization of that group of intellectuals best equipped to become religious critics: the philosophers and religious scholars in universities and in seminaries.

I. The Professionalization of Religious Scholars

The shift of American intellectuals from responsibility to the public to responsibility to the profession began as early as the last decades of the nineteenth century. American students studying in Germany in the 1880s and 1890s envied German professors, who not only earned as much as nine times the salary of a school teacher but were granted high social status. These students returned home with the hope of adopting the new scientific methods of the German professors and simultaneously acquiring their economic and social position. The two seemed to go hand in hand: to elevate academics' social standing, it was necessary to demonstrate the scientific stature of the academic disciplines and of those who work in those disciplines. Soon what Peter Novick calls the common criteria of professionalism were adopted: "institutional apparatus (an association, a learned journal), standardized training in esoteric skills, leading to certification and controlled access to practice, heightened status, autonomy."[8] Gradually through the decades of the first half of the twentieth century, professionalism gained such statute that non-university scholars were called "amateurs" who dabbled in ideas that now "belonged to" a discipline and the university. In the early 1950s, no doubt referring to the particularly extreme local emphasis on scholarship, University of Chicago theologian Bernard Loomer would note that an education for "integrity" (an education that would integrate one's internal and external worlds) had been replaced by an education for specialized competence.[9]

What Clark Kerr called the "great transformation" occurred, however, between 1960 and 1980. It was then, Clara M. Lovett argues, that the model of professionalism, particularly the research-oriented faculty, spread from a few elite campuses to literally hundreds of colleges and universities originally established for other purposes. Lovett contends that it did not seem to matter that only a small minority of faculty actually produced the original research or received significant grants. "It did matter," however, "that *those* faculty activities became highly rewarded and were thought to be the keys to professional standing and mobility." This problem has been compounded by the scarcity of academic jobs and the strategies that scarcity bred. In the process, she argues, the model of "the republican professor," the professor for whom public responsibilities figured large, was all but forgotten.[10]

Bruce Kuklick's ironically titled *The Rise of American Philosophy* functions as a case study of the rise of academic professionalism as much as it functions as a study of the rise of philosophy at Harvard from 1860 to 1930. "Of the six classic American philosophers," Kuklick notes, "five are treated here— Peirce, James, Royce, Santayana, and Whitehead,"[11] omitting only Dewey, because he never taught at Harvard. The book argues that over those seventy years the department replaced these five philosophers, who wrote and lectured intelligibly to a broad cross section of cultured people, with philosophers who wrote and lectured to fellow specialists, who did not apply their ideas to the world beyond their technical areas, and who tended to treat their predecessors as mere popularizers. Kuklick concludes his long book with this short paragraph:

> During the same period in which philosophy became a profession, political and social theorizing continued to occupy a minor place and the philosophic defense of religion began to go out of fashion. Like most academics, philosophers spent their

time in administration, in committee work, in placing graduate students, in organizing conferences, and in running the journals. When narrow professionals turned to their scholarship, they thought of their work as a game. For a few, professional philosophy had become a way, not of confronting the problem of existence, but of avoiding it.[12]

Philosopher of religion Van Harvey argues similarly that contemporary theologians are better seen as professionals than as the victims of secularization that they are sometimes seen to be. Secularization is not a very good hypothesis to begin with; it cannot explain the continuing social importance of religion in America—for example, the rise of fundamentalism that occurred during the very years that the secularization hypothesis was generated by Peter Berger and others. Accordingly, if secularization has not occurred, it can hardly explain why theologians have become intellectually marginalized and thus incapable of speaking effectively to the society at large. The social impotence of American theologians is better understood as a function of their professionalization. Americans tended to accept the German conclusion, reached by Immanuel Kant and Friedrich Schleiermacher, that theology is better suited to the training of the clergy than to basic intellectual inquiry. But unlike German universities, American public universities could not train clergy.[13] So theology was shunted away from the university intellectual center and became a creature of divinity schools. And in the divinity schools, theology became professional in two senses. First, like law and medicine, it was viewed as a training for practitioners rather than an inquiry into basic human understandings. Second, it became professional in the sense described above: it was broken down into narrow disciplines (dogmatics, Bible, church history, practical theology), each of which became so technical that it could not address other disciplines, let alone the society at large.

According to Harvey, two other circumstances conspired to undercut the theological world view that once had been the platform for a more public theology and for what I am calling religious critics and, thus, to further professionalize the theologian. First, Kant, with the collaboration of Schleiermacher, presuming that theology lacked the intellectual authority to propound a metaphysics, left it only the task of commenting on religious experience. Second, the historical-critical methods, pioneered in biblical study and then adopted by other theological specialties, stressed narrow methodological competency and prohibited the intrusion of metaphysics, world views, or even general understandings into technical analysis. Then, increasingly through the twentieth century, many prominent Protestant theologians confined themselves to Christian doctrine, ignoring most questions of science and history. When they bothered to address society at all, they did it lamely—admitting that they were professionally ill-equipped to analyze the social problems they sometimes attempted to analyze. Thus, the worldview and office once so important for, say, a Reinhold Niebuhr, became an embarrassment for the newly professionalized divinity schools; and their theological faculties contented themselves, by and large, with publicly irrelevant commentaries on religious faith. Harvey concludes that now we have dropped, not only worldviews and the moral language of a larger community, but "the sense of what Niebuhr called a 'high religion' and what it might contribute to public life. One does not have to be a Christian to regret this loss or to utter the lament, 'Oh, Reinhold Niebuhr, where are you now that we need you?' "[14]

In "Theological and Religious Sciences," Conrad Cherry corroborates Harvey's explanations for the demise of the religious critic by discussing the rise of religious studies departments in public universities. Despite the fact that most prominent religious thinkers now work in religious studies departments rather than in divinity schools, the trend to increasing professionalization has been sustained. The beginnings of the shift from divinity school to religious studies department lie in the 1960s, when the study of religion exploded. "Between 1964 and 1968," Cherry says, "students in all graduate programs in religion grew from a total of 7,383 to 12,620—in percentages, that meant that graduate education in religion had expanded more rapidly than any other field during the period."[15] At Northwestern University in 1966 Edmund Perry foresaw the imminent end of the dominantly theological approach to the study of religion and understood that to be the end of the Protestant tyranny over departments of religion. Like other scholars decades earlier, the new religious studies scholars sought a kind of scientific neutrality. According to Cherry, these scholars "described their academic posture as that of 'disinterested objectivity,' 'personal detachment,' 'disinterested irreverence,' 'the perspective of the outsider,' and (shades of the late-nineteenth century) as 'nonsectarian' as a way of calling attention to their abandonment of a past and the adoption of a future."[16]

Admittedly, Cherry does not find in the theologians the professionalism that Harvey finds. To the religious studies scholar, in fact, theologians seemed unprofessional, too personally engaged; the question was not whether they should dominate but whether they should be banned entirely from the university. Accordingly, the theologians' preoccupation with "big issues" was supplanted in university religious studies departments by professional preoccupation with specialized study.

Nevertheless, Cherry reaches a conclusion similar to Harvey's: religious studies scholars have become professionalized and isolated from the public. For the religious studies scholar, the politics of peer approval clearly took precedence over the politics of public persuasion. Or, in Cherry's words: "Those occupying the field would measure their task neither by religious trends in the larger American culture nor by the programs of study in the divinity schools. They would gauge their work, instead, by how well it conformed to the acceptable specialties in the contemporary American university."[17] The public implications of religious studies, I presume, hardly mattered. Clearly, there was little room for the serious religious critic in the new religious studies departments.

It is true that, despite their typical indifference to the public implications of their scholarship, religious studies scholars have acquired a measure of public prominence as experts in technical areas. They possess a highly specialized and professionally acceptable knowledge about a specific sort of public phenomena. An ethicist in a religious studies department might be called upon to comment on abortion or on AIDS or other questions of medical ethics. Someone in world religions or religious history might be queried about the power of religion in the politics of Iran, Algeria, or Northern Ireland. Someone in American religious history might be interviewed about the rise of religious cults and mass suicides in Jonesville and Waco. Or they may comment on the strength of fundamentalists in politics.

Whatever their current authority, the newly professionalized religious studies scholars have much to lose from the introduction of poststructural relativism. In the light of poststructuralism, the work of religious studies scholars no longer will be regarded as objective analysis of human phenomena. Rather, it will appear to be the narrow interpretation of fairly atypical citizens—hardly the sort of cachet to be sought by religious critics.

II. Emotions and the Crisis of Authority

I do not argue, however, that relativism alone is responsible for the demise of the religious critic. If relativism is so important, why did earlier historical relativists, such as Carl Becker and Charles Beard, see no incompatibility between their relativism and their willingness as historians to speak and act as public intellectuals—specifically, as social critics?[18]

Many poststructuralists today claim that relativity does not necessarily immobilize the intellectual. It may immobilize only those scholars who seek to authorize their work by contending that it is objective, as religious studies scholars sometimes do. The blockage that supposedly arises from relativism should be traced to such claims, not to relativism itself. Only in the presence of demands for objective truth does relativism look like a villain.

Nelson Goodman, for example, argues that relativism is not about calling anything true you might want to call true but about how claims fit worlds. A world for Goodman is not something objectively known and readymade, nor is it something given, a metaphysical entity that should be known by pure perceptions (perceptions unaltered by earlier conceptions). A world is a framework that may be relative to the person who affirms it; but this does not keep it from being seriously conceived, imagined, constructed, and tested. As modern physicists have demonstrated, worlds can differ significantly; thus, there is every reason to expect that, from world to world, contradictory things might be true. Accordingly, Goodman asks: "How, then, are we to accommodate conflicting truths without sacrificing the difference between truth and falsity? Perhaps by treating these versions as true in different worlds. Versions not applying in the same world no longer conflict; contradiction is avoided by segregation."

Thus, truth is not meaningless, but is relative to some world; what is clearly false is not true in any world." This might, but should not, lead to resignation or that sort of irresponsible relativism where anything can be true. "Neither attitude," Goodman says, "is very productive."[19] Thus, it is not relativity, itself, but such resignation and irresponsibility that are the real threats to those who would be religious critics.

Richard Rorty takes a similar position, asserting that, "except for the occasional cooperative freshman, one cannot find anybody who says that two incompatible opinions on any important topic are equally good."[20] Relativism is a significant problem only to people who want "antecedently formulable criteria for choosing between alternative, equally coherent, webs of belief." Thus, argues Rorty,

> relativism seems a threat only to those who insist on quick fixes and knock-down arguments. To the holist, it is enough to debate . . . in the old, familiar, inconclusive ways . . . bringing up once again all the hackneyed details, all the varied advantages and disadvantages of the two views.[21]

In other words, after you set aside objective claims, you can still sit down and begin to argue that in a particular situation one relativistic, local view yields better results than another; you can hear the counterarguments for a contrary, relative view; you can weigh the arguments; and you can decide for one view or another. After this, you can feel that the entire process was not a waste of time. In short, if you do not begin objectivistically, you can believe that poststructural relativism does not necessarily foreclose judgment or invite despair about what is good for society.

In *Criticism and Social Change*, literary critic Frank Lentricchia quotes Kenneth Burke to endorse a similar view of the poststructural, relativistic, communal world.

> Imagine that you enter a parlor. You come late. When you arrive, others have preceded you, and they are engaged in a heated discussion, a discussion too heated for them to pause and tell you exactly what it is about. In fact, the discussion had already begun long before any of them got there, so that no one

present is qualified to retrace for you all the steps that had gone before. You listen for a while, until you decide that you have caught the tenor of the argument; then you put in your oar. Someone answers; you answer him; another comes to your defense; another aligns himself against you, to either the embarrassment or gratification of your opponent, depending upon the quality of your ally's assistance. However, the discussion is interminable. The hour grows late, you must depart. And you do depart, with the discussion still vigorously in progress.[22]

This is a conversation supported by no objective truth; it is to be swum in for as long as you can. Burke was wary of all those who would argue that conversation makes sense only if there is something fixed, deep down, and extraconversational to give meaning to the conversation. The point is that there is conversation; it offers a surface solidarity; and this is ground enough for pushing on to affirmation and public action. In fact, Lentricchia invokes Burke as the model of a relativist and pluralist who is able to take a social stand—to become, as it were, a public intellectual who is a culture critic.

In short, poststructural relativism and pluralism may explain the public withdrawal of the intellectual, who typically concludes that, if objective truth is impossible, public issues are intractable. But if that two-option demand is dropped, then poststructural relativism and pluralism do not logically lead to the demise of the public intellectual.

More important to the demise of the public intellectual is the pessimism that now accompanies relativism and pluralism and that leads intellectuals to withdraw from the public. This emotion, at least as it now can be found, was not present in earlier, classical American relativists and pluralists—for, while they were pessimistic about large and objective answers, they were not so pessimistic they were unable to perform as public intellectuals anyway. Ralph Waldo Emerson, William James, and John Dewey each rooted his faith in something specific to his own American environment, and each abandoned universal, objective, traditional schemes for making sense of the world—schemes that their contemporaries thought were necessary grounding for personal and public meanings. Emerson revolted from the European hegemony over the American mind and heart; James revolted from the mechanistic structure that made science positivistic; Dewey revolted from the neo-Hegelian idealism in which he and his teachers had anchored their moral thought. Admittedly, this freedom did not lead to optimism—an optimism commonly attributed to each of these thinkers. Stephen Whicher claims "that the 'dogmatic' optimism he [Emerson] vaunted publicly was something of a makeshift cover for the void he felt in private, a too-much-protested (and therefore sometimes callous) faith thrust upon him by 'the ghastly reality of things.' "[23] Bruce Kuklick suggests that "there was in [William] James an awful loneliness. He lived in terrible personal isolation, believing that only individuality counted and that even its joys were fleeting. Much of his optimism was bravado."[24] Steven C. Rockefeller notes that Dewey's poetry "reveals how he wrestled with some of the darker sides of life; the positive attitudes that were controlling in his philosophical writings did not go unquestioned in the inner man."[25] Yet the fact remains that each of these three—despite their rejection of universal truths, their resignation to local truths, their implicit poststructuralism, their little-noted lack of optimism—was able to develop an alternative reading of what is ultimately important, was able to collaborate with his colleagues, and was able to function as an archetypal American public intellectual.

By comparison, many poststructuralists suffer from something that leads to a kind of despair and personal isolation. Although Lentricchia, Rorty, and Goodman believe that poststructural methods do not necessarily lead to despair or to retreat from public involvement, and while they are logically correct in believing this, their methods tend to be followed by people without the resilience of Emerson, James, and Dewey. For much of a generation now, many poststructural intellectuals have adopted the approaches of Burke and Lentricchia, Rorty and Goodman, but have seldom used them to affirm local traditions or to address the public on matters of public concern. Rorty himself has been criticized for his inattention to social concerns.[26] And even Lentricchia's hope for a kind of Burkean social engagement is set within a book that laments the pervasive disengagement of intellectuals, particularly poststructuralist literary critics.

Poststructuralism does introduce cognitive problems, even if not insuperable cognitive problems, for anyone who wants to relate specific inquiry to the public. Relativism, pluralism, and historicism all take away the broad structures through which abstract generalizations work. Like a world clearinghouse, general structures assure that what is drawn here can be cashed there, so that everything from human nature to the meaning of life can be described locally and then applied anywhere. Without these structures, it is not immediately obvious how the words of intellectuals can be translated from a specific inquiry to a public world.

And it is true that the many fashionable writings in neopragmatic philosophy, deconstructionist literary criticism, sociological philosophy of science, new historicism in and outside literature and history departments, and poststructural theology and philosophy of religion do tend to drift toward mere talk. They tend to indulge in talk about the fact that their talk does not claim to be authorized by its correspondence to a world beyond talk, that there are no universal, eternal, structural realities to which their mere talk must correspond to become true. Seldom do these writings issue in answers suitable for public adoption. In a world desperately in need of workable answers, workable answers seem suddenly out of fashion.

One clue to the new avoidance of the public may lie in the fact that most intellectuals today, unlike their predecessors, have been involved simultaneously in professionalism and poststructuralism. Evidence for this explanation can be found in the counter-instance provided by conservatives and neoconservatives who are publicly involved intellectuals but who, in most cases, are neither poststructuralists nor professionalized academics, let alone both together. Since 1980 they have been far more politically effective, particularly during the Reagan and Bush administrations, than have poststructural academic professionals. On most public topics they are far better known to the public: to wit, William Bennett on education, Michael Novak and Richard Neuhaus on religion, Daniel Bell and Irving Kristol on public policy, George Will and Patrick Buchanan on the broad social canvas of the journalist, and William F. Buckley on all categories. Most, if not all, of these people maintain some connection with a religious faith that is traditional, metaphysical, and neither relativistic nor pluralistic nor historicist; in fact, it might be said that they ground themselves outside history. Yet ironically, as public intellectuals, they remain active in historical processes in ways that contrast sharply with the historical inactivity of most poststructural historicists. Add to this the irony that these same neoconservatives and conservatives, with their trans-local structures, affirm their local American context—unlike most poststructuralists, who lack trans-local structures and yet typically ignore the local context they do have, affirming some new mentality found in Paris and Berlin (contexts they do not have). What allows the neoconservatives and the conservatives to be both intellectual[27] and publicly active? I suggest that the explanation lies in their avoidance of the damaging combination of professionalism and poststructuralism.

In the universities, poststructural methods affected those with little confidence in a spiritual culture but much confidence in a professional cohort. Entering this situation, poststructural methods (like house guests who explain themselves only after moving in) unexpectedly undermined a modicum of professional unity with oppositional strategies, undermined a measure of consensus with an argumentative dissensus. And this, in turn, undermined intellectuals' capacity to trust their own conversation. It is these social and emotional reasons, more than anything else, that led to the demise of the public intellectual.

Charles Beard, Carl Becker, Ralph Waldo Emerson, William James, and John Dewey may have been confronted with their own versions of relativism and pluralism, but they had the support of a spiritual culture. But late-twentieth-century academic intellectuals lacked that culture and tended to rely heavily on professionalism. In that setting, relativism and pluralism could stimulate the loss of community and trust and inadvertently promote a kind of public disengagement. To suggest a justification for this account of the disengagement of the intellectuals, I turn to a case study.

III. Dissensus: Peter Novick and *That Noble Dream*

In *That Noble Dream: The "Objectivity Question" and the American Historical Profession,* Peter Novick tells a story about American historians that becomes a story about American academic intellectuals for the last hundred years.[28] The genius of this book (which won the American Historical Association's Albert J. Beveridge Award for the best book of 1988 in American history) is not its description of the objectivity question or its close analysis of American historians but its capacity to work as a synecdoche (i.e., a part representing the whole), where the generations of American historians come to represent the generations of all American intellectuals. Novick makes the historians' dominant methods a reflection of the dominant ethos of the cultural period out of which the historians work, an ethos that affects nonhistorians as much as historians.

Over the last hundred years the American historians moved, more or less together, through a succession of three phases, each time adjusting to a dominant cultural optimism or pessimism by taking an objectivist or relativist stance. In the fourth and last phase, our own period, this process broke down; historians' methods became confused largely because the culture was confused. Consensus was replaced by dissensus, dominant methods were replaced by a chaos of conflicting styles, and, most importantly, the individual historian was left with no clear world view to support discourse about the public.

Novick treats the objectivity question, not as an esoteric issue, but as a nest of related methodological and cultural issues rooted in attitudes of optimism, pessimism, and confusion. His book is more a description of the emotional meaning of America for the American intellectual than a narrow analysis of historical method. It concludes with an account of the emotional obstacles thrown in the way of the American intellectual who would be a public intellectual. To show this conclusion, as well as to provide a glimpse at the American intellectual's recent cultural context, a summary of Novick's phase-to-phase discussion is necessary.

The first and conservative evolutionist phase is objectivistic and lasts from the 1880s into the 1910s. Novick argues that many American academics visited German universities to study the new *Wissenschaft* of *Objektivität,* and then returned home to treat *Wissenschaft* as the "science" of natural science and *Objektivität* as the "objectivity" of sense perception—forgetting that *Wissenschaft* referred to organized knowledge and that *Objektivität* referred to ideal and often nonempirical truths.[29] Failing to realize that German historians would have "reacted with outrage to the suggestion that *naturwissenschaftliche* approaches could be applied within their realm" (*TND* p. 24), the returning American historians not only treated history as a natural science but as a positivistic natural science. In using Leopold von Ranke to authorize a disinterested and factually grounded historical objectivity, they "venerated him for being precisely what he was not" (*TND* p. 28).

The positivistic historicism of this first period was superseded by the progressive historicism which had its roots in the New History of Columbia University in the middle 1910s and was brought to full flower by Carl Becker and Charles Beard in the 1920s and 1930s. Becker's 1931 "Every Man His Own Historian" and Beard's 1933 "Written History as an Act of Faith" were each presidential addresses to the American Historical Association, and each was thrown in the teeth of the objectivists of the earlier phase. They argued that history is interpretation, that it is always influenced by environment, and that it is often arbitrarily selective. They broadened the scope of history and moved behind political history to the social, economic, and intellectual sources of political change. And they argued that historians, typically, not only were not detached but should not be; instead, they should be engaged and didactic partisans, showing how history speaks to the problems of their own day. "Historical thinking . . . is a social instrument," Becker claimed (*TND* p. 98). He went on to criticize his colleagues for first treating enemy ideas as merely relative and then, unselfconsciously, treating their own ideas as absolute (*TND* p. 106). He openly acknowledged that his own theory of progressive relativism was problematic, lacking as it did any fixed standard on which it might be deemed superior.

The consensus historians of the 1940s and 1950s represent the third phase in the career of the objectivity question. With the advent of Hitler, Stalin, and Auschwitz, relativism began to appear repugnant; it seemed to give fascists, Stalinistic communists, and anti-Semites as much worth as their opponents. Becker and Beard were attacked; their relativism was exaggerated by the new objectivists (such as Arthur O. Lovejoy and Maurice Mandelbaum), who implied that it denied all truth claims, even dates and places, and that it was inherently skeptical. Science was treasured for its valiant struggle for objective truth, particularly as described in Karl Popper's principle of falsifiability—Karl Popper, having had, not incidentally, a "life-long revulsion" toward

Marxism (*TND* p. 298). Explicitly linking totalitarianism and relativism, George Orwell could assert that "the really frightening thing about totalitarianism is not that it commits 'atrocities' but that it attacks the concept of objective truth; it claims to control the past as well as the future" (*TND* p. 290). Albeit in a very different global climate and in a much weaker form, this phase was an implicit reversion to the "conservative evolutionist" objectivism of the late-nineteenth and early-twentieth centuries. But now it was recognized that relativism of some diminished sort had to be lived with (as one contemporary put it) "as one lives with eczema: it's not fatal, simply an annoying chronic itch that's best ignored; it only gets worse if you scratch it" (*TND* p. 410). Finally, the new scholarly professional sought to replace passion with professional detachment, contemporary relevance with disinterestedness, political engagement with political neutrality, history for the people with history "for its own sake," even a kind of populist scholarship for the lay audience with elite scholarship for the professional audience. Intellectual history now could be pursued apart from environmental and pragmatic considerations. Perry Miller, for example, in his study of the Puritans uncoupled intellectual from social history and referred glowingly to the life of the mind, as though the Puritan mind for example, might be understood apart from Puritan social life.

Fourth and finally, in the 1960s the comity and polity of the 1940s and 1950s collapsed, and with them the objectivism that had bolstered the fight against totalitarianism. Dissensus, even opposition, among historians became as politically correct as consensus had been in the previous decade. This time the rhythm was broken; there was not a reversion to the relativism of an earlier period (a dominant method reflecting an earlier dominant method). Rather, from the 1960s on, there was to be no dominant cultural style or methodology at all. Quoting the Book of Judges, Novick titles his last chapter, "There was no king in Israel."

Now historians stood on both sides of the objectivity question. A distinctly new relativism did arise and took heart from Thomas Kuhn's *The Structure of Scientific Revolutions*. Objectivists were caricatured by David Halberstam: "Objectivity was prized and if objectivity in no way conformed to reality, then all the worse for reality" (*TND* p. 416). It became important to see things relativistically, so that even the totalitarian point of view had to be felt sympathetically, making it possible to understand, for example, Soviet "concern for security and reconstruction rather than expansion and global subversion" (*TND* p. 448). This relativism, unlike the more personal and individual relativism of the 1920s and 1930s, was a group of relativism that made not every person but every group its own historian. It was more about the status of knowledge (the true is relative) than, as in the progressive period, about morality (the good is relative). Nevertheless, this time relativism was counterbalanced even as it grew in importance. With great energy and a ready audience, opponents of the new historical relativism called it nihilistic and argued that it was riddled with paradoxes.

In fact, most professional historians were experiencing a methodological crisis while remaining relatively unconscious of this fact. "By the seventies and eighties American professional historians' attitudes on the objectivity question were so heterogeneous that it was impossible to identify anything resembling a dominant sensibility" (*TND* p. 593). Further, historians shifted about, not only from objectivism to relativism and back, but from social history to intellectual history, from quantitative history to cultural history.

Again, I describe *That Noble Dream* not to concentrate exclusively on historians but, like Novick, to treat them as representative of American academic intellectuals over the past hundred years. The rhetorical power of Novick's four-phase narrative lies in the fact that he does not take the expected last step. The fourth phase does not reiterate the second phase, as the third phase objectivism had reiterated the first phase objectivism. Novick breaks what could have been a symmetry and argues that recently dominant styles have been replaced by a chaos of styles in the lives of intellectuals. In this last phase there is not even a clear standoff between relativist and objectivist historians; instead, there is something more like an abdication of theory. He does, however, remain consistent in suggesting that, even in this fourth phase, the epistemological situation reflects the cultural situation; method is confused because culture is confused. For example, the new relativists both were and were not relativists; while seeing their opponents' truths as adjusted to their political aims, they tended to absolutize their own truths and saw themselves as innocent of ax grinding (see, for example, Halberstam's presumption above, that he knows the true "reality" that the so-called objectivists avoid[30]). In fact, Novick, himself a creature of this culture, is consistent enough to leave traces of his own confusion in the writing of his book.[31]

I suggest that this epistemological confusion points to an emotional confusion, and it is the latter condition that has made many American intellectuals ineffective in the public world. Novick himself yearned for a way to resolve the objectivism-relativism question at the theoretical level and alleviate the emotional confusion, but none was yet plausible in the 1980s. He cites efforts by David Hollinger and Thomas Haskell to concede the relativism of Kuhn and Rorty without exposure to a Nietzschean relativism, to argue that a kind of disciplinary agreement is still possible without introducing some new kind of objectivity, and to affirm a kind of relativistic realism that will stand beyond objective realism and relativistic nihilism.[32] But, Novick concludes, "as of the 1980s, hardly anybody was listening. Sensibilities were too diverse to be gathered together under any ecumenical tent" (*TND* p. 628). Thus, yearnings or not, the 1980s appeared to be uncongenial to a clear third or middle option, and it is about those times—not about pure possibilities—that Novick is writing.

Nevertheless, Novick's closing contention that "There was no king in Israel" leads to a question about the future of the American public intellectual: Can these bones rise again?

IV. A Way Beyond

The intellectual disorder Novick identifies in our time can be attributed, in part, to the rise of poststructural methods, particularly as they undermined the authority of the professionals. These not only undercut the grounds for generalizations but introduced two other problems. The first was social: dissensus entered the community of scholars and undermined the authority once implicit in the unity of experts. The second concerned a personal sense of plausibility: dissensus impaired a person's willingness to affirm anything. As sociologists of knowledge have said for a generation now, solid social structures contribute to plausibility, particularly to the plausibility of ultimate values, and the absence of those structures contributes to individuals' confusion.[33] Thus, when communal dissensus replaced communal consensus, many intellectuals lost their individual will to believe in ultimate values.

Without ignoring what has been learned through poststructuralism, it appears that the first task is to address the questions of the will and the affections. James Kloppenberg takes just the opposite approach when he asks Novick to extend poststructural theory. Kloppenberg sees Novick leaving readers of *That Noble Dream* "with a bleak assessment of history's prospects in a world in which all knowledge claims are greeted with suspicion." Why cannot Novick be like James and Dewey, Kloppenberg complains, when they "placed their confidence in free-floating communities of inquiry" whose results were always local and revisable and never eternal and universal, but were nevertheless sufficient as a base for intellectual and moral confidence and action? Kloppenberg argues that Novick ignored this American precedent, adopted an epistemological suspicion, and needlessly dismissed third options. Kloppenberg would resolve the problem by invoking Hollinger, Haskell, and a "pragmatic hermeneutics."[34] But Kloppenberg expects Novick to respond at the level of theory. Kloppenberg's pragmatism may be right, but it may not be appropriate as a complaint against Novick, who writes not about right theory but about right intellectual history—arguing that the 1980s failed to offer a social and emotional climate congenial to affirming new theoretical answers. Despite Kloppenberg's implication to the contrary, Novick did not say that third theories were wrong. Nor did Novick say that relativism leads necessarily to skepticism; in fact, he asserted the opposite.[35] Novick's point was not a point about the wisdom of objectivism, relativism, or even middle or third theories. Rather, it was about historical context and its relation to historical interpretation. Historians, he said, simply are not listening to theoretical resolutions of the objectivism-relativism dilemma. They did not listen to objectivists very well in the 1920s and 1930s when there was a regnant pessimism; they did not listen to relativists very well in the 1940s and 1950s when there was a regnant optimism; and in the 1980s, when there was a regnant confusion, they were not listening very well to middle or third theories. The problem is that they were not in the mood to listen, that the current intellectual context failed to provide the requisite social and emotional conditions for getting beyond confusion, for speaking confidently to the public.[36]

Accepting Novick's point, I argue that if intellectuals fail to function as public intellectuals or as religious critics in particular, this may be partly attributable to a breakdown not only of a regnant culture but of community and of the emotional vitality that community might offer.

CHAPTER 3

WILLIAM JAMES, PUBLIC INTELLECTUAL

> Strenuosity, passion, and heroism were all strong re-
> sponses to the metaphysical problems of his earlier
> years; they also served as a jeremiad and solution to the
> social lethargy, to the numbing *tedium vitae* that James
> believed afflicted many Americans in the late-nine-
> teenth century.
>
> George Cotkin[1]

I turn to a case study of William James, who came of age
over a century earlier than today's academic professionals, but
who confronted an emotional and volitional predicament similar
to the one they are experiencing. James resembled today's poststructural academic intellectuals, was no more optimistic than
they are, but was able, unlike his successors, to function as a
public intellectual. But that was only a relatively late development in his life.

As a young man, James was hit from one side with mechanistic materialism and from the other with the abyss of a world
without limits, with the consequence that he could not act as a
public intellectual. The materialism was suggested by the hyper-
trophy of structure (the virtually mechanical laws) in his medical
studies; and the abyss was suggested by the assault on all structure
(the virtual anomie) in his cultural studies. The problem for
James was not, at bottom, cognitive but affective and volitional;
it was about helplessness within an all-determining mechanism
and about vertigo within a world open to everything. And while
eventually he moved to cognitive issues, and then (against all
odds) to a life as a public intellectual and occasionally as a reli-

41

gious critic, his first need was to confront the affectional and volitional problems, even if they were ignored by intellectuals.

I look, then, at James's history, specifically at his movement from emotional and volitional blockage to cognitive answers. After discussing James's history as illustrative of a possibility for our generation, I turn in succeeding chapters to the sort of cognitive issues confronted by someone attempting to function today as a public intellectual, particularly as a religious critic.

I. James as Private

Later to be one of America's great psychologists and one of America's great philosophers, James began adulthood with a sometimes pathetic and lonely fight with depression. He writes of himself being "entirely broken-down before I was thirty."[2] Even in his late forties, still fighting his low spirits, James wrote his wife, "[I] have got it under for a while and mean to fight it out on that line for the rest of my life, for I see that as my particular mission in the world."[3] In fact, it can be said that he spent much of his career explaining the broad implications of that fight.

In his letters James began as early as 1867, when he was twenty-five, to complain of the "hue of stagnation" that lay over his daily life.[4] Causes of this depression were various and complex, as both James's intricate life circumstances and his commentators testify. There is James's failure to participate in the Civil War, making him feel that he would be "judged not to have lived" and provoking him to write about strenuous living and manly virtues and to see sports as the "moral equivalent of war." There is the presence of James's benevolent but domineering father who, not only virtually forced James to abandon his career as an artist, but held before him exalted demands, making him feel unsuccessful and helpless.[5] It is possible that his depression was aggravated also by spending a year and a half alone in Germany in his midtwenties largely unconnected with family, friends, university, or any institution, only to return to four unemployed years in Cambridge.

While not denying the significance of these causes, I focus on philosophical causes, subscribing to Ralph Barton Perry's contention that James's problem was also philosophical and that it was a "personal problem that could be relieved only by a *philosophical* insight."[6] There are parallels between James's late nineteenth-century denial of rational structure, of biblical schemes of history, of natural law and the denial today by poststructuralists of permanent structures of human nature and reason, of received literary standards, of the givenness of scientific law. Equally, there are parallels between the emotional problems experienced by James and by poststructuralist intellectuals. I concentrate on James's bout with depression (described as acedia, anhedonia, or abulia) and treat it as an analogue to the postmodern intellectual's own bout with depression (sometimes diagnosed as aporia). I show how James overcame the predicament by treating it as an emotional predicament, and I use that as a precedent for treating the predicament of today's poststructuralists.

James was presented with a dilemma. He felt the weight of scientific determinism in both his medical studies and current evolutionary thought. In a letter to his friend Thomas W. Ward, he said, "I feel that we are Nature through and through, that we are wholly conditioned, that not a wiggle of our will happens save as the result of physical laws; and yet, notwithstanding, we are *en rapport* with reason."[7] He was haunted by the idea "that those parts of the universe already laid down absolutely appoint and decree what the other parts shall be."[8] But, gradually and partly through the ministrations of Chauncey Wright, James wrenched himself away from that view . . . only then to slide into the abyss of a world without any structure at all. According to George Cotkin, the central source of James's emotional disturbance became "a universe without certitude."[9] It was the vertigo of an indeterminate world, rather than the claustrophobia of a hyperdeterminate world, that drove him to the "panic fear" described in *The Varieties of Religious Experience*. There, putting his sentiments into the words of a fictitious French correspondent, he describes an epileptic patient, "a black-haired youth with greenish skin, entirely idiotic, who used to sit all day on one of the benches. . . . looking absolutely non-human," and confesses that on watching him "something hitherto solid within my breast gave way entirely, and I became a mass of quivering fear." He concludes by noting that "after this the universe was changed for me altogether."[10] Cotkin argues that this quivering fear should be traced to too little structure, rather than to too much structure. It was in this vein that James wrote his brother Henry about

> this awful *Hamlet,* which groans and aches so with the mystery of things, with the ineffable, that the *attempt* to express it is abandoned, one form of words seeming as irrelevant as another; and crazy conceits and countersenses slip and 'whirl' around the vastness of the subject, as if the tongue were mocking itself.[11]

However various the causes and accounts, James was driven into virtual isolation. He traveled in Europe, unattached and mostly solitary, from April 1867 to November 1868. He frequented German health spas for the elderly—because, he said, "thoughts of the pistol, the dagger and the bowl began to usurp an unduly large part of my attention."[12] In January 1868 he concluded a long meandering letter to Oliver Wendell Holmes, Jr., by saying that he had written in "the dismalest of dumps," and that Holmes was "the one emergent peak, to which I cling when all the rest of the world has sunk beneath the wave." Then in a postscript he said, "That is, after all, all I wanted to write you and it may float the rest of the letter."[13] That same month, writing to a friend, he argued that his reputation for possessing "calm and clockwork feelings" was a front. "All last winter, for instance, when I was on the continual verge of suicide," he wrote Thomas Ward, "it used to amuse me to hear you chaff my animal contentment. The appearance of it arose from my reaction against what seemed to me your unduly *noisy* and demonstrative despair. The fact is, I think, that we have both gone through a good deal of similar trouble."[14] In 1869 James received his M.D. and stayed home, unemployed for most of the ensuing three years.

The conclusion of the story is well known. It was anticipated, but only anticipated, in what James told Ward both of them should do: find "a work which shall by its mere *exercise* interest him and at the same time allow him to feel that through it he takes hold of the reality of things—whatever that may be—in some measure."[15] First, decide to act; second, act on an interest that at least gives the illusion of taking hold of reality; third, but only implicit, the rest will take care of itself. James knew that for himself this was possible only if he could free himself from depression's internal control. In his diary on April 30, 1870, he says, "My first act of free will shall be to believe in free will." He amplifies:

> Not in maxims, not in *Anschauungen,* but in accumulated *acts* of thought lies salvation. *Passer outre.* Hitherto, when I have felt like taking a free initiative, like daring to act originally, without carefully waiting for contemplation of the external world to determine all for me, suicide seemed the most manly form to put my daring into; now, I will go a step further with my will, not only act with it, but believe as well; believe in my individual reality and creative power.[16]

James was immobilized by a kind of (Herbert) Spencerian overdetermination and then by a kind of (Friedrich) Nietzschean space sickness. He contemplated suicide but may have lacked even the follow-through to accomplish suicide. He could not go on in life without finding a practical solution to his problem. He developed a practical solution, one that appeared not to be based on any piece of knowledge, one that was put forth as a bold speculation, and one that required that he accept what almost none of his contemporaries (except, possibly, his father) accepted: that beliefs are founded largely on individual actions and interests rather than on evidence or reason. James's world might look like those of the subjective idealist or the idealistic Romantic because it was engendered by the imagination. But it was not like theirs because it came without the assurance that it rested on external foundations. James seemed to have no choice. Apparently he had tried waiting "for the contemplation of the external world to determine all" for him, and this had not worked. So he turned to a world shaped out of imagination and behavior, to what in particular had happened to himself, and to something sufficiently unique that the only generalizations that applied were generalizations about his individual acts of freedom.

From this highly particular situation, James's philosophical, psychological, and religious theories, slowly arose. During truly fast-moving and crucial years in American intellectual history, it took forty years for one of history's most productive intellects to reach, just before his death, a philosophical and theological justification for the unorthodox action he had taken in his twenties.[17] His argument was that a disabling circumstance is best attacked, not by general theories, not by broad methods, but by a decision to act on an interest. This, said James, is what one should do in "the situation of emergency" (to use Frank Lentricchia's phrase).[18] As it happened, his psychology and philosophy gave the theoretical explanation for that approach; that is, his doctrines of radical empiricism, pragmatism, pluralism, and constructivism all, in one way or another, can be seen as theoretical justifications for basing decisions on interests. But that is only incidental; for James's point is that decisions, interests, even impromptu speculations give rise not only to theories but, more importantly, to facts. This is true, James suggested, for intellectuals in any field or for any non-intellectual dealing with any major problem.[19]

James's personal and academic philosophy began in a particular effort to keep from drowning in depression. He saw life as a struggle to survive in the midst of overdetermination and, especially, of underdetermination. To answer the problems implicit in this struggle, he looked to structures offered by philosophy. In 1873 he says, "my strongest moral and intellectual craving is for some stable reality to lean upon."[20] Over thirty years later, James disparaged the desire for "a universe where we can just give up, fall on our father's neck, and be absorbed into the absolute life as a drop of water melts into the river or the sea."[21] Accordingly, he proposed that the solution lay, instead, in his own decision and interest and in the speculations issuing from them.

When this worked in practice, he was left with the question, Why? From this inquiry grew his pluralism, his relativism, his realism, his pragmatism, and, especially, his radical empiricism. In support of radical empiricism, James argued that there was a reason his interests were sometimes worth acting on: although they seemed to arise internally, they sometimes originated in the environment and took shape in a bodily or an affective feeling. Interest, in short, is not simply an internal event but is a mode of perceiving a world external to oneself. How else explain why his own interests had so often meshed with the world? Could it be only accident and luck? Sometimes his interests were simply too trustworthy as guides to the environment to be only self-fulfilling prophecies or only lucky guesses. Rather, interests must sometimes gain insight from contact with the environment, functioning as weak perceptions of the environment. That is, interests must be noncognitive, nonsensuous perceptions, working at a bodily and emotional level beneath the critical intellect and the five senses, discerning something about the environment. This trust in vague knowledge (the reverse of Descartes's trust in clear and distinct ideas) became the major idea behind James's psychology and philosophy. Further, it provided a way to propose how the depressed person's will and affection could interact with the world.

The case of James may be instructive for American intellectuals in the last decades of the twentieth century. Their confusion is not unlike James's; they cannot claim to know deep structures behind history or to know history objectively, simply as it is. More importantly, they lack the will and affections that will allow them to become public intellectuals, let alone religious critics. In such circumstances James decided to act, to follow his interests, occasionally to trust that sometimes those interests read the external world, and to clothe those interests with speculative theories.

II. James and Public Pedagogy

James's decision to address the public was no more predictable in the 1870s than his decision to act on his own was predictable in the 1860s. In the 1860s James was the rich, pampered, neurasthenic, Victorian offspring of a powerful father who had blocked his career as an artist, kept him out of the Civil War, and bequeathed to him low self-esteem and a chronically underdeveloped capacity to decide and to act for himself. And yet, as we have seen, by the early 1870s James's personal autonomy was not only evident but highly exceptional.

Similarly, in the 1870s James was more accustomed to the drawing room, the classroom, and the transatlantic steamer cabin than to public lecture halls and newspapers and semipopular journals. He preferred to meet with like-minded intellectuals in the Cambridge Metaphysical Club or to rub shoulders with the nostalgic, conservative, elitist Mugwumps. Yet from 1895 until his death in 1910, James became the most popular philosopher since Emerson.

An explanation for this transformation is hard to find. Even in George Cotkin's *William James, Public Philosopher,* a book dedicated to describing James as a public intellectual, there is no specific explanation of what drove James to take on a public role; if anything, Cotkin is most persuasive as he tells how James's Victorian seclusion and Hamlet-like indecision augured against any future public role. There was, in short, something unanalyzably particular about James's development, making it not subject to explanation by reference to general patterns or causes. It makes more sense to say that James simply decided to become more responsive to the public, much as, earlier, he had decided to become more responsive to his private circumstances.

Of course, the ground was prepared for this move. James had long pictured the world in such a way that it made the life of a public intellectual important. Although this picture of the world may not causally explain James's decision to become a public intellectual, it makes that decision retrospectively justifiable. His world is "historical" in being open, contingent, and indeterminate, rather than "rational," closed, necessary, and determinate; it is in the making, rather than already made; it is plural and particularistic, broken into many events and many people. This world is more wild than tame, even if it can be arranged by reference to traditions and described scientifically. Most of all, to some small extent the world is literally made by a person's own decisions, not just in how it appears to be, but in what it physically becomes.

It is the last point, particularly, that makes the public intellectual's life seem worthwhile, for it argues that a person's decisions, interests, and speculations do not lie isolated in the separate spirit world of mind or rhetoric, walled off from the matter world, as proposed by the typical spirit-matter dualist. Rather, decisions, even decisions based on little more than faith, have effects on the world. They take possibilities, otherwise dormant, and bring them to life, so that they become historically effective actualities. The life of the public intellectual, then, fit well James's view of the world—for the free initiatives of the theorist have the chance of changing history.

James lived as a public intellectual in at least two ways. First,

he addressed personal and intellectual issues important to individual people, usually under the rubric of moral, religious, and
philosophical problems. Clearly, here he spoke as a religious
critic. He understood how large challenges to his world—whether from the defenders of determinism or from the opponents of
any order whatsoever—had contributed to his personal confusion, particularly to his confusion about values. He assumed that
those who heard him suffered from much the same confusion. He
spoke to student, Chautauqua, and public lecture audiences and
wrote in semipopular journals on people's right to free themselves from stifling determinisms and on their right to invent
truths that would allow them to avoid the abyss of a world
without order. He confronted the popular *tedium vitae* with "the
discourse of heroism."[22]

Second, James addressed issues important to society. I refer
not just to his views, which today would be called progressive in
their defense of the rights of African Americans and of women
and in their opposition to war and to the marketplace manipula-
tions of John D. Rockefeller, but also to his social action. Here
James functioned as a social critic. The vigor with which he
involved himself in social action dispels the view that James was
too emotionally fragile to be more than bookish. Especially during the last twenty years of his life, already steeped in a killing
load of teaching, writing, and lecturing on moral, religious, and
philosophical problems, he still managed to produce a stream of
letters, public testimonies, and proposals on social causes that, on
occasion, were not only unconnected with his intellectual life but
contrary to prevailing intellectual fashions. In 1900 he wrote to
William Dean Howells "I think that '*les intellectuals*' [*sic*] of
every country ought to bond themselves into a league for the
purpose of fighting the curse of savagery that is pouring over the
world."[23]

None of these latter activities made James a prominent social
reformer or agitator, but he was an active citizen and entered the
social and political fray in ways that would be unusual for an
academic intellectual today.[24] He testified at the Massachusetts
State House against licensing of the medical profession—a step
that would outlaw alternative therapies (and, not incidentally,
further professionalize medicine by giving gatekeeper powers to
a technical guild). He argued against militarism, imperialism, and

callous forms of animal vivisection. He argued that the insane were not responsible for their plight. James biographer Gerald Myers said James "corresponded and lectured about lynching, mob psychology, militarism, the tyranny of the majority, international conflicts, alcoholism, responsibilities of Harvard undergraduates, curriculum reform, and the effects of the Ph.D. degree on America."[25] He sent letters to the editor to the *Nation,* the *New York Evening Post,* the *Harvard Daily Crimson,* the *Springfield Republican,* and the *Boston Evening Transcript.* James was most obviously political in his numerous letters to the *Boston Transcript* protesting the Spanish-American war, the takeover of the Philippine Islands, and the subsequent domination of the Filipinos. James's stand against the Spanish-American war most clearly represents James's full development from the depressive young man, virtually in hiding from society between 1867 and 1872, to the social critic acting on behalf of individual dignity.

In arguing for Filipinos—as well as for African Americans, women, the insane, and medically unorthodox healers—he defended the individual oppressed by foreign powers, by white, male leaders, and by medical establishments. In each case the deepest reason for James's defense was not a doctrine of equal rights but the sanctity of the inner life of the individual. James's own radical empiricism had made possible an appreciation of the individual's unutterably private sense of the world. This sanctity of the self had become the basis for his pluralistic world view, for his public philosophy, and for his protest against the trampling of the self by "bigness"—whether the bigness of social forces in America or of imperialistic American actions abroad.[26]

James's concern for the individual exposed him to ridicule. According to Santayana, James's distress over the Spanish-American war was altogether too individualistic. In 1903 James had confessed to a friend, "I am glad you still have the gift of tears about our national soul. I cried, *hard,* when the hostilities broke out and General Otis refused Aquinaldo's demand for a conference,—the only time I've cried in many a long year, and I know one other person who did likewise, a man of 60." Santayana attributed James's upset to his "false moralistic view of history. . . . He cried disconsolately that he had lost his country, when his country, just beginning to play its part in the history of the world, appeared to ignore an ideal that he had innocently expected would always guide it, because this ideal had been eloquently expressed in the Declaration of Independence. But the Declaration of Independence was a piece of literature, a salad of illusion."[27]

Frank Lentricchia defends James, and indirectly acknowledges that James's public philosophy is based on the sanctity of the individual. Lentricchia notes that Santayana is exercising the imperial voice from on high, using a theory of theories to announce what people must really mean in their hopelessly local circumstances, without seeing how his own theory is itself rooted in a highly specific history, even in a personal history. For Lentricchia, James is not a deluded idealist, but an anti-imperialist who holds an anti-exceptionalist theory of America. When James rejected the intellectuals' exalted world, calling it "a kind of marble temple shining on a hill," he stood in a broad line of anti-exceptionalist poets and democratic thinkers. James's figurative mother, says Lentricchia, is the antinomian Anne Hutchinson, thrown out of Winthrop's Puritan community, and his father is the individualistic Emerson, in revolt against all forms of cultural domination. American imperialism in the Philippines and the elite domination of the female, the African American, the insane, or anything unusual, comes down to the tyranny of an abstract power over the concrete individual. There is, in short, no blessing from on high to give Reason, America, or anything else an ahistorical truth to live by. Whatever might guide people is more particular, immediate, contingent, accidental, or, in a word, personal. In the words of *Pragmatism,* "The world of concrete personal experiences to which the street belongs is multitudinous beyond imagination, tangled, muddy, painful and perplexed."[28]

James's support for the individual's freedom led him to what must be called an incipient theory of democracy. Lentricchia argues that

> James's textual metaphor speaks *for* the liberation of the small, the regional, the locally embedded, the underdog: the voice that refuses the elocutionary lessons of cosmopolitan finishing schools. His unfinished (and unfinishable) text of history, au-

thorized by no single author, is the text of American history as
it ought to be—the multi-authored book of democracy in its
ideal and antinomian form.[29]

James, thus, acquired an unannounced and implicitly religious sense of the whole of American history and that served
informally to orient religiously even his social criticism. His
America was a struggling, pluralistic world of individuals, and it
was this that gave a context and an argumentative thrust to much of
his last intellectual work. "What ran deep in James," says Lentricchia,

> and what beyond argument was altogether there in Emerson
> (let's call it the American instinct against the imperial social
> gesture), but which did not surface in James until late in his
> career, after he had been politicized, is a sense of American
> history and society as severely ruptured from its European
> origins and from European institutions synonymous with op-
> pression: the Roman Catholic church, the army, the aristoc-
> racy, and the crown. James named these institutions as the true
> enemy of his philosophic method, which he sometimes late in
> his career associated with a Whitmanesque, unbuttoned, even
> anarchic notion of self-determination.[30]

Clearly, then, James acquired a sense of the American whole
and became a public intellectual. But to make way for this, James
had, first, to confront and to overcome an emotional confusion
and a disregard for the public, which resemble the confusion and
disregard now prevalent among American academic intellectuals.

PART **II**

_____

RECOVERING RELIGIOUS THEORY

CHAPTER 4

RELIGIOUS NARRATIVE AND
THE AVOIDANCE OF NATURE

An artist mediates between the world and minds: a critic merely between minds. An artist therefore must even at the price of uncouthness and alienation from the contemporary cultural scene maintain allegiance to the world and a fervent relation with it.

John Updike[1]

To acknowledge that each of us at the table will eventually be part of the meal is not just being "realistic." It is allowing the sacred to enter and accepting the sacramental aspect of our shaky temporary personal being.

Gary Snyder[2]

The story of William James is a case study in how decision, interest, action, even tentative speculation can overcome depression and reverse the retreat into solitude. His history is instructive for intellectuals whose isolation and confusion undermine their affections and will, thus undermining their potential to perform as public intellectuals.

Although James became a religious critic, and an important one, he was most comfortable speaking from a high podium or issuing a pronouncement in a letter to the editor. Life on the flats, building communities and institutions, developing traditions and myths, was not natural to him. James saw the public as a collection of individuals, not as a present or historic community. Even James's naturalism was virtually limited to individuals; although he studied animals in his pursuit of comparative psychology, he described a world in which significant affections and intrinsic worth stopped where human physiology ended, at the boundaries of the human skin.

James, in short, was not a public intellectual able to reach or discuss the public as a community, especially the public as a community with a slowly evolving tradition. Among James scholars it is clichéd to complain that he was so preoccupied with the individual that he neglected the community. Scarred by isolation and depression, he may have been seduced by the heroic scenario, where true survivors pull themselves up by their own bootstraps. Even his America was a world of individuals, an America populated by people undergoing private religious experiences, finding only fleeting social comfort in momentary, almost promiscuous interactions. Accordingly, although James was a public intellectual, sometimes even a religious critic, his philosophy was marked by its avoidance of community and community traditions.

This deficiency is acute for the American religious critic, who must represent and reconstruct what is ultimately important in a spiritual culture. This very sense of ultimate importance has been developed by a slow communal process, one that grows gradually through traditions that develop around narratives and myths, one that reaches thousands of years behind the European beginnings of America. It is this tradition-making process that James neglects.

Unlike James, today's "narrative theologians" do understand the historic community. Narrative theology originated with Hans Frei's 1973 *The Eclipse of Biblical Narrative,* is currently based at Yale University, and is a powerful contemporary movement in American religious thought. While narrative theologians are interested in the global Christian church, rather than in American Christianity, their approach is instructive to the religious critic who would concentrate on a single spiritual culture. Narrative theologians demonstrate that the religious sense of the whole is developed in communities, and that communities are developed—virtually created—by narratives. Accordingly they show that spiritual cultures are not only the product of communities but that religious communities are formed by religious narratives. This suggests that religious critics also should be concerned with communities and narratives (including the narratives that are myths).

However, narrative theologians tend to avoid nature. By this avoidance and by the rupture it causes in their thought, they inadvertently demonstrate that the religious critic must be concerned with nature as well as cultural narrative, with science as well as the humanities. I will argue that this is the case, even though the idea that religious thought refers to natural history as well as human history is an idea that departs from the mainstream of Western religious thought, certainly from the mainstream of European Christian thought. Nevertheless, if religion is about the sense of the whole, and if the human community is not the whole, then the religious critic must be attentive to a sense of the whole that includes nature. Furthermore, to neglect nature is to be inattentive to certain strands of biblical thought, creating problems for narrative theologians, who typically want to be faithful to the biblical narrative. On these grounds, I will contend that any adequate account of the American spiritual culture should refer not only to human history but also to natural history, not only to the arts and humanities but also to the sciences. It is not enough, in short, to include in religious history everything but nature, as narrative theologians do.

Thus, the example of the narrative theologians is instructive for religious critics. Their narrativism demonstrates the importance of community, narrative, and myth. However, the problems introduced by the narrative theologians' avoidance of nature demonstrate that nature must fall within the vision of the religious critic.

I. The Project of the Narrative Theologians

The Bible, said Frei, is about something real, but this reality is not reached through the detached and critical scrutiny that the modern world takes most seriously. The Bible is about the reality of an imaginative world. To insist at the outset on a critical and detached examination of the biblical reality simply makes that reality impossible to apprehend. To understand the biblical reality, its narrative must be entered as the narrative of a novel is entered.

Not just the community, but the whole world seen from within the biblical narrative looks different, just as the world seen from within the narrative of a film looks different. Most modern scholars have difficulty grasping this elementary truth, Frei believed. They are inclined to ask whether the Bible's claims hold up when examined for their historical accuracy or their rational coherence or for how they embody a general experience; or they are inclined to enter religious sanctuaries and ask immediately whether rituals, songs, prayers, and sermons designed to keep the biblical narrative alive can survive critical examination. Standing in the darkness of that scholarly eclipse, Hans Frei protested the dogmatic modernism of contemporary intellectuals. Within ten years a community of scholars had begun to establish a narrative theology that elaborated Frei's central contentions.

Their objective, it must be stressed, is not to worship the Bible or its narrative, but to understand a religious community and its faith. They argue that the principal contemporary obstacle to this understanding is the neglect of the biblical narrative as narrative. The dogmatism against which Frei and the narrative theologians inveigh is a dogmatism that can deprive intellectuals of the capacity to understand historic, as well as religious, communities. Frei's argument, I repeat, might enable religious critics to function effectively as religious critics in America.

However, if religious critics are to attend to the sense of the whole, they must somehow reflect on the whole of American spiritual culture. Disappointingly, Frei and his colleagues (heirs as they are to a Continental, mind-body, culture-nature dualism) use their biblically-shaped reality to refer only to human mental and cultural phenomena. Like most people related to the arts and humanities, they are remarkably inattentive to the fact that the American public is religiously concerned with and shaped by the world of nature, science, and technology, as well as by the world of culture and literature. The narrative theologians' worthy effort to understand the spiritual culture is flawed by their preoccupation with a cultural history far narrower than the American spiritual culture, which has always mingled cultural and natural history. That is, the narrative theologians' historicism is a humanistic historicism, inadequate to the humanistic-naturalistic religious history of the American public.

Ironically, narrative theology has become so humanistic that it has reintroduced, albeit from a fashionable poststructuralist perspective, just those problems that initiated the modern study of theology. Thus, narrative theology has shown signs not only of superseding but also of preceding modern thought. Modern theology began with the attempt to become nonauthoritarian, to take account of and often to incorporate the full scope of contemporary human opinion—to acquire, in short, a more justifiable sense of the whole. Narrative theology, by sticking to human and cultural history alone, seldom openly espoused premodern notions; but, by ignoring new understandings of the natural world, it lost most of the grounds for rejecting premodern authoritarianism and its supernaturalistic, biblically literal theological teachings. It is just this defect that is evident in George Lindbeck's insinuation of an apparently supernaturalistic eschatology (theory of the end of history) into a sophisticated poststructural theory of doctrine.[3] If someone of the stature of Lindbeck, the foremost narrative theologian, does this, what else might be introduced into a narrativist approach that is out of touch with natural history?

The neglect of nature seems to have allowed Lindbeck (as well as other poststructuralists coming out of a Continental orientation) to reduce science to human culture, to treat science's nature as just another rhetorical gesture. Ostensibly following Thomas Kuhn in treating science as a communal expression, Lindbeck will argue that the division between the sciences and the humanities is collapsing because now it is understood to be only rhetorical; that is, there is no division due to truly different ways of knowing or to truly different subject matters. Lindbeck illustrates his point:

> One hears exacting scholars, as I did at a recent Smithsonian consultation, casually remark with the authority of the commonplace that the epistemological grounding of a physicist's quarks and a Homer's gods is exactly the same. It is rhetorical force rooted in forms of life which gives them different cognitive status.[4]

This comment not only ignores the uniqueness of a form of inquiry, it hegemonically reduces the sciences to a branch of the humanities or to a cultural-linguistic exercise for which, as Paul

Feyerabend has said, "anything goes."[5] It is the sort of comment that prompts otherwise sanguine and religiously sympathetic scientists to say simply, "This is nonsense."[6] Either way, whether by ignoring or by reducing science's own history, narrative theologians may avoid naive, modern objectivism; but, also either way, they preclude the useful critique of religious thought that might come from science or from a religious naturalism.

My point is that entry into the world of mythic literature may be the best way to enter the world of a community. Nevertheless, the narrativist use of the Bible defeats its purpose if it eliminates the naturalistic side of the Bible and ignores the naturalistic beliefs and attitudes of the community that would be reached through the biblical myth. If religious critics are to follow the narrativists' mythic approach in order to reach the public, they—unlike the narrative theologians—should include nature, science, and technology in their narrative. The religious critic, after all, is interested in the religious sense of the whole.

II. George Lindbeck and the Narrative Theologians

In spite of its limited perspective, narrative theology may be the most religiously profound development in the academic study of religion since the Second World War.

The story of narrative theology can be told by reference to its most successful expression, George Lindbeck's *The Nature of Doctrine,* published in 1984. Lindbeck contends[7] that Frei comes closer than other recent religious thinkers to meeting Jeffrey Stout's and Alasdair MacIntyre's criterion that theology must "respond to modernity without becoming either incomprehensible to it or so much like it as to sacrifice the claim to distinctiveness."[8] While narrative theologians are authentic enough to avoid the worst form of apologetics (the effort to satisfy cultured critics of religion by adopting their standards), they also avoid incomprehensibility by responding to modern society, at least at the moral level. They undertake, Stout says, "fruitful conversation and collaboration with nonbelievers on specific issues of common concern."[9]

Lindbeck's project slightly reshapes Frei's mandate, sets it cleanly within history, and offers a more distinct model for the religious critic than Frei offered. Lindbeck states the problem in terms of the Christian ecumenical dialogue, where denominations seek to preserve their distinctiveness even while joining in community with Christians of other denominations and persuasions. At the opening of *The Nature of Doctrine* Lindbeck asks himself this practical question: How do we account for the fact that there is a new reconciliation in ecumenical discussions, even though the participants continue to hold theological beliefs that once caused apparently irreconcilable differences? How, in short, has it been possible to have reconciliation without capitulation? Lindbeck proposes that this development can be explained by the fact that the different denominations were assured that they could share the single Christian narrative without sacrificing their own distinctive denominational beliefs. Reconciliation lies in the recognition that all denominations accept "the" common biblical narrative; avoidance of capitulation lies in the fact that no denomination is required to abandon its specific interpretation of that narrative, even though it might be incommensurable, if not mutually contradictory, with the interpretations of others. They could share a grammar of faith without relinquishing the particular truths they found in that faith.

In answering the problem this way, Lindbeck sets up a model crucially important to the religious critic, a model not only sensitive to communities and how they form around myths but to the specific problem of how, within a broad community, subcultures can retain their specific identities. This model speaks to the particular problem of multiculturism within America, to the urgent problem of how separate cultures within America can be preserved without destroying the American common culture. It could honor the poststructuralist, or postmodernist, sensitivity for the plurality (*pluribus*) within American spiritual culture without denying the sense of the whole spiritual culture (*unum*). Conversely, Lindbeck's approach could explain how the unity of the spiritual culture can be recognized without introducing the tyranny of a dominant tradition, thus eradicating the genuine plurality within the spiritual culture of America.

Lindbeck argues that the problem of reconciliation without capitulation cannot be solved by using dominant contemporary academic approaches, either that of the "cognitive propositionalists" or that of the liberal "experiential expressivists." Both of these groups seek reconciliation through the capitulation of all parties but one: the party that has the right cognitive belief or the right generic religious experience. By comparison, Lindbeck's "cultural-linguistic" approach can solve these problems by acknowledging that religious thought is indelibly stamped by its cultural and linguistic location. According to the cultural-linguistic approach, beliefs of first order language (claims to truth by particular religious groups) are culturally and linguistically relative; they are incommensurable with other beliefs, remain incommensurable, and should capitulate to no one. Reconciliation is based not on such first order beliefs but on narrative. Narrative is represented through doctrines, which pertain, not to truth, but to the "grammar" or the systematic framework, the language of the second order in terms of which first order truth-claims are organized. Participation in a common narrative reconciles Christians as Christians, giving them the basis for constancy through time and for unity across Christian denominations.

Christians are people who understand their lives by relating them to the biblical narrative. This notion of narrative was given a startling rendition by Hans Frei. It is not enough to say that he protected the distinctive (*sui generis*) status of the narrative by refusing to allow it to be reduced to anything else, such as the facts of history, generic human experience, general ideas, or arguments. More importantly, Frei defended narrative's creative role. In his words, "the meaning emerges from the story form, rather than being merely illustrated by it."[10] The consequence is that the biblical stories should be read as the realistic English novel is read, where "the meaning of the realistic stories was taken to be the realistic, fact-like depictions themselves, regardless of their reference, of the question of their factual truth or falsity, or of the 'spirit' pervading the writing."[11] Hence, the distinguishing characteristic of narrative and of doctrine is not that they refer to anything but that they provide a framework of meaning that is real in, of, and by itself.

Following Frei, Lindbeck says, "just as an individual becomes human by learning a language, so he or she begins to become a new creature through hearing and interiorizing the language that speaks of Christ."[12] In other words, "meaning is *constituted by* the uses of a specific language rather than being distinguishable from it."[13] For narrative theology, second order language in the form of narrative and doctrine gives logic and meaning to a particular religious group's first order theological formulations, practices, and moralities. Thus Lindbeck sustains his two points: (1) "the permanence and unity of doctrines," the second order language of narrative that unites denominations and makes them all Christian; (2) the relativity and plurality of their theological formulations, the first order language whereby denominations interpret doctrines.[14]

Here, then, is a model for the religious critic who would attend to a common spiritual culture through recognizing its common myths and traditions, even while honoring the spiritual plurality within this whole. While I do not pretend that this is a wholly satisfactory resolution,[15] I argue that it is useful.

III. The Need for a Wider Historicism

However, as I indicated earlier, the narrativist approach does not quite work as a model for the religious critic for one overriding reason: it concentrates so exclusively on human cultural history that it neglects natural history. Any American sense of the whole or any adequate American narrative or myth cannot be adequate if it neglects that breadth of history that includes natural history as well as human cultural history. Any religious myth will be tested, then, not only by reference to human cultures but also by reference to nature. Rightly, this gives naturalistic testimonies, especially scientific testimonies, a veto capable of overriding traditional Christian narratives and theologies that ignore nature, just as it gives those narratives and theologies a veto capable of overriding naturalistic testimonies that ignore human culture.

The protection of a distinctly scientific testimony is important even for a sociological philosopher of science such as Thomas Kuhn. Although he argues that science is guided by the interpretive, value-laden, personal bias of members of the scientific community, he acknowledges that for science "observation and experience can and must drastically restrict the range of admissible scientific belief."[16] Kuhn does not make science as much a construct of a group's linguistic imagination as George Lindbeck seems to do. While Kuhn makes science largely a social phenomenon, he is enough of a critical realist to give science the right to limit the interpretations human groups might make of nature. Supernaturalism, such as that advanced by Lindbeck, becomes not a casual matter, nor merely the acceptable extrapolation of a congenial world view.[17]

Although Lindbeck includes language about nature in his narrative world, he incapacitates science's distinctive veto by making religious testimonies about nature an instrument of the human community's narrative world—in his case, the narrative world of the Bible. He speaks of religion's narrative world as "all-encompassing," as extended "over the whole of reality," as "able to absorb the universe," even the so-called "extrascriptural realities."[18] This religious captivity of science's language allows Lindbeck in good conscience to advance what he calls a "prospective theory" of salvation, which appears to be a first-century, supernaturalistic theory of the termination of history (eschatology). Lindbeck knows that this will seem "mythological or unreal to those who think science or philosophy makes it impossible to affirm a temporally and objectively future eschaton."[19] He attempts to allay this concern through two arguments. First, he says, "mythological elements (in the technical, nonpejorative sense of 'myth') are indispensable in any religion"; this is undeniably true, if he means that any religion makes implicit or explicit claims about how the natural world works. Second, Lindbeck says that, in any case, "what is real or unreal is in large part socially constructed."[20] Again, this is also true; scientific language is, in large part, socially constructed. However, Lindbeck seems to allow this second point to give Christians license to dismiss the testimony of the sciences. He seems not to inquire about that part of the sciences that is not simply socially constructed; this, in turn, makes it possible for him to treat the astounding accomplishments of science as simply a function of interpretation. (Of course, neither can one give license to those who would take the converse approach, treating the narrative world of Christianity as simply socially constructed, with no remainder, and subject to dismissal by science.)

What is needed is to include scientific naturalism within a historicism wider than a humanistic historicism. Most generally stated, this third option, this wider historicism, this naturalistic-humanistic historicism, would include not only testimony about human history and its meaning but testimony about natural history and its meaning, thus replacing the old dualism of nature and history with a new monism that would make nature one form of history. Nature itself is a thoroughly historical state of affairs; it is not rigidly determined, but, as Charles Darwin has suggested, it is a chain of interpretations that organisms make of their organic environments and that environments make of organisms.[21] It is a chain of mutual interpretations that literally constructs nature as it is. And science itself is a chain of interpretations, constructed by scientists and applied to the chain of nature's interpretations. Thus, without being dualistic, it must be said that science is a distinct chain of historical interpretations that puts its own limits on language, even on the language of human communities. Testimony about natural history not only broadens the historical data but adds new limits to the ways in which cultural narratives of the whole can be formulated—calling into question, for example, the supernaturalistic claims so typical of human cultures.

This wider, more comprehensive, historicism would remain parochial, provincial, and, in its imaginative formulations, relative to a particular society because all testimony of a community, even of the scientific community, is, in that sense, relative rather than universal. This naturalistic historicism would not introduce a new objectivism. But a naturalistic-humanistic historicism would offer a more comprehensive content and method because it would include a more comprehensive range of testimonies and be open to stricter pragmatic tests than those provided by a humanistic historicism alone. It would provide the religious critic with a more adequate sense of the whole.

Finally, this third option (beyond cultural humanism and scientific naturalism), this wider historicism, is useful, not only because it informs a religious sense of the whole, but because it is consistent with at least one strand within the biblical tradition—that tradition from which the American public still derives much of its world view. The Hebrew Bible (the Christian "Old Testament"), on which the narrative theologian draws and by which the public is still shaped, includes a naturalistic dimensions. The American public includes nature in its picture of reality, it can be argued, partly because the culturally powerful scriptural writings have included this dimension.

Two leading biblical scholars, Gerhard von Rad and H. Paul Santmire, demonstrate that, while the Hebrew Bible is not naturalistic in the way Canaanitic religions were, it has a naturalistic dimension nevertheless. Von Rad acknowledges that it took Israel a very long time to connect the idea of creation (commentaries on natural events) with the salvation history of Israel (commentaries on human and cultural events). However, the authors of Isaiah (Is. 1–39) and Deutero-Isaiah (Is. 40–55) finally accomplished this when they argued for the derivation of God's "power over history from his authority as Creator." In other words, God's power over human history was derived from God's power over natural history. Equally, the Yahwist and the Priestly writers (authorial schools of the first five books of the Hebrew Bible) made creation itself a saving act, so that creation provided, von Rad says, "a different foundation" from that described in the earlier (and more specifically cultural) covenants of the Hebrews.[22] Additionally, for the Wisdom literature, "creation was in reality an absolute basis for faith, and was referred to for its own sake altogether."[23] For von Rad, "this wisdom, which we have understood as the primeval world order, as the mystery behind the creation of the world, rules in similar fashion in the non-human creation as well as in the sphere of human society."[24] Apropos those who would confine religion to human history, von Rad contends, "The dualism, familiar to us, of rules for human society on the one hand and rules for nature on the other, was unknown to the ancients."[25]

H. Paul Santmire advances a more deep-running biblical naturalism. He argues that even von Rad makes nature an adjunct to human salvation, so that his theology of nature is anthropocentric.[26] Advancing "an ecological hermeneutic," an ecological theory of interpretation, Santmire lays out an alternative reading of the Hebrew Bible, where the land itself plays a central role and in which, from creation to eschaton, God is also the lord of heaven and earth.[27] Even in the transformed future anticipated by the Apostle Paul, a "new earth" plays a central role. Santmire acknowledges that the metaphor of "spiritual ascent," where salvation involves the human spirit alone, has been predominant in the history of Christian theology and is upheld in the Gospel of John and the book of Hebrews. But he contends that the biblical metaphor of a "fecund earth," in which human salvation is connected to the fate of the earth, should be equally important.

Thus, nature is part of the biblical narrative. By omitting a naturalistic dimension, narrative theologians open themselves to questions about the biblical character of their ostensibly biblical narrative. If the biblical narrative includes in its sense of the whole the naturalistic understandings of its day, how is narrative theology's virtual omission of the naturalistic understandings of its day consistent with the biblical narrative?

Behind this question lies a larger point: if the American spiritual culture refers not only to human history but also to natural history—a point I elaborate in later chapters—then the religious critic who addresses that culture must do the same.

III. Conclusion

I argue, then, that the religious critic is like John Updike's artist: one who seeks to mediate between minds and worlds, thus to surpass the critic who would mediate only between minds.

The religious critic seeks a religious sense of the whole, a view of history in its totality, and thus a sufficient base for a spiritual culture. Religious critics will justify their commentaries by reference to natural history, as well as by reference to human history. Using a wider historicism, religious critics will honor the challenges that come from scientists. Unlike narrative theologians, they will be forced to come to grips with the challenges emanating from sociobiology, from environmental science, from paleontology, from psychology, from sociology. They will be equipped to pursue moral issues typically neglected by the humanist, such as eugenics, environmentalism, and population control. And with this wider historicism, religious critics will be able better to attack problems that most narrative theologians would surely want to attack, such as physiological claims to racial superiority or creationist claims to supernatural intervention in the natural process.

Nevertheless, to return to our first point, narrative theologians offer the religious critic a way to reach communities. They demonstrate that historical narratives and myths give form and meaning to the whole public community, even the public community that includes within itself a variety of subcultures. They demonstrate that the religion of the public community cannot be understood without plumbing its myths.

CHAPTER 5

RELIGIOUS NATURALISM AND
THE AVOIDANCE OF AMBIGUITY

What our intellect really aims at is neither variety nor
unity taken singly, but totality.

William James[1]

The religious critic's task is to extend the search for the
sacred to all of history, avoiding nothing. The religious critic's
temptation is to substitute the part for the whole, to identify the
sacred, for example, with the struggles of the individual, as William James did, or with human history, as the narrative theologians
do. But if the sacred is about the whole, then any substitution of
the part for the whole detracts from the religious critic's task. The
avoidance of community or the avoidance of nature inhibits the
religious critic's efforts to represent and reconstruct the whole
spiritual culture.

I turn to what may be the most American strand of religious
thought, that American religious naturalism that is a religious
empiricism. I ask how it might provide a philosophical or theological basis for the religious critic. Unlike the narrative theologians, these American religious naturalists do not avoid nature and
nature's history. They do not, in effect, protect the meaning of
human history by excluding natural history and the critique that
science might make of the meaning of human history. In fact,
American religious empiricists often give natural history a central
role in religious thought.

Nevertheless, in their own way the American religious empiricists substitute a part for a whole and choose "the better part"
at that. They identify the sacred with the unambiguously good

69

and treat the ambiguities of history as though the sacred does not relate to them. They protect religious meaning by basing it on something pure, on something beyond the ambiguities of history. Religiously stated, these American thinkers are willing to see the power of God affected by, even limited by, nature's powers, but they are unwilling to see the character of God affected by history's evils. In effect, just as James limited sacred history to the history of the individual and the narrative theologians limited sacred history to the history of human communities, these religious naturalists limit sacred history to the history of "the good." While for them the sacred may oppose evil and, in that way, visit the dark side of history, the sacred does not itself reside in the dark side of history. Thus, the empirical theologians, those distinctively naturalistic American religious thinkers, avoid ambiguity just as clearly as others have avoided community or nature. As a consequence they make their approach less than ideal for the religious critic who strives to avoid nothing, to work unflinchingly with a sense of the whole.

Doing this, they speak for an American tradition of thought—a tradition that can be illustrated by reference to American public intellectuals and American strains of thought.

Emerson, for example, may have abandoned the objectivity of European truths, but he did not abandon—at least not most of the time[2]—another objective ground of assurance. Americans, Emerson claimed, want "an original relation to the universe." Even though they have been told that "foregoing generations beheld God and nature face to face," the Americans were unwilling to twist their new world necks to see God through European eyes.[3] Emerson maintained that God was involved even in American history, and that this history should be central to American meanings. And yet, even in this locality, when the "Deep calls unto the deep," "the intellect searches out the absolute order of things as they stand in the mind of God, and without the colors of affection."[4] Thus, while God must be manifest in local history, God also must be manifest as absolute and, thereby, removed from the ambiguities and contingencies of local history.

American immigrants of every era were united in asking whether, within their new and brutish history, they could find a version of God that made particular sense to them. They tended to answer this question by locating their God, consciously or unconsciously, in their history, in the midst of their historical struggle. Whether echoing Emerson the historicist or participating in popular "nature religions,"[5] most Americans were inclined to speak from within the thickness of their history. That is, their God was an actor in their history, including their natural history, and they witnessed to God's presence there. Like the ancient Hebrews, they wandered in strange lands and through strange events; like the Hebrews, they had little choice but to find God in those lands and events. But while their God stood within history, it was not involved in all history. The Americans, like the Hebrews, eventually came to understand their God to be in some respect removed from (independent of) historical evils, particularly from the moral ambiguities of history.

This removal of the sacred from the contaminations of history is paralleled by a similar removal of the Americans themselves. While Americans have not understood themselves to be innocent of history's corruptions, they have seen themselves as God's New Israel, as an historic exception to (independent of) the common historical lot. Both the modern Americans and the ancient Hebrews (at least, some of the time) credited their God with exceptional justice and themselves with exceptional status among the world's peoples; even if they were sinners, they were also God's New Israel. Thus, for both communities, even though God could be found only within history, God's moral character is removed from that side of history that is corrupt; similarly, while these communities are conscious of their moral ambiguity, they are removed from the common lot of historical peoples by their exceptional relation with God. This is the American myth; even if it has been officially abandoned by most Americans today—certainly, by most American intellectuals—it retains much of its original power.

On one hand, historical process seemed pervasive, so that even God was its creature. Americans, jettisoned in a land that was strange and largely uncoupled from the institutions of their motherlands, had little choice but to find themselves and their God in their own historical wanderings. Accordingly, for them, God lived within the natural and cultural history of America. On the other hand, the character of God was uninvolved in (was independent of) the injustices of history. Their God, like nothing in history, was perfectly just. Congruently, the Americans had a special and unambiguous status in history, as God's new chosen people. They were uninvolved in (were independent of) the vagaries of ordinary human relations to God. On one hand, God's power was thoroughly located in history, and that power could be overwhelmed by history, making even human salvation vulnerable to historical powers. Even if others misread them as optimistic, most Americans felt almost naked in the destructive swirl of history and knew that not even their God was altogether clothed. On the other hand, despite this apparently tragic American perspective, the American lot was not quite tragic, for Americans were blessed with an exceptional status.[6]

By their special relation with God, Americans partook of God's unambiguous goodness; they could appeal to ideal possibilities, call them God's will, and proceed with a program that was appropriate to history but that morally transcended what was possible in history. In this respect, Reinhold Niebuhr was their perfect spokesperson, for he would include as a part of his political realism the notion that Christians must pursue "impossible possibilities." Niebuhr argued that it is appropriate to ask history to accomplish what history would inevitably fail to accomplish.[7]

Thus, this American outlook was close to history, even if it stopped short of total immersion in history. It moved God from beyond history to a particular position within history—just that position at which God's power is limited by history's power, while God's character is removed from history's moral and spiritual ambiguities.

This was a vision that grew out of a modern people's struggle with natural and human social forces. Adrift in America, pressed for survival, lacking the steadying pressure of old institutions and old traditions, the Americans were an uncommonly agnostic, a struggling, even a violent people. It made no sense to see history as controlled by an absolute God; there was no alternative but for them to wrest their own survival from the maw of history. But this picture was not merely grim. Something about God's old faithfulness was preserved: through historical reality, but from beyond historical reality, there shone a quality, even a perfection, that could be (or better, had to be) trusted.

Thus, the Americans were not only a violent but a morally

idealistic people—a condition that would seem to explain America's baffling wars in Vietnam and Iraq and its righteous yearning to own guns and to make fighting a spectator sport. Both idealistic and violent, they wanted history to deliver much and knew it could deliver little. This makes for such strange events as, say, the 1972 presidential contest, which pitted George McGovern, who punctuated utopian demands with irresponsibly harsh judgments, against Richard Nixon, who publicly and idealistically heralded America as "number one" and privately and realistically so distrusted Americans that he undermined just those open processes that gave America its best ground for legitimate pride. Nixon understood and embodied this American ambivalence more thoroughly than any recent president. In 1988 he could say that Americans believe that the real causes of global problems are misunderstandings between good and basically similar people, "that conflict is unnatural, . . . that permanent and perfect peace is a reachable goal." Then Nixon could remind these same Americans that "what moves the world for good or ill is power." "This is an immutable aspect of national character." That is, while he understood the strength and pervasiveness of American idealism, he could remind Americans of another side to their own experience and character. Speaking as a realist, he could tell them to "stop feeling guilty about power," "to get in the middle of it" and stop avoiding the frays that inevitably will be presented.[8]

Sacvan Bercovitch in *Rites of Assent* has described America's venerable succession of oppositional radicals who, on one hand, used transcendental standards to excoriate American morals and, on the other hand, hid their own heavy complicity in those very morals and usually forgot to ask what specific historical outcomes they were seeking to achieve.[9] Sidney Hook's *Out of Step* is a long, angry, autobiographical narrative of just such hypocrisies, running from the 1930s to the 1980s; it features, as it happens, academic intellectuals who wanted to be, and in many respects were, public intellectuals.[10] There is evidence, I am suggesting, for that halfway historicism that hobbles just those American intellectuals who would be religious critics. By removing their God and themselves as moral beings from the full corruptions of history, this halfway historicism keeps them from regarding the sense of the historical whole.

II. American Religious Empiricism

The twentieth-century writings of empirical theologians or philosophers of religion begin with Douglas Clyde Macintosh's 1919 *Theology as an Empirical Science,* extend through works by Henry Nelson Wieman, Bernard Meland, and Bernard Loomer, and continue today. These writings are traceable not only to the philosophies of William James, Alfred North Whitehead, and John Dewey but to the essays of Ralph Waldo Emerson, even to the theology of Jonathan Edwards.[11] I focus here on James, Macintosh, Wieman, Meland, and Loomer, describing how their God is found in everything historical . . . everything, I should say, but the ambiguities of history.

When he discussed God, James was involved in an ambivalence more stark than the ambivalence of the empirical theologians.[12] Before writing on God in *The Varieties of Religious Experience,* James had already declared himself a historicist. With the clarity of a convert, James went well beyond his American predecessors in insisting that everything is historical. He amplified his historicism by an empiricism for which everything is known through and tested by historical experience and for which experience refers to values as well as facts. He set forth a world that is historical: plural rather than singular, changing rather than static, and composed of accidents and the innovations of individuals rather than of necessary forces. He developed an evolutionary naturalism in which unpredictable variations make the biological world just as historical as the cultural world is historical. James was a relativist, emphasizing local knowledge and distrusting universal claims. He was America's first almost-thorough-historicist, and he stated his historicism with unequalled vividness.

Yet around the turn of the century he pulled his historicist punch and introduced a history-violating "piecemeal supernaturalism." Uncharacteristically, James stood against the American effort to tie religion to wilderness, science, and the natural world. In the "Conclusion" and "Postscript" of *The Varieties of Religious Experience,* James was confronted with two popular options, neither acceptable: (1) if he accepted a material world determined by mechanical necessity, God could not exist, let alone act in history; (2) if he accepted dualistic "refined supernaturalism," God could exist and be good but would be confined to the world of spirit and, again, not be involved in nature and its history. But James wanted a "real hypothesis" in which God could act in history. Accordingly, he declared himself a "piecemeal supernaturalist." James allowed God occasionally to act in history, if that meant that God's character could be kept as good as the refined supernaturalists had wanted it to be.

Why, in this way, would James, in both senses, finish off his most influential book? First, he had deftly opposed the idealistic and mechanistic reductions of history and had adroitly practiced his own historicism; then, anomalously, he had introduced a piecemeal supernaturalism. On one hand, he was an original promulgator of philosophical historicism; on the other hand, he subscribed to a crude violation of natural history. I suggest that James permitted this contradiction in order to preserve, in his own pragmatic way, the goodness of God. James appreciated the goodness of God preserved in refined supernaturalism, but he did not appreciate the historical ineffectuality of refined supernaturalism's God. If God's goodness was to be effective and pragmatically meaningful, then God had to act in history, and piecemeal supernaturalism appeared to be the price James had to pay. There was no way for God to achieve good effects, except through miracles that defied both mechanistic materialism and refined supernaturalism. James's great book concluded ambivalently: on the whole, God would work through the natural psychological processes, empirically observed (this is the main burden of the *Varieties*); but when God's goodness was at stake, God would have to act with uniform goodness, even if this meant God would violate natural processes.

A similar ambivalence can be found in the concept of God developed by the empirical theologians. They merely extended in new ways, I argue, the historicist approach already implicit in American religious thought. They insisted that God act in history and be known through history, natural as well as cultural history; nevertheless, they set a limit to the historicizing process and removed God from part of history. They contended that God has a character that is everywhere the same and that is perfect in the way that only something removed from (independent of) the full ambiguities of history can be perfect. That is, God simply is not fully present in the dark side of history, and this leaves the goodness of God uncompromised.[13]

On the one hand, the empirical religious thinkers confined God's power to what is historically possible, rejecting that classical, God-world dualism according to which God's extrahistorical grounding made possible the violation of the laws and limits of history. These classical theological traditions, the empirical theologians claimed, entered Western religious thought out of a largely mistaken loyalty to ancient Greek dualism and were developed in modern European philosophies that revived that dualism. The empirical theologians affirmed the interdependence of matter and spirit, nature and culture. God could be found in both science and literature. They saw God as historical in the sense that God's power worked entirely within the limits of ordinary historical process—although, like James, Macintosh did hold that God could and would do virtually anything to save deserving people, even if that meant miracles.

On the other hand, the empirical religious thinkers repeatedly argued that the value realized in history could not be explained by reference to ordinary historical forces alone. History is marked, or vectored; it bears the stamp of something; it is valuable in ways that cannot be explained except through postulating the influence of something perfect on the course of history. Although the empirical theologians grimly acknowledged the inescapable moral ambiguities of history, they claimed that history, nevertheless, suggests something beyond ambiguity. Thus, even if history does not conform to a power beyond history, that does not mean it moves in no direction at all. History is influenced by a perfection within the imperfections of history, a perfection with which people might cooperate to make history better than it otherwise would be.

The empirical theologians amplified this claim about history by using language about God. God is a creativity within history that encourages history, as much as anything finite might encourage history, to become qualitatively better than it otherwise would be. God is the inexplicable vector in history, coaxing it to greater value. God is absolutely good, so that God's moral guidance is absolutely good (relative to nothing evil) and, thus, always should be honored and served. Admittedly, for Loomer, God is not absolutely good, as I will note in Chapter 8. However, Loomer reserved for God an absolute character of another sort: God is absolutely beautiful, even if not absolutely good; God has apparently absolute aesthetic stature, even if not an absolute moral stature. The absoluteness of God's character is preserved by the empirical theologians in the only way possible: by making God's character independent of, and thus not truly interactive with, the dark or ambiguous side of history. Thus—even if God does not, because God cannot, control history—God is a perfectly moral or aesthetic persuasion operative within history but, in one sense, removed from the whole of history.

In associating God with history's moral or aesthetic advance, the empirical theologians, as well as William James, remain fundamentally consistent with Hebrew and Christian scriptures and, in that respect, consistent with the American culture still influenced by those scriptures. Typically, the Hebrew scriptures see God as the central but not overriding determinant in the history of Israel's spiritual, political, and military life and see the nation as religious to the extent that it reacts to history as if it were guided by God. Equally, the Christian scriptures see God as the central but not overriding determinant in the history played out in the life of Jesus and in the history preceding, surrounding, and succeeding Jesus; and one is religious in a Christian way to the extent that one sees God acting in the life and history flowing to, through, and from Jesus.

Nevertheless, the American religious empiricists' ambivalence about God's relation to history makes them mixed guides for the religious critic. First, when the American religious empiricists adopt a postdualistic world—one that includes natural history and science as well as cultural history and the arts and humanities—they adopt a wider history, and their God operates within natural as well as cultural history (including the history of doctrine and the church). They deal with just that wider history that would provide religious grounds for an American religious critic. Second, when the empirical religious thinkers protect God's character from the contaminations of history, they partially dissociate God from the dark side of history and thus from the whole history to which the religious critic would speak. If public action occurs in history, and if American religious empiricism places the locus of religious value beyond the problematic side of history, how is the religious critic to use that value to address the whole history?

The empiricists' veneration of a nonhistorical structure of divine goodness ill-serves the intellectual who wants to be plausible to a late-twentieth-century poststructuralist world. In aiming to discover God's absolute, perfect, and uniform character as it operates throughout all history, American religious empiricists conform to the modern, not the poststructuralist, spirit. They aim to discover the structure of God's will as it already operates in all history; they seek to work out human meaning by reference to the givenness of that will; and they ask people to conform to that will. Here the religious imagination can only discover and never construct; it has no fundamentally creative power or cash value. The religious imagination becomes only a fixture in what William James calls a mere game of private theatricals. What people do cannot alter values; it can only play out the already implicit, eternal and perfect values. People are useful only to the extent that they copy the absolute good already fixed in history.

This structuralism of the American religious empiricists bears little relation to the recent canard that how we know affects what we know. American religious empiricists exclude the possibility that people can have any effect on the character of "the Deep" underlying history's tragically ambiguous course. Ironically, at this point empirical theologians follow classical Christian theologians: where the character of God is concerned, American religious empiricists affirm the classical aseity (independence of being) of God. The character of God is relative to nothing. To put it another way, American religious empiricists accept rather completely what the poststructuralists call the modern "myth of the given."[14] God's moral purposes are there for discovery but not for creative interpretation, if creative interpretation means that the interpretation alters the identity of the interpreted.

I am suggesting that religious critics who would work within the poststructuralist intellectual environment will not receive all the help they need from this side of American religious thought. They will rightly suspect that ongoing historical atrocities suggest that the deepest (the divine) character of history is morally ambiguous after all, and that any mature philosophy of religion will recognize that. This will mean that any responsible religious critic will not passively worship the moral "perfection" of God but will seek to alter history's deepest and imperfect character through reinterpretation. But more of this later.

III. James's Theological Historicism

There is, I have argued, a deep American ambivalence about history, and this shapes American thought about the sacred. First, Americans, through most of their history, have tended to see themselves as, in one respect, removed from, independent of, the common lot of humanity. They have understood themselves as a people distinguished from other historical peoples by a special divine blessing, a blessing that made them exceptionally valuable. Second, Americans have thrown themselves completely into history, seeing themselves as a people who had historically to invent themselves because their cultural landscape was too barren to give them a cultural location, and they were too isolated to sustain the heritages of their lands of origin. They were historicist in contriving their history through their historical imaginations and then locating their God within this contrivance. William James's willingness to invest God with supernatural powers and thereby to place God beyond the workings of natural history reflects the first of the above tendencies; and the perfect divine character reflects the same tendency for the empirical theologians. And James's and the empirical theologians' pragmatic naturalism represents the second of these tendencies.

I am suggesting that a more consistent historicism would offer a better model for the religious critic. A historicism trimmed when the seas get high, a historicism that invites people, just when historical responsibility is most needed, to look for outside help, cries out for revision—a revision that would make for greater consistency and for the greater personal responsibility that would accompany that consistency. It calls for a historicism in which not only powers but values are functions of historical decisions, in which not only the sacred capacities to effect quantitative change but the sacred capacities to effect qualitative change are worked out in history. Admittedly, it is logically possible to go the other way—that is, to drop historicism altogether in the hope that supernatural causes determine everything. But James, as well as the empirical theologians, likely would have seen this as the wrong move, even the wrong religious move, because it would mean falling into the attitude of the prodigal son, according to which we can abandon responsibility, fall on our father's neck, and melt as a drop of water into the sea.[15]

The question remains, How can such a thorough historicism, in which all is subject to historical determination, be religious? Uncannily, James anticipated an answer.

Over the years 1889 to 1900, James had delivered in Edinburgh the lectures that led to *The Varieties of Religious Experience;* in the spring of 1908, James delivered another set of lectures to another British audience, this time at Oxford. In the later lectures, which would lead to *A Pluralistic Universe,* James abandoned the earlier heroic stance, where he taunted European idealists and iconoclastically defied the new mechanistic science by suggesting supernatural rescue. In the intervening years he had become the sensitive, aging, terminally ill American seeking a God answerable to the desire for sympathy and intimacy, even if not to the desire for religious rescue. He had read Bergson's 1905 *Creative Evolution* and gravitated to Bergson's world, not one made of atomic pieces, subject to piecemeal analysis, but a world in the making, modeled organically rather than atomistically.[16]

James's concern in 1908 was to correct, not the idealists' refined supernaturalism, but their sense of history and what that implied about God. The problem, James now saw, was that his idealistic audience "confined itself too exclusively to thin logical considerations,"[17] thereby ignoring the thick complications of particular histories and the ways in which God might be involved in those histories. The idealists proposed a God who is absolute and who, as absolute, is the keystone in the grand monistic arch spanning all time and space. Everything that will happen in history already has been comprehended by and included in this God, so God is beyond historical limitation and historical suffering. The idealists' God "escapes from having an environment,"[18] with the consequence that it escapes not only environment but history (life affected, in part, by environment). Most importantly, God escapes us, who, incorrigibly, are historical beings. In *A Pluralistic Universe* James says that idealism pictures "the deepest reality of the world as static and without a history, it loosens the world's hold upon our sympathies and leaves the soul of it foreign."[19] In other words,

> *As* absolute, then, or *sub specie eternitatis,* or *quatenus infinitus est,* the world repels our sympathy because it has no histo-ry. . . . What boots it to tell me that the absolute way is the true way, and to exhort me, as Emerson says, to lift mine eye up to its style, and manners of the sky, if the feat is impossible by definition? I am finite once for all, and all the categories of my sympathy are knit up with the finite world as *such,* and with things that have a history.[20]

James went on to replace this absolute God of a hierarchical world with a finite God of a pluralistic world. A finite God cannot escape the limits of natural history or act supernaturally, not even in a piecemeal way. To state it more theologically, in *A Pluralistic Universe* James defends a pluralistic pantheism, a notion prob-ably to some extent dependent on his obscure ally, Benjamin Paul Blood.[21] James abandoned the earlier dualistic, monarchical the-ism of the "Conclusions" and "Postscript" of *The Varieties.*[22]

James now saw himself defending the popular Christianity of his day, not by supporting supernaturalism, but by sticking with history. Popular Christianity, James argues, has long re-jected monarchical theism and the absoluteness of God and found God "an essentially finite being *in* the cosmos, not with the cosmos in him, and indeed he has a very local habitation there, and very one-sided local and personal attachments" to David, Isaiah, or Jesus.[23] Here God may be finite but now is able to pertain to the whole without violating the meaning of the whole—something superhuman but not supernatural.

Here God conforms to the historicist idea "that *nothing* real escapes from having an environment" or that "nothing in the universe is great or static or eternal enough not to have some history."[24] Now, reversing himself, James harshly described the theistic God as

> not heart of our heart and reason of our reason, but our mag-istrate; and mechanically to obey his commands, however strange they may be, remains out only moral duty. . . . [T]he most we can do is to acknowledge it passively and adhere to it, altho such adhesion as ours can make no jot of difference to what is adhered to[25]

James's God now lives entirely in history and out of historical resources. It is not a God whose moral commands we are helpless to affect. Instead, it is a God whose *very moral commands* depend, apparently, on our interpretations and on how we choose to act. James's discovery (if it can be called that, rather than an outright invention) is that one can be religious without leaving history. One can be religious even while including the sacred in all aspects of history and one's identity in all aspects of history.

In effect, James contended that a true historical sensibility was a sense of the whole, that God represents an ultimacy entirely within history and referring to all aspects of history.[26] Yet even James did not move on to ask whether the immersion of God in history required that even God's character, evident in God's commands, is contaminated by the ambiguities of history. He did not directly say that all our interpretations, good or evil, and all our actions, right or wrong, also affect God's commands—although that would seem to follow. He did not say how the dark side of history has its role in shaping God's moral commands. Nor did he say how people are to survive religiously when their values no longer rest in something pure.

Answers to these questions bear on the religious critic who would operate out of a sense of the whole. They suggest a magnitude of responsibility not typically envisioned: societies must take responsibility, not only for fulfilling their deepest, sacred mandates, but for constructing them.

CHAPTER 6

THE RELIGIOUS THINKER
AND THE ACCEPTANCE OF HISTORY

We are, as it were, introduced into a world beyond this world which is nevertheless the deeper reality of the world in which we live in our ordinary experiences.

John Dewey[1]

Like William James, the religious critic will accept that "I am finite once for all, and all the categories of my sympathy are knit up with the finite world as *such,* and with things that have a history."[2] Religious sympathies cannot be knit up with the finite world as such unless the sacred pertains to everything—not everything but the community, not everything but nature, not everything but ambiguity, but everything. The religious critic attempting to ascertain a sense of the whole in society will be inclined to avoid nothing, not even the ambiguity of the sacred. That is, the religious critic will find history sufficient.

This suggests an historicist pantheism (or, to use William James's and, recently, Nancy Frankenberry's term, a "pluralistic pantheism").[3] I use the word pantheism not to identify God with the world, which would be to make "God" a meaningless term, better replaced by the word *world*. I use *pantheism* to indicate that ultimate meanings refer to everything in history, to indicate that from whatever is ultimate no historical things can be excluded. If, as was suggested at the close of the last chapter, a historicist pantheism requires that God be morally or aesthetically ambiguous, that may be the price paid for a concept of the sacred that a religious critic can use in the public world. As James

83

appropriately asked nearly a century ago, What is the point of having a God that cannot be used?

In this and the following two chapters I ask how the sacred can be understood so that it refers to the whole of history. Initially in this chapter, I discuss two religious critics, Cornel West and Gordon Kaufman, who have related the sacred to the whole of history in a more or less poststructuralist way. West is notable for relating the sacred to social crisis, while Gordon Kaufman is recently notable for relating the sacred to nature. Each refuses to exclude certain dimensions of history from involvement with the sacred; equally, each has a notion of the sacred that deliberately avoids nothing in history. Their work is innovative partly because they adopt poststructuralist modes of religious thought, West doing this as a neopragmatist and Kaufman doing this as an evolving Kantian. Both abandon the structuralism that would describe universal, eternal, ahistorical structures and tie God to those structures. While in these respects each is a poststructuralist, neither has accepted a poststructuralist skepticism about moral and religious language. Each is, in certain respects, a realist (believing that religious language refers to conditions external to the knower), although neither is a foundationalist or an objectivist. For each, religious terms refer to something resident in but not "given" to history. Neither relies on argument, and yet neither is a fideist, willing to stop inquiry when approaching the door of faith. Each entertains mystery but rejects supernaturalism. Each has innovatively redefined the sacred so that it fits a new intellectual climate and, in the process, has developed a notion of the sacred that applies to all aspects of history. In a word, each is an historicist, recognizing the sheerly historical origin of everything and yet refusing to honor historical precedent because it is precedent.

I conclude this chapter by asking whether historicists like West and Kaufman, who heavily deemphasize questions of how we know (epistemology), may leave their approach open to abuse. Without revelations from beyond history, relying so heavily on sheer imagination as a source for the meaning of the sacred, such a historicism can entertain virtually any characterization of the sacred. I ask whether guidelines for knowledge of the sacred might be provided, not by supernatural revelations, but by a specific "sense" (in this instance, an awareness rather than a meaning) of the whole.

I. Cornel West and the Social Dimension of History

West has followed John Dewey in relating religious thought to social problems. Although Chicago School theologians, with their sociohistorical method,[4] described the social origins and functions of religious beliefs with more sophistication than Dewey, it was Dewey's comments that made the greater social impact. In his 1934 *A Common Faith,* Dewey described how the religious is rooted in the social imagination and how it functions to relate a people's ideals to its social practices. And Dewey was always conscious of how American society gives a local meaning to the religious. In *The American Evasion of Philosophy,* West has translated some of Dewey's methods to fit the poststructuralist intellectual and social context; and in his social and political writings, West has begun to develop a kind of poststructural Deweyan public philosophy,[5] particularly with the publication of the well and widely received *Race Matters.* While West may criticize Dewey's social program for the ease with which it adopts "the flavor of small-scale, homogeneous communities,"[6] he shares Dewey's desire for a religiously based public philosophy that would reconstitute the society.

For both West and Dewey the intriguing social unit is the nation, and the nation to which most attention is given is America. Unlike exceptionalist thinkers, Dewey and West do not gravitate toward any simple concept of America; they accept the diversity of plural, relative, and pragmatic American worlds. Nevertheless, they entertain and develop a vision of how the relativities and pluralities might be united in some new and unifying national way. Theirs is a socially based, not a metaphysically based, unity.[7] While West shares the poststructuralist animus against premodern metaphysics and modernist structuralism, he is not so possessed by that animus that he interdicts all talk about unity. He believes that a vision of social unity is required if the new opposition to absolutes is not to devolve into historically detached, methodological talk with no public significance.

West, an African American, argues that even questions of race must be considered in a national context. He chooses to "speak a moral language that transcends race," to see the issue of race in the context of all forms of bigotry, and to see bigotry in the context of the "common good" of all Americans. "From this view," he says, "racism is not simply a moral failure of individuals, but, more important, a national dilemma that once again threatens the future of our grand, though flawed, democratic experiment begun in 1776."[8] His reputation as a champion of African Americans notwithstanding, West still seems to subscribe to Dewey's notion of a "state consciousness": "the idea that the state life, the vitality of the social whole, is of more importance than the flourishing of any segment or class." He would support Dewey's belief in "the necessity of maintaining the integrity of the state as against all divisive ecclesiastical divisions"—if it is remembered that here "state" refers, not primarily to a political or economic reality, but to a historical and cultural reality.[9]

West sees the failure to appreciate the national whole as, in part, an intellectual problem, one that religious thinkers must address if they are to be what I am calling religious critics:

> Rarely have Americans seriously probed into their own circumstances in order to meet new theological challenges—with the glaring counter-examples of Edwards, Channing, Emerson, Dickinson, Bushnell, Rauschenbusch, and the Niebuhrs exemplifying this rarity.
>
> Instead, Americans have tended to rely on European sources, especially German ones. Yet after Hitler, concentration camps, and national partition, German theology has had little energy to confront the problems of race, gender, and war. Encapsulated French Catholic thought and mutilated British theologies have provided few guides. In short, the European well has run dry, leaving most American theologians holding an empty pail—hence easily seduced by the mirages of a golden past and a revolutionary future.[10]

The emphasis here on national identity, I repeat, is not patriotic in any exceptionalist or triumphal sense. Rather, it responds to the quite unglorious fact that there is no community-neutral way of understanding anything; all theory must be communally and historically grounded. Therefore, any significant philosophy, including public philosophy, must be explicitly and critically involved in the history from which it inevitably issues. This is not simply an American point; it applies to philosophers everywhere.[11]

West couches the same message in his plea for what Antonio Gramsci calls "organic intellectuals," as distinguished from "traditional intellectuals." West explains Gramsci's two intellectuals this way:

> To put it crudely, the former are those who, because they are organically linked to prophetic movements or priestly institutions, take the life of the mind seriously enough to relate ideas to the everyday life of ordinary folk. Traditional intellectuals, in contrast, are those who revel in the world of ideas while nesting in comfortable places far removed from the realities of the common life. Organic intellectuals are activistic and engaged; traditional intellectuals are academic and detached.[12]

West recognizes that organic intellectuals and the public to which they speak are afflicted with a pessimism, even a nihilism. West and his poststructuralist intellectual colleagues are denied the assurances that may have still worked at a subconscious level for John Dewey, who began study as a neo-Hegelian. Unlike Dewey, West arrived at college "primarily motivated by the radical historical *conditionedness* of human existence."[13] He was vulnerable to the full implications of Friedrich Nietzsche's nihilism, particularly as it was developed by post–World War II philosophers. Early in his career West set forth the negative Nietzschean heritage as it is elaborated by American philosophers: (1) antirealism in ontology, as propounded by W. V. Quine, Nelson Goodman, Richard Rorty, and Thomas Kuhn; (2) the abandonment of the Myth of the Given in epistemology, as propounded by Wilfrid Sellars and Rorty; and (3) the dismissal of the transcendent mind as a sphere of inquiry, as propounded by Quine and Sellars. West argues, however, that Nietzsche believed that such moves lead to "a paralyzing nihilism and ironic skepticism" unless they are augmented by some new world view or countermovement.[14] West's thesis is that "postmodern American philosophy has not provided such a 'countermovement.'" Instead, it has offered "updated versions of scientism" as found in Quine and Sellars, "an aristocratic resurrection of pluralistic stylism" as found in Goodman, "a glib ideology of professionalism" as found in Kuhn, and "a nostalgic appeal to enlightened conversation" as found in Rorty. Apocalyptically, West concludes that postmodern American philosophy has become "a dead, impotent rhetoric of a declining and decaying civilization."[15] It is fair to say that earlier public intellectuals, including Dewey, had not anticipated the destructive implications of relativism, pluralism, and pragmatism, all later witnessed by poststructuralists. Yet, the poststructuralists lacked Dewey's own capacity to build a countermovement. These new circumstances, West appreciates, have compounded all efforts to persuade a public that there are grounds for common action.

A similar nihilism undermines the poor, particularly the poor African Americans, West argues. While their plight flows both from the systemic failure of American economics and politics much discussed by liberals and from the lack of private responsibility much discussed by conservatives, their plight should be seen also as a cultural problem, particularly as a breakdown of families, schools, churches, synagogues, mosques, and media. But more important, and not unrelated to the cultural problem, is the personal breakdown that follows the social breakdown and that threatens the very existence of black Americans, a breakdown that West describes in dramatic terms: "the murky waters of despair and dread that now flood the streets of black America," "the monumental eclipse of hope, the unprecedented collapse of meaning, the incredible disregard for human . . . life and property in much of black America," "the profound sense of psychological depression, personal worthlessness, and social despair so widespread in black America."[16] Of course, African American youth do not worry about how recent philosophy has undermined "rational grounds for legitimate standards or authority." Rather, their nihilism is a problem of "lived experience," properly addressed by a "politics of conversion."[17] Because it is lived, rather than technical and philosophical, does not mean that it is a problem the religious critic cannot address at the level of theory—for example, urging African Americans to rise above what West calls commodification and hedonism.

West's religious criticism, in short, underlies his social and cultural criticism. The despair and nihilism to which he points are rooted in the absence of a felt sense of ultimate meaning. His analysis here is guided by what he calls the prophetic pragmatism of the Christian tradition. This tradition is pragmatically true for him in two ways. First, it meets his personal need for a countervailing optimism. "On the existential level," West explains, "the self-understanding and self-identity that flow from this tradition's insights into the crises and traumas of life are indispensable *for me* to remain sane."[18] West contends that his "own left Christianity" is "in part a response to those dimensions of life that have been flattened out, to the surfacelike character of a postmodern culture that refuses to speak to issues of despair, that refuses to speak to issues of the absurd." By comparison, he finds "Christian narratives and stories *empowering and enabling*."[19] Second and at an instrumental level, this tradition allows him, as no mere cognitive approach can, to understand the poor. West contends that, although it is not necessary to be religious to understand the poor, "if one is religious, one has wider access into their life-worlds."[20] In fact, says West, "the severing of ties to churches, synagogues, temples, and mosques by the left intelligentsia is tantamount to political suicide; it turns the pessimism of many self-deprecating and self-pitying secular progressive intellectuals into a self-fulfilling prophecy."[21]

Thus, for West, a Christian philosophy of religion can be useful, though not any Christian philosophy of religion. Academic theologians who "nested in Barthian cocoons or emulated logical positivists and linguistic analysts" simply missed the importance of history.[22] Liberation theologians, such as Gustavo Guitierrez, Mary Daly, and James Cone may be "politically engaged and culturally enlightening" and understand history, but they are "lacking in serious philosophical substance."[23] In the early works of Daly, "neo-Thomist metaphysics loomed too large," and in Cone's writings, "Barthian Christocentrism was too thick." These philosophical inadequacies, West suggests, have been demonstrated by Schubert Ogden and John Cobb, Jr. An adequate philosophy of religion should deny both transcendental objectivism and subjectivistic nihilism and affirm a concrete, local, emotionally laden, "thick" historicism and moral sensitivity, especially the capacity to see the world through the eyes of victims.

Yet, the question remains: Can West's personal, existential approach to black prophetic Christianity, coupled with a pragmatic reaction to nihilism, provide a sufficient basis for a religious critic? Certainly, West—along with Richard Bernstein, Frank Lentricchia, Jeffrey Stout, and many others—makes an important move toward a neopragmatic public philosophy. This is a public philosophy that rises from a historical tradition rather than an extrahistorical presence; it is evaluated by its social consequences rather than by its correspondence to a foundational reality; it is invulnerable to postmodern strictures against foundationalism and epistemology. West's religious version of this philosophy may be unique, for neither Bernstein, Lentricchia, nor Stout see in religion a viable base for public affirmation.[24] Yet West's religious commentary pertains directly only to the individual person and to the human community. It does not develop a distinct concept of the sacred (although he does protect the mystery of the sacred) or a religious naturalism or a religious epistemology. Here West departs from Dewey, who ventured a concept of the sacred, an American religious naturalism, and an "immediate empiricism" that gave to religious knowledge an (albeit weak) empirical referent. While Dewey's "religious meaning of democracy" is about the democracy of all living things, West's is about the democracy of humans. West does not discuss how the sacred might be experienced—this despite the fact that an affective, noncognitive epistemology was crucial to the classical pragmatism out of which West's own work springs.

I say this only to indicate how not even West has laid complete grounds for the religious critic—nor should that be demanded, since he has never (at least not to my knowledge) claimed to write constructive religious theory.

II. Gordon Kaufman and the Natural Dimension of History

Gordon Kaufman's recent enlargement of his concept of the sacred can be appreciated only after recognizing that it comes after a career-long odyssey that at times seemed headed in another direction. He began in 1960 with a healthy Kantian distrust of theological claims to objective and universal knowledge; he put God behind a veil mostly impenetrable by human ways of knowing; and he coupled that with a neo-orthodox trust that the God revealed in the Christian Bible is sufficient if reinterpreted to fit our ways of knowing.[25] With this Kantian skepticism, he could be sympathetic to and not overwhelmed by the new forms of relativism and pluralism he was to encounter in the following decades. That is, he was better able to agree that knowledge is relative to history and that it varies from history to history, and to do that without undergoing the nihilistic shock felt by those who approached postmodern literature still hoping for objective truth.

Then, as his trust in neo-orthodox notions of revelation began to dim, he gave new emphasis to how history shapes religious thought. Now it became clear that people not only reinterpret but reconstruct their God to fit their history. He replaced the neo-orthodox test of revelation with a pragmatic test of truth.[26] Thus, in his 1981 *The Theological Imagination*, Kaufman describes theology as "essentially a constructive work of the human imagination"; in fact, Kaufman says, "our awareness and understanding here [with regard to the reality of God] is gained entirely in and through the images and concepts themselves, constructed into and focused by the mind into a center for the self's devotion and service."[27] And in *Theology for a Nuclear Age* he talks of "Christian theology as imaginative construction."[28] Now, for him, revelation not only begs the question but illicitly imposes the conclusions of an earlier history on a later history (much as John Dewey thought "religion"—as opposed to the "religious"—was the imposition of an earlier people's adjustment to its environment on a later people's new task of adjustment). Given his Kantian skepticism, the importance of imagination, and the pragmatic test, any claim to direct knowledge of God appeared to Kaufman to be unnecessary, even presumptuous.

At the same time, the inescapably physical effects of war (especially, possible nuclear war) and attacks on the environment caused Kaufman to argue that moral questions about nature must have a role in religious thought. Here he departed from the Kantian tendency to separate cleanly nature from spirit. He began adroitly to introduce an American, post-Lockean naturalism into his theological work, particularly into his concept of God. He placed himself partly in line with the naturalist tradition of American religious empiricism, without abandoning the epistemological skepticism derived from the Kantian tradition. God became not just a source of human value, but "a cosmic movement"[29] or a "hidden creativity"[30] in nature as well as in human subjectivity. Not only was Kaufman now able to protest on religious grounds the twentieth century's two greatest threats to nature (nuclear war and environmental devastation), he also provided religious grounds for religious critics to speak on naturalistic issues.

Kaufman's evolving position, most definitely set forth in *In Face of Mystery*,[31] represents an enormous contribution to the balance, sensitivity, and public relevance of American religious thought. Specifically, it develops a poststructuralist, constructivist, historicist, and realist concept of God, and relates God to the whole of history, including natural history. This provides theological grounds for the sense of the whole that would inform the religious critic. Nevertheless, it leaves the religious critic with an unanswered question about epistemology, a question that is practically important.

III. The Experience of the Whole of History

It is not as though any value-laden sense of the whole is acceptable, for—as both Cornel West and Gordon Kaufman recognize—there are value-laden meanings of the whole that are finally deficient. It is not as though, for example, a Hitler or a Stalin entirely lacks some sort of sense of the whole; they hoped, after all, to advance a rather comprehensive interpretation of history. Thus, the sense of the whole must be critically evaluated. In the American religious context I am exploring, that critical evaluation is pragmatic, assessing an idea for whether and how it works in society. However, as John Dewey and William James recognized, an idea is more likely to prove pragmatically acceptable if some consideration is given to *how* the idea is known. Apart from such an epistemological consideration, there is no clear way to distinguish in advance those few propitious estimates of the whole that might be advanced from those hundreds that are sheer accidents, mere projections of wishes, or simply self-interested objectives.

This is a problem John Locke discussed 300 years ago. Locke's 1690 *An Essay Concerning Human Understanding* was written not primarily to locate universal criteria or universal starting points, as some have claimed of the British Enlightenment.[32] It was written primarily to warn against undue reliance on subjective knowledge. The apparent moral objective of the *Essay* is to induce "the busy mind of man" to "stop when it is at the utmost extent of its tether,"[33] to encourage people to be skeptical of belief (which is only possibly true) or enthusiasm ("a warmed or overweening brain"). Locke advised the reader that ideas should be logically related to each other and that they should agree with *"actual real existence."*[34] It is through such scrutinized ideas that people can "communicate with a greater, and in others with a less, number of particular beings."[35] Here, said Alfred North Whitehead, is Locke's "new doctrine of ideas."[36] The total neglect of the origin of ideas, Locke insisted, left them too much to the isolated subject. Nevertheless, Locke acknowledged that even an effort to ground an idea in knowledge yields only a "tacit proposition" about the world.[37]

For the religious critic, John Locke's question was: What keeps enthusiasm or bias alone from selecting those ideas that would provide one with a sense (meaning) of the whole? His answer was to propose that one pay attention to reports of the five senses. The American radical empiricists of the twentieth century amplified Locke's suggestion by arguing that one should pay attention not only to sensuous perception but also to non-sensuous perception, particularly to the nonsensuous perception of the whole.

People do have a vague and largely nonsensuous intimation of the meaning of, say, a national community—analogous to their perception of the distinct meaning of a marriage, a family, an orchestra, or a classroom of students. Somehow they are able to deal with more than particular sensuous phenomena; and they are able to deal with totalities that are more than the quantitative sum of separate entities and their mutual relations. Sometimes they can legitimately claim that their idea of the "whole" is based on some awareness of the whole, that it is not a blind construct produced by the private imagination. Naturally, there is good reason to be skeptical of any and all intuitions, adumbrations, and feelings for wholes, but skepticism can be overblown. It is possible that new attention to an empirical sense (awareness) of the whole may foster a better sense (meaning) of the whole.

Admittedly, the claim to have an empirical sense of the whole cannot determine whether the meaning of the whole that issues from it is true. One cannot prove the truth of an idea by tracing how it came to be known.[38] However, that does not close the issue. Awareness may not necessarily by worth nothing. At least this was the belief of the founders of pragmatism, particularly James and Dewey, who concluded that it simply was not pragmatic to rely on pragmatics to the exclusion of epistemology. They knew that the effectiveness of an idea is not unrelated to how the idea came to be known. Today it seems clear—current fashions notwithstanding—that, for example, how politicians know the world (cynically, naively, with bias?) suggests how they will act in the future. Why else would we ask for the politician's life story? It seems clear that, given their experience, female and minority leaders are probably more capable of writing discrimination policy than white males are. Equally, affirmative action policy assumes that an employer's knowledge of a wide applicant pool is likely to influence his or her hiring decision. And which rap you get for murder depends on whether it was premeditated. And educated guesses are taken more seriously than lucky guesses.

Knowledge of the source of an idea has something to do with whether an idea is likely to be pragmatically true. Drop all considerations of the sources of an idea, and one functions like a cook without memory and without recipes. Imaginative construction becomes simply a wild guess, no more likely to work out pragmatically than any other wild guess. Accordingly, without experience, proposals about the meaning of the whole are simply arbitrary or random, which is not to say that with experience proposals are assured of pragmatic success. Recognizing this need for perceptive awareness, William James, John Dewey, Alfred North Whitehead, and the empirical theologians developed a radically empirical theory of knowledge. They argued for a partial reliance on the full breadth of experience rather than on the five senses alone—on nonsensuous perceptions (the indirect, vague, and highly fallible experience of relations, values, affections) as well as on sense experience.[39]

There is a question of the philosophy of history here. The standard choice has become the choice between a copy-theory epistemology and no epistemology at all. In effect, this was a choice between a deterministic way of knowing (copy the truth mandated by reason or the facts) and an aleatory, or dicey, way of knowing (just hope you hit on an idea that pans out). Finally, the first is mechanistic and denies freedom, and the second is accidental and arbitrary. In the context of this discussion, this becomes a choice between a deterministic historicism and an aleatory historicism. Richard Rorty, for example, denies copy-theory epistemologies, eschews any third option, and is driven to say of Galileo's hypotheses, that "he just lucked out."[40] To avoid this awkward outcome, classical pragmatists and empirical theologians have introduced a kind of contingent historicism where unpredictable choices are made, but in response to a context. Taking a view of history similar to this, Stephen Jay Gould, speaking as a paleontologist, says, "This third alternative represents no more nor less than the essence of history. Its view is contingency—and contingency is a thing unto itself, not the titration of determination by randomness."[41] And, although Gould does not say this, it is apparent that contingent historicism gives experience a role to play and makes evolution more than merely repeated throws of the dice.

Classical American pragmatism did not require the abandonment of epistemology, although it did require the abandonment of direct epistemological justification. William James, for example, was a pragmatist, but he was also an empiricist. That is, while he acknowledged that successful consequences make ideas true, he also insisted that nonsensuous perception contributes to the selection of which ideas get to be likely candidates for truth. The "that" received from the past, James said, is the seedbed for the "what" that we test. "The 'that' of it is its own; but the 'what' depends on the 'which'; and the which depends on 'us.' "[42] My point is that the "which," while it depends on us, is selected from the "that." Accordingly, James was deeply interested in experience as a source of hypotheses, and his radical empiricism set forth his broad and original notion of how experience hooks onto the world external to the self.

When experience is disregarded, Jesus or Martin Luther King become just statistical freaks; they have this incredible lucky streak, stumbling from one lucky spiritual choice to another. The verdict of the Nuremberg trials would have to be that the World War II criminals were just extremely unlucky, introducing one spiritual monstrosity after another. In neither case can we introduce the religious individual's experience. Forget Jesus' Jewish upbringing, King's schooling in religion and in a racist society, and the personal histories of the war criminals.

Dewey, James, and Whitehead, along with Henry Nelson

Wieman, Bernard Meland, and Bernard Loomer (the empirical theologians who took those three philosophers most seriously), moved beyond the dichotomy between a bad epistemology and no epistemology. They ventured an empiricist epistemology that gave status also to nonsensuous and affective perceptions: James called it "radical empiricism," Dewey called it "immediate empiricism," Whitehead referred to "causal efficacy," Wieman referred to a kind of mysticism, Meland called it "appreciative awareness," and, at least in conversation, Loomer used stories to acknowledge something beneath the directly known world. This epistemology was joined with the hypothesis that the world is just as spiritual as it is material, not because it is a blending of the material and the spiritual, but because it is a world more complex than subjects, objects, or both added together. Sometimes James summarized that third reality as relations between facts; Whitehead argued that the experience of relations lies at the heart of aesthetic appraisal.

It was Dewey who said it best for our purposes. In *Art as Experience* he claimed "we are never wholly free from the sense of something that lies beyond." Any limited and definite experience always is felt in a larger context. "But however broad the field, it is still felt as not the whole; the margins shade into that indefinite expanse beyond[,] which imagination calls the universe."[43] We might talk of a "quality" pervading the many particulars; this quality is not "known" but only "emotionally 'intuited.'" Because intellect knows only what is definite, this whole cannot be intellectually grasped. It can, Dewey says, "only be felt, that is, immediately grasped." When this intuition is particularly intense, we might call it "mystical."

In one way or another, art and religion specialize in this experience of the whole, and they cannot be accounted for apart from an awareness of the whole. Art and religion, Dewey said, work directly to appreciate the "world beyond this world which is nevertheless the deeper reality of the world in which we live in our ordinary experiences." But, as always, Dewey is not content to tuck this away in the categories of art and religion and be done with it. Rather, the sense of the whole is practically important because it offers the deepest context for judgments of importance and relevance, thus serving as a "guide to our reflection." For this reason, it is this alone that makes particular experiences sane and coherently related to other experiences.[44]

I am arguing, then, that without this sense of the whole, religious critics work at a disadvantage. Without any awareness of the whole, the religious critic's theory of the spiritual culture is merely arbitrary.

On the other hand, by emphasizing the sense of the whole, I do not make the religious critic merely an oracle for an intuited whole. Kaufman is right to claim that "imaginative construction" always contributes its own element to the creation of a present picture of the world. Accordingly, any particular religious critic's sense of the whole always outruns what is given; the perceiver always contributes an independent spontaneity, so that any sense of the whole includes an independent interpretation of the whole, an unpredictable (but not utterly blind) "spontaneous variation." And the sum of variations, past and present, literally composes the environment that is the whole.

Thus, imaginative interpretation of the whole contributes to the very evolution of the world interpreted.[45] Interpretations compose not only views of the whole, but the substance of the whole itself. In this way, then, religious critics not only read the spiritual culture but, in their readings, contribute to the very construction of that culture. We are left, then, on the threshold of what in the Introduction I called "conventionalism." Imaginative constructions of what the whole might be, if they are accepted, enter history and become actual constituents of the whole itself; they become living conventions.

A last word: the role of imaginative construction by religious critics looms most important just at those crucial junctures when the sense of the whole is changing. While spiritual traditions about the sense of the whole are important, they become less important when society is changing so rapidly that tradition is failing. Then the religious critic's new sense of the whole becomes crucial. Walter Lippmann could announce in 1929: "For ages when custom is unsettled are necessarily ages of prophecy. The moralist cannot teach what is revealed; he must reveal what can be taught."[46] Thus, the crucial moments for the religious critic come not in those quiet circumstances that permit the virtual reiteration of traditions about the sense of the whole. Such moments may be a time, in fact, for religious critics to remain silent. It is the exceptional moments, when historical change requires departure from tradition or custom, that are, in the words of Ecclesiastes, "a time to speak."[47]

PART **III**

GROUNDING RELIGIOUS THEORY

CHAPTER 7

THE REALITY OF CONVENTIONS

> In the realm of truth-processes facts come indepen-
> dently and determine our beliefs provisionally. But
> these beliefs make us act, and as fast as they do so, they
> bring into sight or into existence new facts which re-
> determine the beliefs accordingly. So the whole coil
> and ball of truth, as it rolls up, is the product of a
> double influence. Truths emerge from facts; but they
> dip forward into facts again and add to them; which
> facts again create or reveal new truth (the word is
> indifferent) and so on indefinitely. The "facts" them-
> selves meanwhile are not *true*. They simply *are*. Truth
> is the function of the beliefs that start and terminate
> among them
>
> William James, *Pragmatism*[1]

In speaking thus, William James affirmed, not only that the
factual world has its role in creating what we believe, but that
what we believe has its role in creating the factual world. What
we believe is an interpretation, a construct; but an interpretation
can grow from an empirical intimation of the past and it can
become a social fact that affects our future beliefs. Our interpretations or constructs become conventions, where a convention is not a fantasy internal to the subject but a historical reality
external to the subject. James's constructivism led to a new realism. He was not simply a conventionalist, but the great American
ur-conventionalist. As James boarded the twentieth century, he
described what many recent American poststructuralists are attempting to describe before that century drops them off.

In James's discovery lies a way around the dilemmas of the

101

religious critic in America. James offers a way of saying how the sacred is a construct that becomes a convention, which, like any other convention, lives within and emerges with history and yet remains capable of changing history. This, in turn, provides a poststructuralist way of understanding how spiritual cultures, which are formed around sacred conventions, themselves evolve. Further, if conventions, including sacred conventions, begin as constructs, then whoever contributes to the formation of these constructs contributes to the formation of spiritual cultures. Specifically, if religious critics specialize in analyzing and reconstructing sacred constructs, they have an important role in contributing to sacred conventions, to spiritual cultures, and to society itself. Conventionalism, I will argue, offers a poststructuralist way to account for a public sense that something sacred works through a people's spiritual culture, that it expresses a people's scriptures and traditions, that it fosters and judges a people's spiritual culture, and, most importantly, that the sacred is real, that it cannot be reduced to mere projections of a people's hopes and fears.

In this chapter I lay grounds for a conventionalist concept of the sacred by defining the idea of the convention and by illustrating that idea by reference to American philosophic and scientific thought. In the following chapter, I will attempt to explain how the sacred can function as a convention.

I. Conventionalism

In 1987 the American intellectual historian Thomas Haskell wrote "The Curious Persistence of Rights Talk in the 'Age of Interpretation.'" Haskell points to this paradox: the very intellectuals who insist that things are important only if people say they are, also insist that human rights should be important even to those who deny they are. On one hand, these intellectuals talk like relativists, saying that things exist and claims are true only in relation to certain situations; on the other hand, they talk like absolutists, saying that the rights of humans exist everywhere and are defensible everywhere, regardless of the situation. If this contradiction continues to arise, and Haskell believes it does, why then is it allowed to live on? It is to explain this curiously persisting contradiction that Haskell puts forth his theory of conventionalism.

The question of universal human rights continues to be an unresolved question. For example, in the June 1993 World Conference on Human Rights, it was argued that "human rights" may not apply to many less developed nations, who may be more interested in protecting "economic rights" even when they jeopardize human rights.[2] Or in the United States many conservatives and feminists have argued that individual rights are so stressed that they overwhelm group rights, such as the right to be protected from pornography.

Haskell deals with such issues at a theoretical level. He knows full well that a kind of lighthearted subjectivism and relativism are fashionable. But, he asks, how we are "to reconcile this lighthearted image with the heaviness of heart we all feel upon reading, say, the reports prepared by Amnesty International."[3] It is too late to eradicate all subjectivism and relativism, just as it is too late to introduce absolutes in order to defend human rights.[4] Nevertheless, Haskell finds that even he is willing to defend rights over against what any particular individual or group prefers, despite the fact that he cannot point to an authority other than what individuals and groups prefer.

Haskell concludes that this sense of contradiction is fueled by a hidden premise and that it might be overcome if this premise were exposed and eliminated. The premise is that rights, to be meaningful, must be supported by universal structures. Because we accept this premise, we tend to honor two contradictory voices: (1) the voice of the political theorist Leo Strauss, who claims that morals will crumble if they are not supported by universal structures; and (2) the voice of the philosopher Friedrich Nietzsche, who claims that because such universal structures have died, morals are indefensible. The Straussians say that universal structures for morals must be defended to avoid moral anarchy; the Nietzscheans say that, because universal structures for morals cannot be defended, a kind of moral anarchy is acceptable.

Haskell argues that each side is simply historically wrong and suggests that these errors stem from a preoccupation with universal, extrahistorical structures, to the neglect of actual history. First, the historical fact is that many people who have no universal structures, or foundations, for morals go right on defending universal human rights—paradoxically, in this age of interpretation. Thus, "Strauss was wrong: neither rights nor the practices they authorize need foundations sunk deep into the heart of nature."[5] Second, the persisting historical fact is that this structureless rights talk successfully rejects anarchy, so that Nietzsche also was wrong.[6] Thus, in actual history, relativity and rights talk can and should co-exist and do so in the absence of universal structures and bad conscience.

These history-based reflections led Haskell to describe what he thinks has happened historically. Even after the demise of metaphysical structures and objectivity, even after the introduction of relativism and pluralism, people still make nonsubjective moral affirmations, and do so, wittingly or unwittingly, by appeals to a third kind of reality—that is, to conventions. Conventions are social traditions developed through several generations, as opposed both to universal structures and to arbitrary acts of the subjective will enforced by the arbitrary exercise of power.[7] Conventions offer less than the authority of the absolute and more than the authority of the isolated individual. While they offer no more than temporary and local authority, they can stand, nevertheless, over against the mere arbitrariness of the individual will. Thus, human rights talk can be defended in an age of interpretation by grounding that talk on conventions. As a society, we have not overthrown those conventions and do not intend to do so, even though we have no universal structures on which to secure them. Social conventions, then, are the basis for a third and positive reality, one which answers the question about the curious persistence of rights even in an age of interpretation.

To summarize what appears to be Haskell's conclusion: human rights can be authoritative for a society if those rights are fixed in conventions formed by a long string of legal and moral precedents in favor of rights and if they are currently reaffirmed. Thus, people living in societies where human rights are normative can, in good conscience, defend them as norms, even for people in other societies, and do so without abandoning their relativism, without introducing absolute norms, and without being inconsistent.

Conventionalism, I add, is consistent with recent forms of pluralism and relativism; after all, conventions are created by local cultures. Further, without using an old-fashioned foundationalism or structuralism, conventionalism can explain one kind of old-fashioned realism—where, pragmatically, to have social effects, as conventions do, is to be real. Conventionalism explains the coherence of what happens in most Western societies today, where normative worldviews are affirmed even though universal grounds for those worldviews are not. It offers an answer to those who believe that to abandon universal grounds for truth is to invite nihilism. Further, there is nothing in conventionalism to block intercultural conversations. After all, societies can advance their relative and normative conventions in intercultural interactions, let them be criticized, and then revise them—all without finding anything contradictory or doing anything imperialistic.

A convention, in short, lives through time as a tradition, but as a tradition that is continually augmented by new criticisms and precedents. A convention is a reality apart from its causes, even though its causes contribute to it. Like any organism, it is more than what caused it, just as a child is more than what its parents and its environment would make it. Pragmatically stated (where meaning is determined by effects), the independence of a convention from its causes is evident in the fact that a convention can have effects different from the effects that would be predicted if one knew everything that contributed to the convention. Equally, a convention is a reality apart from its effects, so that it is not simply what it is interpreted to be, even though what it is interpreted to be can alter its identity. What a convention is, in itself, is a mystery, just as a person or the sacred is a mystery. Although these analogies with persons are instructive, a convention is not a person or a subject of any sort, nor is it an object. Rather, it is a social, or relational, reality that exists not only in time but through time.

It is this independent effectiveness that makes a convention public. The convention is public because it transcends, works beyond, those private persons who invent it. The public impact of the convention suggests that religious critics, who help shape religious conventions, can foster public meanings. Conventionalism explains how religious critics can be relativistic, pluralistic, and historicist and yet be realists and work publicly. Even as poststructuralists, they can help to criticize and reconstruct the spiritual culture of a nation.

Further, conventionalism can provide the model for a concept of the sacred and its impact on a spiritual culture. To model the sacred on the idea of the convention is to locate the sacred thoroughly within history but not to make it entirely the creature of historical forces. Conventionalism allows the sacred, or God, to be real and to exercise a distinct function, to act as well as to be acted upon.

Conventionalism, as I treat it, bears strong resemblances to "the social construction of reality" discussed by Peter Berger and Thomas Luckmann in their classic book by that title. They discuss ways in which "habitualization" becomes "institutionalized" and how what is institutionalized by one generation can be "objectivated" and confront the next generation as a separate reality. "In other words," Berger and Luckmann say, "the institutions are now experienced as possessing a reality of their own, a reality that confronts the individual as an external and coercive fact."[8] Although I recognize the similarity between social construction and conventionalism as I am interpreting it, I do not discuss below Berger, Luckmann, or other sociologists of knowledge for three reasons. First, what I say is so obviously sociological that to support it by citing sociologists could seem redundant; that is, the case for conventionalism is most persuasively made by nonsociologists (although, if sociologists were considered, sociologist Anthony Giddens's notion of the "constitution of meaning" would be relevant).[9] Second, I am most interested in a history wider than that used by the sociologist of knowledge, one that includes natural conventions as well as human conventions. Third and most important, Berger and Luckmann treat objectivations as genuine social accomplishments but insist that they are nothing but social constructs; to forget this, and treat the social projections "as possessing a reality of their own," is to "reify" the projection and to make a mistake. For them, the sophisticated observer recognizes that what appears to be an "external reality" is really nothing but a human construct. The sophisticated observer does not allow the objectivated construct to become a reification (a projection falsely treated as a separate reality). "In other words," they say, "despite the objectivity that marks the social world in human experience, it does not thereby acquire an ontological status apart from the human activity that produces it."[10]

Conventionalism, as I am describing it, gives the convention just such a separate ontological status. While conventionalism acknowledges that some projections are only that, it also recognizes that some projections take on a life of their own and become more than a sedimentation of human projections. In short, conventionalism moves beyond Berger's and Luckmann's two ontological options (either subjective or objective, so what is not truly objective is merely subjective) and treats the convention as a third option. (Ironically, Berger's and Luckmann's two options are a perfect case of the false reification of human projections; they have taken a Continental subject-object dualism and falsely treated it as a settled ontological limit.)

Finally, the historical character of the convention suggests that any explanation of conventionalism should rely on history rather than on abstract talk about method. If the convention is not a historical reality, no methodological talk can make it plausible. To state it circularly, if conventionalism is a defensible notion, it should itself be a convention. Accordingly, I define conventionalism on the basis of history. Also, because conventionalism, like anything historical, has no essence, only something like historically developed family traits can be discovered.

II. Epistemological Conventionalism

Conventionalism makes its initial appearance as a theory about how social decisions affect "known history." It denies that "real history"—the history out in the world, beyond knowers, their knowledge, and their known history—can be reached objectively; it also denies that real history is simply whatever the subject believes it to be. It affirms that the history that is known is a convention. Known history is an interplay between the knower's subjective beliefs about history and the limits and opportunities provided by the real history itself. Conventionalism is here an "epistemological conventionalism" because it makes the known history a convention; it is not an "ontological conventionalism" according to which the real history, beyond the known history, is a convention. In fact, for all epistemological conventionalism knows, the real history is unaffected by human conventions.

Ludwig Wittgenstein, to take perhaps the clearest case, sets forth epistemological conventionalism in *On Certainty*. Refusing to choose between utterly static and universal metaphysical truths and utterly fluid and local truths, he suggests a third position, particularly in his discussion of that picture of the world that influences everything else a community knows. Such a picture is never proven, but is "the inherited background against which I distinguish between true and false."[11] It is not as though this background ever came in the form of explicit rules that were learned; rather, it came as "a totality of judgments," "a whole system of propositions" that a child, for example, comes to treat as reliable.[12] This background describes a "world-picture, which might be part of a kind of mythology." It might function like the rules of a game, rules that are picked up in the playing of the game rather than learned in advance and by themselves. Propositions that become rules can slide from a non-rule location in society to a rule location and back again: "the same proposition may get treated at one time as something to test by experience, at another as a rule of testing." Introducing the analogy of a river and its river-bed, Wittgenstein said that propositions can be hardened, become world-pictures, and serve "as channels for such empirical propositions as were not hardened but fluid." It also happens that this relation can change in time, so "that fluid propositions hardened, and hard ones became fluid." "The mythology may change back into a state of flux, the river-bed of thoughts may shift. But I distinguish between the movement of the waters on the river-bed and the shift of the bed itself; though there is not a sharp division of the one from the other."[13]

These rulelike, river-bed, world-picture truths are neither static and universal nor momentary and local but, like conventions, operate over a period of time and in a variety of circumstances and their status derives from their social function. Like conventions, they have enough authority to continue through a variety of circumstances and to warrant respect. There may be no eternal truths, but there are temporary truths that serve as grounds for other claims. This suggests how a society may be deprived of transhistorical truth but still have norms and thus escape sheer subjectivity, plurality, and relativity, or the utter arbitrariness of everything.

Wittgenstein seems to stop at an epistemological conventionalism because (particularly in his later philosophy) he was oriented toward what is known through language ("that whereof we can speak"), rather than toward a world less susceptible to linguistic analysis. Wittgenstein was not opposed to ontological conventionalism, and at times he seems to defend it (when he suggests that facts might buck one out of the saddle).[14] Nevertheless, Wittgenstein seems on the whole to have been agnostic about what I am calling ontological conventionalism. Whatever real history might be was, for him, shrouded in mystery.

Epistemological conventionalism has far earlier origins than Wittgenstein. In the early 1920s, when Wittgenstein was still in search of language that would correspond to an objective world beyond language, Rudolf Carnap in his earliest writings was arguing that scientific theories are unverifiable and unfalsifiable claims, based, in part, on free choices. Thus, the history of the sciences might have taken other routes, with other theories describing the world in equally valuable but quite different ways. As Edmund Runggaldier explains, Rudolf Carnap in both his doctoral dissertation, *Der Raum,* and in his "Habilitationsschrift," *Der logische Aufbau der Welt,* (Part I; Chapters I–VII) was a conventionalist. The *Aufbau,* Runggaldier explains, "is undoubtedly grounded on the strong positivistic standpoint that sense impressions are, so to say, the 'rock bottom of knowledge,' but also on the standpoint that the allegedly certain sense perception is actually an unconscious synthetic construction."[15] It is this emphasis on synthetic construction that makes Carnap a conventionalist. Runggaldier argues that Carnap at this point was not yet a typical logical positivist and also that Carnap's conventionalism could not be explained as an implicit idealism.[16] The early Carnap is far closer to Kant than has been thought, in that Carnap saw everything as interpreted through a screen rather than in its rawness. However, for Carnap the screen (for example, the notion of causality) is the result of a convention rather than, as with Kant, a necessary, universal, a priori human category. On the other hand, while conventions depend on free choices, they are not sheerly arbitrary but depend on "the practical principle of the greatest simplicity ('Einfachstheit')."[17] Yet Carnap's conventionalism is epistemological rather than ontological, in that it points to the effects of conventions on sense perceptions rather than on the world beyond sense perceptions.

Carnap acknowledges that the conventionalist stance in his first article (1923) "was influenced by Poincaré's books. . . . "[18] Henri Poincaré's 1905 *Science and Hypothesis* argues that geometry is not really deductive; nor are its conclusions derived from experience; nor is it entirely arbitrary. *"The geometrical axioms are therefore neither synthetic à priori intuitions nor experimental facts.* They are conventions. . . . In other words, *the axioms of geometry . . . are only definitions in disguise."* Consequently, it is meaningless to ask whether Euclidean, or any other, geometry is true. "We might as well ask if the metric system is true, ... "[19] Poincaré went on to argue that scientific principles also are conventions. They are based on our own definitions, and our definitions are preferred when they are convenient, which is to say, confirmed by experiment and practice as "fertile." Experience itself, Poincaré said, "leaves us our freedom of choice, but it guides us by helping us to discern the most convenient path to follow."[20] Poincaré was enough of an empiricist to deny nominalism; that is, he refused to concede that our definitions make the external world what it is, leaving nature no independent voice. Further than this, he argued that scientific law was itself quiet unaffected by our conventions.[21] Thus, while he was an epistemological conventionalist, he was not an ontological conventionalist (one who would allow the world to be shaped, in part, by human conventions).[22]

Conventionalism was extended into the sciences by Arthur Stanley Eddington, who argued that science is conventional in that the claims of physics depend largely on the concepts of the scientist. Scientific concept are like fishnets: "real" fish are those too big to slip through the holes; smaller fish are treated as unreal. Our concepts select those parts or aspects of the physical world we will observe; because those concepts originate subjectively, Eddington calls his notion "selective subjectivism."[23] Eddington compares the scientist to a college bursar who knows nothing of his institution but what his account books tell him. One day he "discovers" this about the college: that "for every item on the credit side an equal item appeared somewhere else on the debit side. 'Ha!' said the Bursar, 'I have discovered one of the great laws controlling the college. It is a perfect and exact law of the real world.'" Eddington also argues that, because we like permanent things, we "discover" the law of conservation, neglecting whatever does not conform to this law. These illustrations do not necessarily reduce the law of conservation, permanent things, balanced books, or large fish to mere figments of our imagination, for some imagined things do not work in practice. A thing's "practical importance depends," says Eddington, "on our knowing that which obeys it."[24] Thus, "the physical universe is neither wholly subjective nor wholly objective—nor a simple mixture of subjective and objective entities or attributes."[25] Instead, Eddington puts forth a third position that carries many of the earmarks of conventionalism. Eddington sees society as contributing to the definition of the only nature we know; nevertheless, he appears to stop short of arguing that nature is itself a social convention.

Thomas Kuhn and Nelson Goodman also are epistemological conventionalists, for they argue that the meaning of the natural world is a function of how the natural world is known, and that how the natural world is known is a function of social conventions among scientists and others.[26] Kuhn's 1962 *The Structure of Scientific Revolutions* is not a book about nature, nor a book specifically about scientific ideas, but a book about how scientists in groups reach agreements.[27] When within any particular science new ideas conflict with accepted ideas, scientists eventually reach a new consensus that circumvents a stalemate and allows cooperative work to continue. Usually they select a new reigning paradigm (a new exemplar or model of the world that sets new methods and styles, and determines what counts as plausible scientific work) which will replace the earlier reigning paradigm, under which conflicts had arisen. Kuhn sees the matter sociologically; social turmoil in scientific societies is resolved by a new paradigm, one that finds room for new interpretations while holding onto as much of the earlier interpretations as possible. In the wake of these social agreements difficult social adjustments occur: people are read out of and into scientific societies and positions of leadership; new seminal thinkers are identified and former seminal thinkers are discredited; popular textbooks are scrubbed and replaced by new textbooks. Kuhn's analysis is itself revolutionary partly because of steps it refuses to take. The new truths created by these revolutions are not objective readings of nature, reflecting a change in nature, nor are they merely subjective conclusions (for Kuhn asserts that the new paradigms must be experimentally workable). Rather, his point is that science, as it constructs a known world, is a social tradition; and it is a tradition that has real effects on the work that science and technology do on the world beyond the mind of the scientist. That is, science is a sequence of social conventions.

Equally, the "worlds" of Nelson Goodman should be seen as social conventions. In *Ways of Worldmaking,* Goodman asserts that the rightness of worlds does not depend on truth, but truth on the rightness of worlds; and the rightness of worlds itself depends on social conventions. Worlds are fundamental ways of organizing things, and these ways are themselves determined by social traditions which come and go:

> Without the organization, the selection of relevant kinds, effected by evolving tradition, there is no rightness or wrongness of categorization, no validity or invalidity of inductive inference. . . . Thus justifying such tests for rightness may consist primarily in showing not that they are reliable but that they are authoritative.[28]

Goodman is explicit about the importance of conventions: "And so we may regard the disagreements as not about the facts but as due to differences in the conventions. . . . "[29] Like Kuhn, Goodman does not argue that worlds are merely arbitrary or subjective, for Goodman recognizes that theories, whatever the strength of their social authority, must also work somehow in practice.[30] Also, like Kuhn, Goodman does not advance an ontology; neither man is an ontological conventionalist, claiming that worlds beyond worlds are themselves made of conventions.

Alfred North Whitehead's epistemological conventionalism is so enlarged that it affects the very workings of nature and the laws of nature. And, yet, he draws a sharp line between his own epistemological conventionalism and a truly ontological conventionalism. Whitehead came by conventionalism late. He had risen to prominence as one who would show (in his collaboration with Bertrand Russell in *Principia Mathematica*) not the conventional but the necessary, the logical, foundations of mathematics. Nevertheless, at the end of his career, Whitehead was to become a conventionalist in mathematics as well as in science. In *Modes of Thought,* he argued that mathematics describes "a process and its issue," rather than Plato's "eternal mathematical forms," and he acknowledged that the process is social and temporal and involves nonhuman as well as human societies. He contended that "the laws of nature are merely all-pervading patterns of behavior, of which the shift and discontinuance lie beyond our ken."[31] In these ways, Whitehead was a conventionalist, dropping his insistence that what we know is a function of a universal logic or an objective reflection of a fixed condition beyond ourselves. Yet he avoided mere subjectivism, contending that the known and constructed "laws of nature" do refer to the present known world because they work experimentally.

Nevertheless, Whitehead retained universal structures, making nature "a complex of the more stable interrelations between the real facts of the real universe"[32]—where the *real* facts of the *real* universe are the metaphysical uniformities he describes in *Process and Reality*. It turns out that conventions, even though they may affect the very workings of nature in any given cosmic epoch, are mere selections from a static deck of cards held permanently by God and arranged and guided by God's own eternal preferences. Thus, the importance of social conventions, even in history, is limited after all. While prevailing laws of nature may be conventional, they are selected from an eternal, universal, and nonconventional range of eternal and universal possibilities. In Whitehead's words: "A society does not in any sense create the complex of eternal objects which constitutes its defining characteristic. It only elicits that complex into importance for its members, and secures the reproduction of its membership." Therefore, "When societies decay, it will not mean that their defining characteristics cease to exist."[33] In effect, Whitehead travels to the borders of ontological conventionalism, but refuses to become an ontological conventionalist.[34]

III. Ontological Conventionalism

Subtly different from the epistemological conventionalisms in logic, math, and the philosophy of science are the cosmological or ontological conventionalisms arising in the natural sciences. While they do not use the terms "convention" or "conventionalism," some physicists and biologists argue, nevertheless, that nonhuman nature is a product of processes that work like conventions. They talk not primarily of objective worlds or of subjective readings but of how innovations initially "proposed" by a nonhuman entity are then "accepted" generally in a space-time location or in an environment. That is, they have understood the natural processes they study to be truly historical; these processes are contingent on particulars and are not overridden by eternal and universal laws or by human minds observing them. The ontological conventionalists have described convention-making in nature and have suggested that nature, itself, is a history of conventions. This account has general, metaphysical, cosmological, or ontological implications.

I believe that ontological conventionalism is needed because, without it, epistemological conventionalism is not fully intelligible. It is not clear how known histories can be conventional if real histories are not conventional. What sense does it make to affirm the openness of epistemological conventionalism if convention-making humans are bound and gagged in the machinery of nature? How can the imagination work or express itself if it is housed in rigid atomic or cellular processes? If people's very brains are robotic or locked in robotic bodies, then how can their minds be free to propose and develop those novelties that lead to new conventions? If the very muscles of the throat are strictly determined by mechanical causation, how are a person's "free" decisions to be given voice? Secondly, if the environments in which people live are causally determined, what chance is there that free and indeterminate conventions can take hold in those environments? Conventional forms of knowing, it would seem, must occur in a world that is itself conventional; otherwise, the imagination that would offer new conventions can have no effects in the world beyond imagination and, thus, no pragmatic meaning. Thus, it can be argued that any sensible, defensible epistemological conventionalism simply requires an ontological conventionalism.[35] I will explore the possibility of ontological conventionalism, not metaphysically, but naturalistically, not through claims about world structures, but through discussion of recent science.

Most scientists are not ontological conventionalists; the majority remain reductionistic and mechanistic. (The same dualism that allows intellectuals working in the arts and humanities to ignore the scientists' materialism permits most scientists to ignore the freedom and responsibility presupposed in the arts and humanities.) Nevertheless, there are new voices in the scientific choir. I cite two illustrations, not to rest my case on them, but to illustrate growing themes in science: the quantum theorists of the physics section and the neo-Lamarckians of the biology section. These are unusual voices; neither is quite ready to solo, let alone serve as the recognized leader. But these unusual scientists are aware of the dominance of objectivism, mechanism, determinism, and reductionism in the sciences; and they deliberately oppose those orthodoxes with theories analogous to conventionalism. They are not from the lunatic fringe of physics and biology; they represent broad and growing trends within the sciences and an increasingly historical understanding of nature.

Conventionalism within quantum physics is best represented by John Wheeler.[36] His approach can be understood by reference to the uncertainty principle. For Wheeler that principle does not refer to mere technical difficulties of knowing (how, for example, measuring one thing screws up measurements of another thing). Rather, working out of the Copenhagen interpretation of the uncertainty principle, he argues that there simply is no reality apart from observers and observations and that all entities, not just humans, are observers. Wheeler puts it this way: "no elementary phenomenon is a phenomenon until it is a registered phenomenon."[37] While here the qualifier "elementary" confines that particular dictum to microphysical worlds, in other writings Wheeler extends it to the macrophysical world. The universe, Wheeler argues, is a "self-excited circuit." He asks, "Is the architecture of existence such that only through 'observership' does the universe have a way to come into being?"[38] And he answers affirmatively, contending that the very existence of the universe depends on the existence of observers. In short, the observer's interpretation not only affects what is known about what is, but what is; he elevates observership from a principle of knowing to a principle of being. Yet he has done this without becoming a subjective idealist, making the world a figment of a person's imagination. That is, while the observer's interpretation may be a necessary condition for what is, it is not a sufficient condition. Reality is not simply a function of a projecting mind, for the world is somewhat independent of any observer. God does play dice; there is a world-based unpredictability about "what measurements will disclose, about what 'answers nature will give.' "[39] Thus, reality is determined neither by the observer's interpretation alone, nor by the thing observed alone; rather, what is real is the unpredictable chain of interactions between the observer's interpretation and the thing observed as it impinges on the observer—which is to say that reality is determined neither by the subject nor by the object, nor by the sum of the two, but by conventions.

Wheeler's conclusions can be understood more specifically in the context of the "delayed-choice experiment."[40] This experiment builds on the double-slit experiment, where photons can be read either as waves or as particles depending on what apparatus is used to read them. The double-slit experiment confirmed the principle of "complementary," according to which two seemingly incommensurable meanings are said to augment, or complement, each other. Now Wheeler went beyond the double-slip experiment when he proposed a different experiment using a different apparatus: if, after a photon has registered as a particle on a particle-registering apparatus, the same photon (on the same flight, an instant later) were read by wave-registering apparatus, the second apparatus would make the "same" past different, changing outright a particle past to a wave past. Strangely, one registered history would be literally changed into a different registered history. More importantly, because no phenomenon is a phenomenon "until it is a registered phenomenon," Wheeler's thought experiment suggests that real history is partly a function of observation.

In fact, Wheeler's comments only extended an earlier discussion, one best expressed in 1964 by "Bell's theorem,"[41] which is John S. Bell's response to the Albert Einstein, Boris Podolsky, Nathan Rosen article of 1935 (the EPR paper).[42] The EPR paper had argued for the independent reality of events in "local space" (that is, for the idea that observed events can be isolated from observer influences). Independence could be defended, Einstein, Podolsky, and Rosen argued, by observing the behavior of one of two corresponding and "correlated particles, localized in regions A and B far apart."[43] They pictured an atom emitting two photons, flying off in opposite directions with exactly opposite polarizations. By observing the polarization of the first photon (in region A), they could predict the opposite polarization of the second photon (in region B), proving that photon B can have its own, local, real polarization, even though it has been "observed." That is, B has a specific identity that exists independent of its being observed through the actions of photon A. The locality (independence) of photon B is assured because it moves apart from photon A at the speed of light, so that any observer action on photon A could not reach and thereby affect photon B, for nothing travels faster than light. Their point was that it can be known that a bit of history exists independently and has its own identity, unaffected by other observer-actions in the universe.

Bell responded thirty years later through calculations that demonstrated that, if the photon located in area B were described by examining the correlated but far distant photon in area A, photon B would be affected after all—despite the distance between the two regions. That is, an act of observation affects *any* event about which information is learned, despite the fact that there is no known way, given the absolute limit of the speed of light, in which the observation (of A) can affect the learned-about event (B). That is, there simply is no "local space" or "local time" as Einstein and his colleagues had argued; all spaces and times are nonlocal, so that, it would seem, no reality is independent of observer-affects, and any event is what it is, in part, because of its relations.

Bell's 1962 theorem was only a weakly confirmed[44] thought experiment (and Wheeler's 1978 and 1979 claims that registration gives to the past a specific identity were only speculations), until Alain Aspect of the University of Paris-South at Orsay and his colleagues developed an experiment in 1982 (the "Delayed Choice" experiment). Aspect found a way to emit a single photon which registered as a particle, then to introduce midway in the photon's flight a wave-registering apparatus, and then to see the same photon register as a wave.[45] That is, the photon *became* a wave in the most basic sense: it was observed to be a wave. As Wheeler had said it would, the wave-reading apparatus reached into the "past" and changed it, despite the fact that there is no mechanical way to explain how that could happen. The experiment does not suggest that the existence, itself, of the past depends on the observation, for all agree that some kind of real photon was introduced at the beginning of the Aspect experiment. But the experiment does say that the past's specific identity is a function of an interaction between the observer and the observed.

The delayed-choice experiment seems to point to an ontological conventionalism because it indicates that relative and subjective readings have real and historical effects. The experiment denies that identity is: (1) determined in advance by some rigid, extrahistorical law or essence imposed on entities; (2) contained within or local to an entity; or (3) exists only within the mind of the observer. Instead, these ideas affirm that history is relational, that it is an interaction between a real past and a present interpreter. Admittedly, this rendition of the delayed-choice experiment extends the meaning of "observer," applying it to nonhumans (like the microphysical photon A and the particle or wave detectors). But that is only to take seriously the notion that all things register other things (which is implicit in any field theory, such as gravitational theory), and that there seems to be uncertainty in how things register other things (which is implicit in quantum physics). This moves conventionalism to a more portentous, less commonsensical level: it is not just that observations nudge things in a slightly different direction; it is that specific identity simply is not determined prior to observation.

This theory of Wheeler and this experiment by Aspect are not only about how we know and how our interpretations affect our knowledge (epistemology); they are about what is, the very thing that is known (cosmology or ontology). It is not only about known history but about real history. What is known is a convention: it is not an object, not a subject, not the mere sum of the two; it is a relation between the two, and that relation is partly determined by observer choices and the traditions that those choices create. Aspect's experiment suggests that, in highly sensitive situations, whether the photon is a particle or a wave can be determined by the observer. On the other hand, his experiment does not affirm that either particles or waves are entirely determined by the present observer or that they are entirely unlawful. What is known is not simply what the subject says it is. Rather, what is known is a tradition (or heritage) of previous observer-observed interactions from the past, *as it is affected by* the present. The known particle or the wave is not an instantaneous creation, even if whether it is a particle or wave is instantaneously determined. The known particle or the known wave is determined primarily by an old, but slightly flexible, traditional of photon phenomena. It is this tradition that is the principal convention; the present observer, the point is, creates a slightly altered convention for the future.

The workings of nature's traditions are better seen when Wheeler moves from microphysical ontology to macrophysical ontology. Time is not unlimited but bounded, says Wheeler. Time makes no sense in black holes, before the big bang, or after the big crunch; thus, physical laws, which operate in space and time, are neither universal nor eternal. Some laws come to be almost instantaneously, others are distilled out of initially lawless interactions between observers and things observed. Still other laws are developed through continuous and sometimes slightly unlawful interpretations of the traditions of law. To put it in Wheeler's terms, the macrophysical universe itself, not just the microphysical photon, is "participatory." If, at the smallest level, reality is determined by the interaction of observer and the observed, so must be the totality of such interactions, even as they develop the world regularities which we call laws. Wheeler finds such interactions in the development of genera and species, based as they are on innumerable mutations. Even the patterned organization of living things is "of nothing but higgledy-piggledy origin." Equally, Wheeler says of the laws of physics: "in what can they have their root but billions upon billions of acts of chance?" Thus "events beyond law" are what build law.[46]

This lands Wheeler in neither meaningless chance, nor objectivism, nor subjectivism. First, Wheeler qualifies what might appear to be meaningless acts of chance by calling them "the statistics of billions upon billions of acts of observer-participancy each of which by itself partakes of utter randomness."[47] To call an individual act random is to say it is not predictable, that it is not determined by law. But unpredictability is not equivalent to meaninglessness; if it were, then all human choice (even the choice to accept meaninglessness) would be meaningless. Accordingly, random decisions within observational procedures do not make those procedures meaningless. Second, Wheeler is not an objectivist. As he explained, there is no objective world that observations must passively copy. Rather, the world beyond the observer is itself always in part an ongoing function of observational decisions, and the present observer merely continues that process. Third, because he does not disregard the existence or the strong influence of the past, Wheeler is not a subjectivist.[48] He is saying, instead, that past interpretations work within a context that is virtually lawful. Traditions, or laws, of nature are composed of particular decisions, but over time these decisions form traditions that are so strong they work almost like eternal laws.

How the world involves the past but also chance and subjectivity is best explained by Wheeler's analogy of the old game of twenty questions.[49] In the orthodox version of twenty questions there is a right answer (a universal structure) determined in advance by the players, and the "it" person must discover the players' right answer before having asked twenty questions that get a negative answer. In Wheeler's version there is no right answer agreed to in advance; rather, each player begins with his or her own private answer. But each individual player's answers must evolve during the course of the game because each new question by the it person and each new response by other players limits in unpredictable ways the range of possible answers. Thus, in the course of the game, players must change their answers to fit the ever-changing history (the evolving tradition) created in the earlier acts of observer-participancy. Eventually, Wheeler testifies, a single right answer, on which all players agree, can be reached. (Others also, myself included, have played it and seen the "right" answer reached by all the players). The key here is that decisions are reached subjectively and random elements operate, but they do not destroy the reality or the meaning of the game. Wheeler's game of twenty questions illustrates that the historical tradition of observer-participatory creates a range of possible answers, imposes a limit to possible answers, and keeps the observer from imposing just any answer. Ranges of possible answers are limited, so that only one good answer may be left, thus explaining why and how there are, in fact, real temporary orders in the universe. Traditions work; they become reality-defining conventions at a point in time and space. But then, traditions also are open.

The convention can be identified at each moment, as it is inherited by each player. It lies in the observed world as it is being shaped, in part, by each observational choice, by each higgledy-piggledy random gesture. Wheeler's world is determined by neither blind physical chance, nor by predetermined law, nor by subjective arbitrariness. Wheeler makes nature historical and traditional. It is a slowly changing and indeterminate tradition of interactions between present interpreters and an interpreted past. It depends on random or decisional events that have real consequences and make real worlds. Nature is a convention that precedes and makes possible a human, epistemological conventionalism.

Thus, the aptness of Darwin grows clearer. Darwin's world is the product of conventions rather than foreordained structures. However trivial, each new variation spontaneously proposes to its past world a new interpretation of the natural order; each natural selection of a variation is a decision by a local environment to accept that interpretation into the natural order. What began as a variant internal to a particular living thing is rejected by the world external to that thing or it is accepted (thus altering that world's local order). The original proposal is not a copy of something eternal or universal, somehow essential but not yet actual; rather, it is spontaneously (Wheeler would say, randomly) posited by the particular living thing. The acceptance of the variation by the environment, although it is rare, means a change in the present and future order of the environment. This environment changes from one without "variant X" to one containing "variant X." Darwin is a conventionalist in that the natural order he finds is neither a foreordained structure given to the world, nor a fiat imposed on the environment by the subject, but a sequence of prevailing social agreements between organisms and environments, each moment of which depends, in part, on the spontaneity of the organism. To use Wheeler's language, the structures of living systems are built out of individual observations of the environment by particular living things; but when observations are accepted, they change the observed. Natural laws are not ahistorical and eternal laws; even if they change much more slowly than cultural fashions, they are just as historical and conventional as culture is historical and conventional.

It is particularly this characterization of the laws of nature that troubles most scientists. They object with good reason to any simple dismissal of these laws as local and temporary. First, it appears that Wheeler's interpretation not only exaggerates the fluidity of natural principles but treats extreme instances as standard. Newton's law of gravity (that every particle in the world attracts every other with a force directly proportional to the product of their masses and inversely proportional to the square of the distance between their mass centers), it is asserted, seems to hold everywhere and always, even minutes after the big bang. Study of spectral lines in remote regions of space and time virtually demands that atomic behavior be described by fundamental constants (the speed of light, the mass of the electron, the mass of the proton, Planck's constant, Boltzmann's constant, to name a few). Calculations about the size and age of the universe and the composition of the stars proceed on the quite uncontroversial assumption that principles remain constant. Astrophysicists assume that they can look at a remnant heat and describe the extent of the expansion of the universe or that they can explain the presence of radiation by arguing that it was formed in the radiative recombination of protons and electrons in the early formation of hydrogen. Even within quantum physics, it is assumed that, while individual events remain uncertain, the envelope of probabilities is certain.

However, none of this effectively nullifies Wheeler's belief that the randomness of events may tell a larger tale not subsumable beneath universal and eternal principles. That is to say, these objections do not overthrow Wheeler's claim that his paradigm is the more basic and more accurate paradigm, just as Einstein's relativity is more basic and accurate than Newton's mechanics—even though Newton's laws of gravity are so close to accurate for most purposes that they are used in space flights today.

Further, I acknowledge that the way I have spoken of Darwin violates current neo-Darwinian rhetoric, in which Darwin is treated as a mechanist, a successor to Isaac Newton, a proponent of classical causality. The neo-Darwinians tend to see the world, not as though it were formed as convention (partly through the interpretations of the organism), but as though it were formed mechanically (where the interpretations of the organism either do not exist or have no affect on outcomes). Neo-Darwinians believe that mutations are random, that they occur independently of both the environment and anything like the organism's choice, and that they can be predicted statistically. For them, "spontaneous" and "random" do not mean unpredictable (as they do for Wheeler) but blindness to both environment and the organism's intention (if the organism has an intention). Evolution is driven by the mechanical fit between genetic capability and environmental niche. In the last decades of the nineteenth century, arguing with Herbert Spencer, William James clearly saw the disturbing social implications of such mechanistic selectivism; he went on to emphasize variationism as a kind of protoconventionalism.[50] But among biologists, Spencer has been the winner, an unacknowledged champion of such widely varying biological commentators as Richard Dawkins, E. O. Wilson, and proponents of the Gaia theory, all of whom have nonhuman species (and, sometimes, humans) mechanically controlled by a combination of random mutations and environmental selection.[51]

Nevertheless, conventionalism can be found in biological theory—specifically in the theory of "directed mutations." This theory argues that certain bacteria develop a larger than predicted number of adaptive mutations when presented with a hostile environment and that this arises somehow in response to the environment. The theory is neo-Lamarckian (after the Chevalier de Lamarck, 1744-1829), not in the strict sense that it argues that *all* mutations arise in response to environmental pressures and are heritable, but in the weak sense that *some* mutations arise in response to environmental pressures and are heritable.[52] That is, these neo-Lamarckians differ from the neo-Darwinians, who argue that mutations arise in complete independence of environmental pressures, blindly presenting genes from which an environment can select. I am calling the theory of directed mutations a form of conventionalism because it argues that a genetic construct can arise within an organism and then enter the stream of history as a living tradition and, further, that the construct arises from something analogous to observation and decision— that is, interpretation.

Directed mutation is best explained in "The Origins of Mutants" by John Cairns, Julie Overbaugh, and Stephan Miller, published in *Nature* in September 1988. They argue that when E. coli (Escherichia coli) bacteria are introduced into hostile environments, they mutate adaptively; that is, their mutations are directed rather than random and merely spontaneous. Cairns and his colleagues contend that E. coli, as a consequence, are able to adapt to a hostile environment at a rate higher than neo-Darwinian probabilities allow. Startlingly, they say, "we describe here a few experiments and some circumstantial evidence suggesting that bacteria can choose which mutations they should produce."[53] They argue that the belief that mutations abide by probabilities irrelevant to environment is "a doctrine that has never been properly put to the test." Further, they argue that S. E. Luria and M. Delbrück, whose work is so important in the defense of orthodox theories of blind spontaneity, never seriously tested whether responsiveness to the environment could figure in the bacteria's mutation. Luria's and Delbrück's experiment killed bacteria before it was possible to explore fully whether or not they might "choose" an adaptive mutation.[54]

The literature around this and subsequent publications by Cairns and his colleagues is rapidly growing, and it is both critical of and supportive of directed mutation.[55] Of course, the use of the word "choose" by Cairns and his colleagues is controversial, particularly when they provide no explanation of how choices to increase the rate or the propriety of mutations are made. Further, there are reasons other than directed mutation that might explain why mutations appear to be directed.[56] Nevertheless, Cairns and his colleagues contend that their experiments work in support of the romantics, who would allow whole bacteria to choose, and against DNA reductionists, who would reduce all mutations to the physics and chemistry of smaller parts of bacteria. Cairns, as well as Patricia Foster, have continued to argue for some kind of directed mutation; the critics of directed mutation have continued to argue that the unexpectedly high mutation rate can be reductionistically explained. The argument is, at this point, unresolved.

Still, there appears to be a new openness about whether biological change can be explained, not mechanically (through predetermined and probabilistic laws and blind spontaneities), but through something analogous to interpretation, where organisms at the simplest levels in some way experience and decide about how to react to environments. When E. coli mutate, they literally transform themselves and, in effect, their relation to the environment—from an inhospitable relation (that would kill them) to a hospitable relation (that allows them to survive). The consequence is a new tradition of hospitable relations between some new form of E. coli and its environment. Thus, real history is changed by how it is observed.

Theories of directed mutation could contribute significantly to the notion that there is something analogous to historical behavior at the bacterial level. Further they could suggest that bacterial "decisions," as they link bacteria and environments, can create something analogous to new conventions and that these are passed on and change the bacterial world—all of which is analogous to the way social conventions work in human societies.

This is to say that natural history, in at least two ways, may be affected by conventions. This raises the possibility that natural history can be seen as a tradition built of conventions, always presently augmented by new conventions. And this suggests that real history, at its most elementary level, is conventional, thus allowing history, at its most sophisticated and human level, to be conventional.

IV. Conventionalism and Values

For religious critics the theory of conventionalism clarifies a responsibility. The meaning of the whole implicit in the spiritual culture is, like so much else, neither given nor static. Rather, it arises through an empirical sensibility and grows as a convention. Because of this, religious critics can help, not only to analyze those spiritual conventions, but to develop new conventions to meet new conditions. Religious critics, in that sense, can change history and can be understood to do so without violating what has been learned through poststructuralism—nay, can capitalize on the end of structuralism. This presents a new menu of responsibilities.

But while conventionalism gives to religious critics clear responsibilities, it also places them in a moral quagmire. If a society's conventions originate in imagination or in something analogous to biological variation, and if imaginative constructions become conventions because they gain social approval, then all permanent moral criteria for conventions are lost. It appears that whatever is locally accepted and socially instituted simply becomes true or, in the case of ethical conventions, good. Does this not permit virtually anything to be named true and good for a society? Does this make conventionalism a dangerous paradigm for the work of the religious critic?

The historian Kenneth Cmiel raises this sort of question when he argues that poststructuralist methods put historians on the moral fringe. Historians Hayden White, Dominick LaCapra, and Hans Kellner are inclined, Cmiel says, to reduce history to a rhetorical construction—to whatever language makes it. They have not clearly explained how evidence and moral value shape the work of the historian. Nevertheless, Cmiel notes, even these new historians are not content simply to reduce history to fiction. Nor do they "countenance historians making things up."[57] For them it is not acceptable to say that the Holocaust never happened. They are methodologically skeptical and, at the same time, committed to something like the true and the good. Add this irony: White and LaCapra cast themselves as fierce defenders of the historian's public obligations, yet their newly professional poststructural methods are so dense that the public cannot read them. So Cmiel concludes by asking, "In what ways can one combine being a professional with being a human being and citizen?"[58]

Thomas Haskell, in many ways a poststructuralist himself, acknowledges these important questions but argues that conventionalism can answer them. He responds to historian David Brion Davis, for whom conventionalism tends toward relativism, eliminates moral grounds, and sanctions any social bias so long as it is a social convention.[59] Like Richard Rorty and Nelson Goodman (see Chapter 2), Haskell argues that the elimination of absolute moral grounds need not lead to moral irresponsibility. Historians are not helpless before their preferences; despite the relativity of their knowledge, they have the capacity and the obligation to gain critical distance on what they study—even if they often fail to do so. To avoid this obligation, to declare themselves incapable of imagining an opponent's stand, to yield to the conclusion that every claim, even one's own, is equally selfish and blind, so that no comparative judgments can be made, "is to turn a blind eye to distinctions that all of us routinely make and confidently act upon."[60] Historians are obligated, Haskell believes, to read texts with "that vital minimum of ascetic self-

discipline" that people commonly practice as they seek to overcome wishful thinking, to accept verified bad news and avoid
unverified good news, and, most important of all, to "suspend or
bracket one's own perceptions long enough to enter sympathetically into the alien and possibly repugnant perspectives of rival
thinkers."[61] So Haskell argues that conventionalism, despite its
modified relativity, does not prevent a modified critical objectivity. In effect, he argues for retention of the historical realism that
is part of conventionalism properly understood; and he opposes
the sheer subjectivism and relativism that some poststructuralists
or critics of poststructuralism would make of conventionalism.

Thus, Haskell's position on the morality of conventionalism
offers no clean, clear, third option, no quick fix in the postmodern quagmire. He suggests a behavior of criticism—a
groundless, ad hoc, contingent, self-critical, muddling-through
mode of behavior—as a way of replacing the unequivocal answers of objectivism or the utterly equivocal answers of relativism. Charles Taylor in "The Politics of Recognition" takes a
similar stance. Taylor sympathetically describes both the liberal
formalistic objectivism that would affirm the equal worth of all
truth claims and the multicultural subjectivism that would defend
local claims against the invasion of general claims. But, finally, he
opines that "there must be something midway between the in-
authentic and homogenizing demand for recognition of equal
worth, on the one hand, and the self-immurement within ethno-
centric standards, on the other." Thus, without denying our commitment to our own tradition of values, we tend to believe that
other traditions, even traditions we abhor and reject, should be
heard and learned from. We are not driven into isolation, and we
can be open to other traditions. This behavior is underwritten by
a kind of humility: "an admission that we are very far away from
that ultimate horizon from which the relative worth of different
cultures might be evident. This would mean breaking with an
illusion that still holds many 'multiculturalists'— as well as their
most bitter opponents—in its grip."[62]

American historian James Kloppenberg contends that pragmatism provides a specifically American approach to this relativity issue. Kloppenberg's pragmatic hermeneutics subscribes to
the "more sophisticated versions of historicism" found in the
writings of Richard Bernstein and Richard Rorty and in the

classical pragmatism of William James and John Dewey.[63] Partly because these thinkers find it impossible to discover foundations beyond social consensus, they authorize that consensus; but they also test the morality of social consensus pragmatically. Kloppenberg not only connects conventionalism to neopragmatism and to classical American pragmatism but argues for a nascent movement of historians who are conventionalists, including Haskell, David Hollinger, Gordon Wright, and William H. McNeill, all of whom call for a value-laden historicism.[64]

Kloppenberg's use of American pragmatism as a key to conventionalism can be vindicated by an example. Many of the conventionalists I discuss above cite William James, the popularizer of pragmatism. Not only did Ludwig Wittgenstein read James's *Varieties of Religious Experience* at a crucial point in his own development (1912), but his river-riverbed analogy is eerily close to James's analogy in *Pragmatism*.[65] Commentators on the life of Niels Bohr (who in some respects is the father of John Wheeler's "participatory universe" described above) frequently cite Bohr's dependence on William James.[66] Wheeler cites James as an ally.[67] Among historians, Kenneth Cmiel sees James introducing the needed sort of third option.[68] Hollinger first discusses Rorty's "conversation of the West" and then shows its similarity to James's "interlocking set of traditions that make up this conversation."[69]

An additional concern for Kloppenberg is to show how academic conventionalists have been morally effective. His *Uncertain Victory: Social Democracy and Progressivism in European and American Thought, 1870–1920* demonstrates how the implicitly or explicitly pragmatic philosophies of James, Dewey, Wilhelm Dilthey, Thomas Hill Green, Henry Sidgwick, and Alfred Fouillée affected progressivist and social democratic politics. At bottom, Kloppenberg suggests, we make conventions because we want to change society, not because we want merely to describe ideals or even local circumstances.

Kloppenberg not only defends the morality of conventionalism but suggests a moral mandate for religious critics. Conventions, it would appear, not only arise from private imaginations and take form in past social agreements; they are realities that intellectuals can and should themselves forge, thereby to change society. Conventions are not static objects, nor are they socially useless private relativities. They are hypotheses that have social consequences. It would follow that the religious critic should imagine, project, and defend hypotheses that can become social conventions in order to institute social change for the good.

Finally, however, Cmiel and Davis and others are right in warning that conventionalism is morally problematic. While conventionalism in the hands of the right historian or religious critic may call for a new style of moral responsibility, it is also a gate through which moral irresponsibilities can march.[70]

CHAPTER 8

THE REALITY OF THE
SACRED CONVENTION

> Surely all this is not without meaning. And still deeper
> the meaning of that story of Narcissus, who because he
> could not grasp the tormenting, mild image he saw in
> the fountain, plunged into it and was drowned. But
> that same image, we ourselves see in all rivers and
> oceans. It is the image of the ungraspable phantom of
> life; and this is the key to it all.
>
> Herman Melville, *Moby Dick*[1]

Melville acknowledges that "the ungraspable phantom of
life" may begin as our own reflection, but everything he says in
Moby Dick points to the fact that the phantom of life far exceeds
mere reflection. It takes on an uncanny force of its own, restlessly
working in the natural history of the great waters and in the social
histories of those who sail on those waters.

Like Melville, the religious critic recognizes that our images
of the sacred may begin, like Narcissus's, with what comes from
ourselves but that eventually they exceed anything we can control. They become realities. Unlike Melville, the religious critic
lives in a poststructuralist society and needs an explicitly historical understanding of the sacred. To help answer that need, I am
proposing that the sacred be understood as a convention, a reality
operating in a society's spiritual culture.

I am not arguing that language of the sacred (or of the
divine) is indispensable. Perhaps artists, for example, can criticize
the spiritual culture only if they avoid the language of the sacred.

131

Many Buddhist and mystical forms of thought are conducted without using God language.

Nevertheless, I do argue that in American culture, on the whole, language of the sacred, even language of God, can be pragmatically justified. It allows people to use the religious traditions they have inherited, even if they reject most of the literal claims of those traditions. Using these traditions, people are better able to respond seriously to the moral and aesthetic and religious challenges that arise in their path.

People have questions about the meaning of parts of their history, and seem unable to answer those questions unless they acquire a sense of the whole of their history. Religion refers to a people's sense of the whole; religion refers to that appreciation for the whole that gives an adequate context to parts of people's personal or public history. The sacred is whatever charges that sense of the whole with evaluation; the sacred is understood to be ultimately important and, as such, is the source for religion's normative claims. The sacred provides the narrative direction, the thrust against which, and in collaboration with which, a person's deepest emotions gain and expend their energy. None of this requires that the sacred is a being or is supernatural or that the word "God" is anything other than a term of reference pointing to whatever it is that accomplishes those functions.

The sacred, I propose, is analogous to the point that ties together the loose ends of a very subtle story, giving to the parts of the story a sense and purpose otherwise absent. Eventually, this point to the story works, not only in the story, but in the life of the story's reader. The sacred is that which ties together the unresolved questions in a people's historic traditions. The sacred is an answer that works, first of all, within the story of those traditions. And yet, it is an answer that finally points beyond the tradition to a people's present history in all its manifoldness, making the tradition an answer to what otherwise is unanswered but most important in that history. As such, the sacred is that on or about which people are "absolutely dependent" (Friederich Schleiermacher) or "ultimately concerned" (Paul Tillich); it is that which is "maximally important" (George Lindbeck) or is "the ultimate point of reference" (Gordon Kaufman) or is that which allows life "to achieve some end other than extinction" (John Cobb, Jr.).[2]

The sacred so understood should help people function in what they perceive to be a purposeful way and without which they tend to drift. With language of the sacred, people can more easily see how, in the whole of their history, they are accomplishing something. The sacred is, in that sense, useful even for those who, out of a justifiable cultural or intellectual caution, refuse to use the term.

Yet, if the sacred understood as a convention is to be useful for the religious critic, it must survive, not only the legitimate intellectual objections to most conceptions of God that have arisen in the West in the last three hundred years, but the post-structuralist objections raised in the last three decades. Admittedly, in attempting to defend the language of the sacred, one is well advised to proceed with a kind of religious agnosticism, acknowledging that, on such matters, no one knows truly whereof he or she speaks. Religiously, this is a claim for the mystery of the sacred. Aesthetically, it recognizes the inevitable and usually unintentional absurdity in being a religious thinker or a religious critic. As Gordon Kaufman argues in *In Face of Mystery*,[3] this ignorance means that, despite their claims to the contrary, all thinkers about religion have no choice but to construct God and see whether or how it works.

I. The Sacred as a Convention

If the sacred is a religious convention, it is composed of images of what is ultimately important as they are carried by the spiritual culture of a people. The sacred, I am proposing, is a living and evolving convention about what is ultimately important. Although it is continually reinterpreted, the sacred is not just passive to the influence of a people's interpretations of what is ultimately important. It is also active, influencing a people's estimate of what is ultimately important. The sacred, so understood, is partially independent of a people's interpretation; it influences an emerging sense of ultimacy in ways not anticipated by those whose images have contributed to the sacred. The sacred's independence is implicit in the fact that the effects of the sacred convention exceed the effects that might be predicted by reference solely to the images about ultimate importance that contribute to that convention. The sacred, like any socially constructed reality, can turn back on society and act in ways that were not originally intended. Nevertheless, this sacred activity is a thoroughly historical activity. The sacred, then, is a living tradition of agreements about what is ultimately important, is continually reinterpreted, is partially independent, and is thoroughly historical.

The sacred is real, as a living tradition of conventions is real. Like any living tradition, it embodies a society's deepest imaginings but becomes, to some limited extent, independent of those imaginings. Any religious tradition begins in imagination, which is an empirical sense of the whole (as discussed in chapter 6). The tradition is real both in that it has effects in the society in which it is located and in that it works in ways that cannot be strictly predicted, no matter how much is known of the past. The sacred understood as a convention has the ontological status of a social convention, not the ontological status of an objective reality (such as a divine and supernatural person), not the ontological status of a subjective reality (such as the projection of a wish).

The sacredness of the sacred, the divinity of God, depends not only on the partial independence of the sacred but on the fact that it involves what is ultimately important. It responds to a people's deepest unanswered questions and suggests answers that purport to be ultimately important.

Conventionalism offers not only a model of the sacred but a key to understanding the religious thinker as a religious thinker. When intellectuals seek to interpret the largest context of their own work, they involve themselves in conventions about the sense of the whole—that is, in religious conventions. To the extent that questions of ultimate importance enter their sense of the whole, then their conventions about the whole depend on the sacred. Religious critics are not only "frameworkers," criticizing the public framework of meaning, but "religious frameworkers," people who assess the adequacy of the ultimate meaning implicit in the public framework. As such, they both represent and seek to reconstruct the spiritual culture of a society.

Conventionalism is a way of describing the sacred, a model for understanding what God is. Just as the sacred has been understood to be the reality behind scriptures or universal and eternal structures or great rites and ceremonies, it can be understood as the convention that represents what is ultimately important in the sense of the whole. As such, conventionalism does not reject scriptures, religious ideas, and religious ceremonies but sees them as public conventions about a sense of the whole. While conventionalism does not treat those scriptures, ideas, and ceremonies as historical mirrors of a God beyond history, conventionalism is in its own way conservative, for any convention about what is ultimate stands in the line of past conventions. Any current convention is tied on a fairly short leash to the history of previous conventions. Further, while religious conventionalism does not accept the metaphysician's extrahistorical grounds for a sense of the whole, it affirms, nevertheless, a particular society's own, relative picture of the whole. That is, religious conventions about the meaning of the whole can be grounded in a society's spiritual culture, rather than in an extrahistorical foundation.

Conventionalism is compatible with a form of social relativity, but its social relativity is no more extreme than that of many other religious theories. As Shailer Mathews or Shirley Jackson Case and a line of sociohistorical students of church history have argued (in the 1920s and 1930s, decades before the sociology of knowledge was developed), all ecclesiastical interpretations of God and of Christ have been adjusted to meet the social needs specific to particular cultural situations. That relativity does not keep religious beliefs from being normative within a community, nor does it keep a community from being critical of those norms as it tests them by their success or failure within a community or in interaction with other communities. Nor does that relativity keep a group from judging its religious beliefs in the light of the beliefs of other religious communities.

In making the sacred relative and, to some extent, formed by a people's interpretations, conventionalism differs from classical theology and modern theology, which treat God as an objective reality. Taking an objectivist stand, classical Western theology has prized God's independence *(aseity)*, the fact that God is a self-moved mover, one who creates all and is created by nothing. As such, God has been seen as something given to societies, rather than as partially constructed by societies. And as a given, God guides the world, intervenes in its processes, or lays ground rules in terms of which the world must operate. Modern theology, it is true, goes beyond classical understandings by locating God within, rather than beyond, natural, rational, or existential forms of life. Nevertheless, most modern religious thinkers understand God to be that which gives the world the rules it has. Whether orthodox, liberal, or fundamentalist, modern religious thinkers tend to argue that the world is the way it is because God makes it that way and that this can be discovered through observation, reason, religious experience, scripture, or some institutional authority as it operates in the world. Except for process, empirical, and historicist theologians, modern thinkers seldom talk of how the world might contribute to God.

To put it in language about types or reality, what is distinctive about conventionalism is that it works out of a model of neither the object, nor the subject, but out of the model of the convention. A convention is a public construction, always formed by an objective public past interacting with a current subjective creativity, but it is not reducible to either of those causes or to their combined effects. A convention is as real as the American Constitution is real. Like the American Constitution, a convention is never reducible to a written document, nor to the inventive interpretations of every session of the Supreme Court; it is never reducible to the text the framers intended or to the interpretations of innovative jurists.

The reality of a convention is found in the fact that, like the American constitution, it turns one day and acts in unpredictable ways—uncannily, it takes initiatives. In this independent action and in this mystery lies the distinct reality of a convention, certifying its status as a third, rather than a middle, term. To put it in pragmatic language, the meaning of a convention lies in its effects, consequences, and outcomes. Because the convention supersedes its causes, takes on a life of its own, and is not entirely predictable, its meaning can be discovered only in its consequences. Analogously, the evolving life of the American constitution has been unpredictable, and its meaning can be found primarily, if not only, in its social effects. No public convention can be reduced to its causes—not to past traditions and not to reinterpretations of those traditions, and not to any combination of the two.

The sacred convention is a concrete, evaluative thrust living and operating in a society. It has a life of its own, just as a whole organism has a life that cannot be reduced to the lives of its parts.

Its life is, finally, inaccessible through analysis of all that caused it or of all that interprets it. It cannot be observed, just as a universe cannot be observed. Yet it operates. The sacred provides the deepest normative drive in a society as that society works out of its religious sense of the whole. It lives as a convention lives; it is not an object, and it is not reducible to a subjective projection; it is historical and active and real, and yet it is subject to alteration. It seems to be impossible to explain exactly how the sacred exists or how it functions; the battlefields of theology and metaphysics are strewn with failed explanations. To recognize this is to recognize the mystery of the sacred even as it is seen from a particular cultural standpoint. I am proposing that to believe in God is to believe that something like this is happening in one's society. And I am proposing that that belief makes a difference in how a people understands itself and, particularly, in how it reforms itself.

The sacred conceived in ancient Israel or in modern America is, to some extent, generated by the interaction between the Gods of earlier traditions and the local community of faith. The sacred, thus understood, is no less real and independent of people than the Constitution is real and independent of people. The life and mystery of the sacred become evident when the sacred acts in unpredictable ways, something the ancient Hebrews well understood. In this life beyond the control of the past and the present lies a glimmering of what came to be called God's aseity (the ontological independence of God). But the sacred, thus understood, is also relative in a way William James recognized when he said "mental interests ... help to *make* the truth which they declare."[4] Recognizing both relativism and realism, James said, first, that religion, if it is not to be a game of private theatricals, must affirm that our efforts count, so that "God himself, in short, may draw vital strength and increase of very being from our fidelity" and, then, that "god is real since he produces real effects."[5]

In the biblical religions these forces of independence and relativity combined to form a divine law, prophet figures, a Christ, and a God. To treat the sacred as to some extent a function of Israel is consistent with new directions in biblical studies. Of course, for centuries biblical scholars have said that the Hebrews were the passive recipients of divine actions and laws that enter history from beyond history. But during the last 150 years of Hebrew Bible (Old Testament) scholarship, it has become increasingly evident that the Hebrew biblical writers and rabbis imaginatively constructed their religious world.[6] Through a chain of interpretations, creatively shaping and reshaping their tradition to voice new needs and address new problems, the ancient Hebrews reinterpreted their covenants with their God and/or their God itself. The implication is that the sense of ultimacy can affect ultimacy itself, just as any image can move from subjective construct to objective condition. The Hebrew God, like any convention, is altered by an imagined image that becomes socially effective. Of course, some theories of God never become conventions; in Israel, false prophets were censured and had little affect on the traditions of ultimate importance. At the same time, it is also true that the God of Israel is, finally, more than the sum of Hebrew interpretations of God. Thus, even though they may have constructed their God, many Hebrews have continued to be baffled and dismayed by their God—right up through the Nazi Holocaust.

Equally, for centuries Christian scholars have said that the first Christian community passively received a new revelation. But again, today most New Testament scholars argue that the New Testament motifs, including the understandings of Christ and of God, were imaginative reconstructions of a variety of ancient Near Eastern influences. In short, they point to how popular images went on to contribute to sacred conventions.[7] Much of the excitement over the Dead Sea Scrolls is the excitement of seeing to what extent the New Testament authors and communities they represented formed their own conventions and to what extent they conveyed earlier conventions.

This reimagination of Christ and of God in light of subsequent social environments continues through the history of the Christian church, as Shailer Mathews and Shirley Jackson Case so well demonstrated in their histories of Christian thought fully two generations ago.[8] Interpretations both reflected earlier conventions of Christian communities and altered those conventions for the future.

Theories of religious construction and convention do not necessarily undermine the reality of the God of the Jews and of the Christians. After all, to acknowledge that language to some extent constructs its referent does not, by itself, prove that the referent is unreal. Not only can invented terms refer to heretofore hidden realities, they can construct new realities. (Or, as John Dewey argued, the telegraph did not exist before Morse imagined it, and the locomotive did not exist before Stevenson imagined it, yet each now clearly exists.[9])

Admittedly, theories of convention appear religiously wrong-headed from the vantage point of a specific sort of objectivism, where an account can be called true only if it replicates what caused it and where the faithfulness of its replication is tested by something like the clarity and distinctness of its ideas. Peter Berger, an eminent sociologist of knowledge, seems to have accepted such objectivism in *Rumor of Angels*. Involving himself in a two-option fallacy, he treated the social construction of God as a groundless reification (treating a projected thing as a real thing) and juxtaposed that with only one other possibility—that God must be "*an other reality* ... which transcends the reality within which our everyday experience unfolds."[10] To save his supernatural God, Berger resorted to a rationalistic exercise, the search for "signals of transcendence," which are "experiences that appear to express essential aspects of man's being" and, at the same time, transcend "the empirical sphere."[11] Thus, although Berger acknowledged that projections and signals sometimes arrive at the same conclusion, he assumed that they point to quite different realities, one merely historical and invented and the other extrahistorical and given. This omits entirely the third kind of reality to which conventionalism points.

A reconception of the sacred by reference to the conventionalist model can yield two ideas: first, that the sacred is an imaginative, social construction that becomes conventional and public; and second, that the sacred is real in the sense that it is more than, or independent of, the sum of imaginative constructions about the sacred. When conventionalism makes God a convention, it does not reduce the sacred to the sum of social constructs, although it acknowledges that the sacred is, to some extent, affected by those constructs. It follows from these two ideas that the sacred is neither an objective reality given to and disinterestedly observed in the known world, nor a merely subjective projection; it is a convention.

II. The Moral Ambiguity of the Sacred

A third implication follows from the use of the conventionalist model: that the sacred is morally ambiguous. This conclusion seems appropriate, given the foregoing definition of how the sacred comes to be and of the pragmatism implicit in conventionalism. First, if the sacred is a convention about what is ultimately important, and if that convention is fueled by ambiguous human images of ultimacy, then the sacred, itself, must be ambiguous. Second, if a people's images of what is ultimately important are affected by the sacred and if their images are ambiguous, then, reasoning pragmatically (from consequence to cause), it could be argued that the sacred cause is, itself, ambiguous.

Of course, these arguments are not conclusive. So long as one insists on the mystery and on the independence of God, no historical cause or consequence can prove anything about the sacred reality. I have contended that the sacred cannot be reduced to social conditions that caused it or to interpretations made of it. Thus, however ambiguous the human estimates of what is ultimately important, these do not provide sufficient grounds for declaring the sacred reality ambiguous. The fallibility of the pragmatic argument is particularly apparent. Just as children can cause terrible divorces and still be innocent or citizens may occasion robbery and still be innocent, so the sacred reality operating in history may lie behind the motives of those who perpetrate the terrors of history and still be innocent. Nevertheless, there is a point beyond which such innocence seems implausible. Admittedly, Elie Wiesel in *Night* did not have proof that God could be associated with the crimes of Nazi death camps; yet, I contend, that he had good reason to cry out when he first set foot in one of those camps and heard of the crematory: "The Eternal, Lord of the Universe, the All-Powerful and Terrible, was silent. What had I to thank Him for?"[12] Accordingly, the misery of human histories would seem to provide an adequate, though inconclusive, justification for believing that the sacred is in some sense implicated in that misery.

"The moral ambiguity of God" is an idea with several meanings. First and as a symbol, it affirms that moral ambiguity goes all the way down, that it is so basic and so pervasive that it is escaped by nothing, not even by the sacred. Equally, it denies that in the idea of moral perfection there is a deeper wisdom or that a society benefits from hearing that moral perfection somewhere exists; it affirms, in fact, the opposite. Second, the moral ambiguity of God is an idea that attempts to describe what is, rather than what ought to be, to account for the actual "meaning of the whole," rather than call for something good, humane, rational, or ideal in the whole. Here language of the divine is to describe the historical process (not to grade it) or to respond to the mystery (not to seek the ideal). This is to follow Luther, Calvin, and Paul Tillich as they acknowledge the strangeness of God, rather than to follow the more irenic theologians of the Christian church. In American religious thought, it is to follow religious thinkers such as William H. Bernhardt, Bernard Loomer, and, today, Elie Wiesel, Fred Sontag, and John K. Roth.[13] It is to deviate slightly from the American naturalism that identifies God as perfect, as one to be worshipped, or as the creative good, especially in the writings of Alfred North Whitehead, Henry Nelson Wieman, Charles Hartshorne, David Griffin, and, most recently, Jerome Stone (who, in representative language, acknowledges that transcendent creativity is ambiguous but identifies God with transcendent creativity only "in so far as" it is creative of good).[14]

The connection between conventionalism and the moral ambiguity of the sacred can be described through a comment on John Dewey, who, in several respects, is a conventionalist but who assumes, like most Westerners, that God, to be called God, must be good. God, says Dewey, "is that unity of all ideal ends arousing us to desire and actions."[15] This makes God not only a construct composed of human ideals but a construct that acts somewhat independently on human communities. Dewey sees a world that would disintegrate were it not for a force creating harmonies, and he calls that force God. For Dewey, God is not a being, but a convention—a stream of traditions about the ideal, fed by imagined ideals, and operative in and on the world. And as a convention about what is ideal, Dewey's God is unambiguously good.

Further, Dewey sets his God within a consideration of "the whole." In *Human Nature and Conduct,* a book on ethics published in 1922, well after Dewey had abandoned Hegelianism, he reaffirmed an apprehension of the whole. The sense of the whole permitted Dewey to avoid the amorality of pragmatism, for which Randolph Bourne had criticized him.[16] With a sense of the whole, Dewey could argue that pragmatic success should refer not to just any result but to results that foster a sense of the whole community of interests. In that book he repeatedly refers to "a sense of the whole," "the sense of an enveloping whole," "the sense of this effortless and unfathomable whole" that is appreciated only after our activism in a world of pluralities is exhausted.[17] After affirming that the religious is about "our being in its entirety," Dewey virtually concludes *A Common Faith* by invoking "the community of causes and consequences in which we, together with those not born, are enmeshed," "the mysterious totality of being the imagination calls the universe." God, Dewey affirmed, is that specific unification of all relevant ideal ends, giving normative unity to the whole. God is "the unity of all ideal ends arousing us to desire and action,"[18] prompting people to harmonious action within the whole; this action tends to convert dissonances that threaten the meaning of the whole into harmonies that preserve the meaning of the whole.

For Dewey, God is not itself the whole[19] but is that process whereby a unity of ideals reconciles disparities, making an otherwise fragmented world into a whole world. As a radical empiricist, Dewey argues that this unity is grasped through imagination, not as a fantasy, but as knowledge: "the reflex of the unification of practical and emotional attitudes." This unity of ideals becomes a "heritage of values" that acts on people. So God is real for Dewey: "In reality, the only thing that can be said to be 'proved' is the existence of some complex of conditions that have operated to effect an adjustment in life, an orientation, that brings with it a sense of security and peace."[20] Thus, Dewey claims God is known through those events that appear to be consequences of a mysterious process, and thereby echoes William James's "God is real since he produces real effects." In all this, Dewey's God is a convention.

Dewey's God, however, is an unambiguous force for goodness. "For it [God] involves no miscellaneous worship of everything in general. It selects those factors in existence that generate and support our idea of good as an end to be striven for."[21] Never is Dewey's God implicated in social evil. In this, Dewey is not unsubtle, and he does not simply forget his own relativism when he claims God is good.[22] Nevertheless and after all is said and done, Dewey's God stands as unambiguously good.

But if Dewey had adhered more completely to his own conventionalism, he would not have called God good. Dewey did recognize, even emphasized, the moral ambiguity of organized religion[23] but failed to acknowledge that "the unity of ideals" that prompts people to do what otherwise they would not do becomes, in historical practice, just as ambiguous as religion. It is obvious that those specific harmonies based on "the unity of ideals," and once judged to be good, very often turn out to be perverse. This suggests that the God who is that operative unity of ideals is ambiguous, for God is known by its effects. Often historical societies prompted by a theological unity of ideals recognize—sometimes almost immediately—their impropriety. Some Israelis, for example, have sincerely invoked their religious ideals as their reason for manipulating Palestinians in Israel; and many Israelis now call that manipulation evil. Or Christians have invoked their specific religious ideals as the reason for elevating the Christian faith over all other faiths; and many Christians now call that elevation evil. Equally, Western religious traditions have used their religious ideals to proclaim the inferiority of women and blacks and now call that evil.

As the exception that proves a rule, Dewey's apparent mistake indicates that a thoroughly historicist and conventionalist analysis leads to the moral ambiguity of the sacred. If the sacred is a historical convention about ultimate importance, and if conventions (no matter how ideal at the outset) turn out to have morally ambiguous effects, then the sacred is itself morally ambiguous. (Of course, Dewey or anyone else could qualify their claims about divine goodness by saying that whenever the unity of ideals issues in immoral behavior, it must not have been the real unity of ideals and thus not the unity of ideals that is truly sacred. But this is to reduce theology to second-guessing.) Conventionalism leads to a recognition, not just of the moral ambiguity of religion, but of religion's God. This is conventionalism's strength, not its weakness, for, in the last analysis, it lends historical realism to religious thought and encourages people not to rely entirely on the sacred and to be more responsible for religious developments.

While the idea of a morally ambiguous God may deviate

from much mainstream Western tradition, certainly it can be found in that tradition. Theodicy is the name for the form of arguments that attempts to vindicate the goodness of God in face of the question: How can God be good, if God is omnipotent and the world is plagued with evil? The long history of theodicy suggests that its task has never been quite accomplished.

"The attempt to defend God's honor," James Crenshaw argues, "prompted the very first human speech within the Bible, Eve's response to the serpent, and persists to the last canonical book and beyond."[24] Nevertheless, Crenshaw goes on to argue, biblical theodicies are undermined by their own unfairness. They excuse evil by: (1) underrating human suffering, (2) blaming the human victims, or (3) invoking the *deus absconditus*.[25] Crenshaw's *A Whirlpool of Torment* retells five Hebrew Bible stories where God's goodness is successfully challenged: God's demand that Abraham kill the innocent and long-promised Isaac; Jeremiah's claim that God has seduced and abandoned him; Job's conviction that God has treated him unjustly, capriciously murdering his family, his servants, and his cattle; Ecclesiastes's conviction that the God of creation has replaced order with meaningless chance; and Psalm 73's witness of the prosperity of the wicked.

Crenshaw does not suggest that faith in a morally ambiguous God is either self-contradictory or nonreligious. Although divine betrayal is "a genuine feature of biblical faith," the ancient Hebrews denied that this leaves them "alone in the world."[26] The reality of God and a relation with God were affirmed despite God's moral ambiguity, allowing God to remain ultimately important for the society's development.

Judith Plaskow, a Jewish feminist theologian, offers a contemporary argument for the moral ambiguity of God. She introduces the God who devoured Aaron's sons for offering "strange fire" (Lev. 10:1), who killed Uzzah for putting out his hand to steady the ark (2 Sam. 6:6–7), and who warned the assembled Israelites not to come too close to the base of Sinai lest they die (Exod. 19:12–13). She criticizes feminist theology's adherence to "the 'niceness' of God," particularly as it divinizes "the so-called female virtues of nurturing, healing, and caretaking."[27] In effect, she argues, the denial of divine ambiguity is a denial of the real ambiguity of human experience or promotes a God unconnected with that experience. "One of the things I have always most valued about the Jewish tradition," Plaskow says, "is its refusal to disconnect God from the contradictory whole of reality. 'I form light and create darkness, I make weal and create woe—I, the Lord, do all these things,' Isaiah announces (Isa. 45:7)."[28] In Plaskow's approach there is an implicit empiricism: language about God must reflect, first of all, the experience of history in its entirety. Her empiricism is rooted in the experience of ultimate importance, the creative power of God, rather than in the experience of the goodness of God. Like Isaiah 45, she points to a God active through all phases of history, rather than to a God active only in the redemptive phase. In effect, for Plaskow the relation with God begins before normative thinking can exclude God from the dark side of humanity's raw, pre-moral, and concrete experience. Hers is a radical empiricism, a radical historicism, a full accounting of history; and it attests to a fully ambiguous God. In this, she agrees with Paul Tillich when he denounces the truncated Hebrew prophetic interpretation that ended in "the identification of holiness with moral perfection."[29]

The New Testament and the history of Christian thought also recognize divine ambiguity, even if in a minor and neglected key. I refer to the Jesus who said, "I have not come to bring peace, but a sword" (Mt. 10:34), and then ignited violence, even against himself, as well as to Calvin's and Luther's ominous recognition of God's power and how this gave God a leading role in the dark side of history. The maturity and boldness of this religious reflection is its willingness to find God, or whatever is ultimately important, not only in a sanitized portion of the whole of history, but in the whole of history.

This was not an idea that Dewey or his liberal intellectual colleagues, whether religious or secular, took seriously. Dewey's bias for the scientific and cognitive "method of intelligence" made it difficult for him to account for the nonscientific and noncognitive sense of importance. He neglected the spiritual significance of disharmony—both religiously and aesthetically.[30] Instead of giving empiricism free rein, he fixed the game, normatively restricted the inquiry, and then treated part of the sacred as the whole of the sacred. The problem, I am suggesting, is that, although Dewey claimed that religious questions grew out of "the sense of the whole," he limited the sense of the whole to the sense of the good.

By contrast, Bernard Loomer, in his *The Size of God*, suggested another direction for American liberal religious thought. Emphasizing, not Dewey's aesthetic harmony, but aesthetic contrast, Loomer described that restlessness in the whole body of creation, that wildness that breaks orders and pushes the world into uncharted waters, that energy that introduces variations so deviant from tradition that further deviation would destroy society, and names it God. Loomer contended that this divine energy, like human energy, fosters evil consequences just as surely as it fosters good consequences. Loomer's effort, like Plaskow's, amounted to the "refusal to disconnect God from the contradictory whole of reality."[31] God "may exemplify itself as an expansive urge toward greater good. It may also become a passion for greater evil that, however disguised or rationalized as a greater good, also has its attractiveness."[32] Loomer explicitly sought adequacy to the whole and argued that this is a more realistic standard than rational perfection (which he characterized as more abstract than concrete, more about divine cleanliness than divine historicity).[33]

In all this, however, it should be noted that Loomer did not identify God with what is worshipful; in effect, he argued that God should be worshipped only to the extent that God serves goodness as we understand goodness.[34] Or in my language, if the sacred is seen as a factor within the whole, then it is, first, to be understood for its role in the whole, not for its moral improvement of the whole. The empirical problem is the adequacy of the concept of the sacred to the whole; the specific reaction to the sacred is something for human deliberation. The task of religious critics is, first, to understand the whole, including the part played by the sacred convention, and second, to foster the community's reconstruction of the sacred in order to morally improve the whole.

One way to explore the moral ambiguity of the sacred is to cite less theoretical and more historical writings. There is in the Holocaust writings of Elie Wiesel, John K. Roth, Richard Rubinstein, and Irving Greenberg a whole literature on the moral ambiguity of God.[35] But, because the astonishing Holocaust literature tempts people to treat raw evil as exceptional rather than as normal, I turn instead to the utterly quotidian world of American professional sports. The moral ambiguity of something as normal as sports, particularly when sports is seen as a religious metaphor, suggests the inescapability of ambiguity, even of the ambiguity of the sacred.

Joyce Carol Oates is convinced of the metaphorical meaning of sports[36] and the moral ambiguity of sports. She is drawn to professional boxing because it "is the only major American sport whose primary, and often murderous, energies are not coyly defected" by devices like pucks and balls. Boxing is, she claims, as ritualized and bound by traditions "as any religious ceremony." Yet, it is utterly blunt and unvarnished: two men, nearly naked, climb into an area the size of an animal pen and, symbolically, only one will climb out alive. Boxing is "a powerful analogue of human struggle in the rawest of life and death terms"[37] (or, conversely and humorously, "life is a metaphor for boxing"[38]). She attacks those who dismiss boxing because it is so primitive—"as if inhabiting the flesh were not a primitive proposition, radically inappropriate to a civilian supported by and always subordinate to physical strength: missiles, nuclear warheads."[39]

Sports events may be more about the evil of defeat than about the good of victory. The single most important moment of a basketball game may come when men—moments earlier a seated but angry crowd—exit the arena, shoulder to shoulder, down canyons of stairs. Some must attempt silently to come to terms with the humiliating defeat just administered to their team, even as they are surrounded by opposing fans. Boxing, Oates asserts, "is about failure far more than it is about success."[39] Sports fans sometimes dwell on the defeat of others, as well as on their own. I will not forget sitting in remote and cold bleachers at the 1992 Indianapolis 500 race and watching Michael Andretti coast with a blown engine into the third turn in the 189th lap of that 200 lap race, which he had led for 160 laps and "deserved" to win. Nor will I forget feeling the fans packed closely around me suddenly come to life, rise to their feet, and cheer with derision. In their most significant moments, sports columnists are moral advisors, concentrating on personality and story rather than on the technical or physical side of sporting events, dwelling on stories of defeat rather than success.

Because of its moral degradation, some argue boxing should be banned. Why not ban auto racing too, which exposes men to far greater danger (in the 1992 Indianapolis 500, 21 out of 33 drivers did not finish, 13 crashed, eight went to the hospital, and one died attempting to qualify)? Why not football, which may be far too violent for viewing by the electorate of a democracy with the nuclear weaponry to eradicate all higher forms of life? On the other hand, it might be argued that sports is religiously too important to be banned. In professional sports lies one of the last public places in America where the brutality of everyday life is ritually dramatized.

Too often American theology and public philosophy do what they can to isolate ultimate values from such evil and, thus, to isolate religion and public philosophy from history. As Oates argues, "In the brightly lit ring, man is *in extremis,* performing an atavistic rite or *agon* for the mysterious solace of those who can participate only vicariously in such drama; the drama of life in the flesh."[41] She closes *On Boxing* with this sentence, "Boxing has become America's tragic theater." For Oates, boxing is ambiguous, not only a "rite of cruelty, sacrifice," but also of "redemption."[42]

III. The Aesthetic Character of the Sacred

If the sacred is to be modeled on the idea of a convention, how does the sacred convention operate in the spiritual culture? I propose—as a highly speculative extension of an already speculative chapter—that the sacred convention operates as an inspiration that prompts action. As such, the sacred may be analogous to a musical composition. Compositions are neither something discovered in the objective world through disinterested observation nor something sprung full grown from the composer's subjective mind. Instead, compositions are conventions: they are real expressions of the composer's interaction with his or her musical and nonmusical environment, and they both deconstruct and build on those environments, particularly on the musical environment or tradition. Those compositions can affect those who listen. Similarly, the sacred is neither something objectively given nor something simply projected out of imagination; the sacred is the product of imagination in interaction with environment, and it affects those who receive it. And the sacred, as a living tradition of ultimate importance, can enliven a people, inducing them to do what otherwise they are incapable of doing.

Accordingly, in the American context, God is often felt as a steady temporal urge, a tropism, toward aesthetic complexity. God is felt through an imagination, which itself grows from an empirical sense of what is ultimately important in the whole. From Jonathan Edwards through the Transcendentalists, through the classical pragmatists, through the rise of American relativism, pluralism, radical empiricism, and historicism, the religious impulse has often been treated aesthetically.[43] To paraphrase Whitehead, God's power lies in persuading the world to enjoy richer forms of experience. Stated historically, the sacred can be seen as a unified tradition of conventions about what is ultimately important to the public; it is continually reinterpreted but partially independent; and it works aesthetically to inspire new complexities in new circumstances. It functions, I am proposing, to inspire aesthetically richer relations between ideals and environments. That such a tropism toward complexity exists in natural history, admittedly, is disputed and worthy of much critical investigation.[44] But even Stephen Gould, a strong contemporary critic of grand theories of greater complexity, does not end, in fact, by denying the presence of increasing complexity in those living systems that survive arbitrary destruction.[45]

I am proposing that conventionalism can make this practical argument: the sacred is that which, through the creatures' empirical sensibility, stimulates their new interpretations. There are creatures who otherwise could have been as addicted to repetition as they have become addicted to aesthetic novelty.

Finally, a comment on how the reality of the sacred convention might affect the religious critic. If the sacred convention in the spiritual culture can be represented and reinterpreted, the religious critic is the intellectual who makes that work his or her special responsibility. With conventionalism, American religious critics can understand how the formation of religious conventions is possible and important. Recognizing that the sacred convention is morally ambiguous, the religious critic attempts not only to appreciate but to morally reconstruct the sacred convention. In the spirit of Reinhold Niebuhr, however, it should be noted that any such reconstruction is likely to introduce its own, grave problems in the spiritual culture.

PART IV

RECLAIMING AMERICAN CULTURE

CHAPTER 9

THE RELIGIOUS CRITIC
IN THE THIRD SECTOR

Philanthropy is a tradition, "a sequence of variations
on received and transmitted themes," as Edward Shils
put it in *Tradition*. It is not a body of laws, nor is it a
fixed set of institutions. As a tradition it has common
roots, themes, practices, and values. As a tradition it is
also dynamic and changing, and the themes, practices,
and values change so that even tracing the roots becomes a continuing problem. It is "the social history of
the moral imagination" (to borrow a wonderful phrase
from Clifford Geertz's *Local Knowledge*) or at least
one prominent thread in it.

Philanthropy in some organized form appears in
all the major cultural and religious traditions, and it
might be argued that *philanthropy is an essential
defining characteristic of civilized society.*

Robert L. Payton[1]

It is one thing to point the finger at intellectuals, blaming
them, in part, for the lack of a mature American spiritual culture.
It is another to ask whether it is possible for intellectuals to affect
the public, even if they wanted to. Stanley Elkins argues that the
American Transcendentalists of the 1850s, although they were
fervent abolitionists, had little chance of making their abolitio-
nism effective because they were not connected with institutions.
Elkins presupposes

that institutions define a society's culture, that they provide the
stable channels, for better or worse, within which the intellec-

153

tual must have his business—if, that is, his work is to have real consequences for society and if he himself is to have a positive function there.[2]

But the Transcendentalists of Brook Farm, the leading intellectuals and religious critics of their day, not only lived in an institutionally underdeveloped society, they were themselves dogmatically anti-institutional. Consequently, their opposition to slavery had little chance of either ending slavery or averting the most brutal war in American history.

It is necessary, that is, to go beyond the definition of the public task of religious critics and to ask whether there are institutions through which they might criticize and reconstruct conventions about the sense of the whole, the sacred, and the spiritual culture, in order to reach the public and, thereby, function as religious critics. If religious critics are again to develop and proliferate that spiritual culture through which society's fragmentary pursuits are to be integrated, then other questions must be answered: Where, in what institutional venues, might intellectuals be understood and supported as religious critics? How, through what institutional vehicles, might their proposals more effectively reach the spiritual culture and the society at large?

Of course, religious critics, like most American intellectuals, tend to be housed in institutions of higher education—or, in shorthand—in "the university." But do the universities provide the best venue and vehicle for the religious critic? Are the university's ideals and interactions with society the best the religious critics can hope for? I argue that religious critics are more likely to be socially effective if they give their loyalties to virtually any institution in the society's third (nongovernment, voluntary, not-for-profit) sector *except* the university, even if they work in universities. That is, even though the university is the customary, expected, and preferred home and instrument of intellectuals in American society, it is the nonuniversity, voluntary organizations within the third section that offer religious critics the better home and the better instrument.

By "the third sector," I refer to the independent, the nonprofit, the voluntary sector of American society, as opposed to the government (the first) sector and the for-profit (the second) sector. I recognize that *third sector* suggests an imagery that, on the one hand, urges an unrealistically simple, geometric division of the society and, on the other hand, neglects the important social complications and dynamics of class, race, and gender. But the term is at least better than "independent sector" (for government or market influences abound here), "nonprofit sector" (for very often a profit is earned even if it is not distributed to board members), and "voluntary sector" (for many workers are paid staff). James Douglas defines the third sector by showing that it fills a space not otherwise filled:

> Western civilization has developed two great systems for the allocation of resources. These can be symbolized conveniently by their most distinctive mechanisms: the market and the ballot box. Both have been extensively studied, in both descriptive and normative terms—the market sector of commercial enterprise by economists and the government sector by political scientists and theorists. There are, however, a host of organizations that fit tidily neither into the public, or government, sector nor into the private, or commercial, sector.[3]

The third sector includes, for example, churches, arts organizations, political movements, social action agencies, gender- and race-based rights groups, charitable organizations, foundations, and universities which, in most cases, cannot be properly called either for-profit or governmental (although university research projects often may be chattel to the market or to the government).

These third sector organizations are broadly effective. Many of their ideas, policies, and practices are ultimately adopted by government and by business. Many government welfare ideas and most public education policies can be traced to the third sector. Many of the products and services now located in the second sector originated in nonprofit and voluntary organizations (for example, in religiously sponsored hospitals and counseling services, in YMCA and YWCA recreation facilities, in not-for-profit art galleries, and in garage-based scientific research).

Third sector organizations are social conventions, as I am using the term; they take on the form of particular institutions. That is, these organizations can be traced to an originating imaginative construct, usually some vision of how a social value might be fostered by a voluntary organization; they come into life when that construct becomes an actual institution. In Robert Payton's language in the epigraph above, third sector organizations are best seen as the result of evolving traditions, with common roots, themes, practices, and values; they are particular embodiments of "the social history of the moral imagination."

In the United States, any third sector organization is virtually mandated to see itself as indirectly serving the whole society rather than any narrow objective. If it is to attract monetary contributions or voluntary service, a third sector organization must formulate an internal mission statement that justifies its objectives, often in light of what is good for the whole society. In addition, to best attract monetary contributions, a third sector organization must qualify for tax-exempt status, making some effort to justify that status in light of society's needs. These exercises prompt a consciousness of the organization's worldview, its moral objectives, sometimes even its "sense of the whole." Accordingly, most third sector organizations at least pretend to be philanthropic, and some (including many nonecclesiastical organizations) qualify as religious, as I have defined the term in preceding chapters. If they are religious, they seek to contribute in some way to the spiritual culture of a society. Accordingly, religious critics, whose primary task is to analyze and develop a society's religious conventions, can find a home and an instrument in third sector institutions.

This, of course, does not guarantee that the third sector, in fact, actually contributes to the spiritual culture, but only that, more than the other two sectors, it must give attention to that culture. Equally, just because the government sector is preoccupied with order and the for-profit sector is preoccupied with earnings does not mean that either of them must fulfill its objectives to qualify as belonging to its sector. In short, to claim that the third sector pertains to the spiritual culture does not guarantee that it actually benefits that culture. It does suggest, however, that the sector is likely to be more imaginative and critical in its attention to that culture. It is for that reason that I suggest that the religious critics should find their venue and vehicle in the third, rather than the first or second, sectors and in the non-university parts of the third sector, rather than in the university itself.

Of course, when I nominate the third sector, but not the third sector's universities,[4] as the best home for the religious critic, I recognize that the university seems to offer the obvious place and instrument for religious critics. After all, academic intellectuals are already located in universities and colleges and have, it would seem, only to use their occupational resources for public work. Overriding this is the fact that the university's professionalism works against the religious critic—at least for the time being, until poststructuralism effectively undermines professionalism.

I. The Problem

Turning for the moment from religious critics in particular to public intellectuals in general, I argue that it is no accident that academic intellectuals seldom become public intellectuals. Most academic intellectuals live within the mystique of academic professionalism and tend to think in terms of an academic agenda, while public intellectuals (whether social critics, culture critics, or religious critics) tend to think in terms of what might be called a public agenda. Both types of intellectuals fondly hope for those few moments in their careers when they will work in ways that qualify them as creative intellectuals, when they will lend a hand in the construction of theories or policies that alter the future, in whatever small way. But most academic intellectuals aim to alter an academic discipline, while public intellectuals aim to alter the public. Accordingly, academic intellectuals seldom become public intellectuals. I recognize that not all academic intellectuals should become public intellectuals and that not all intellectuals teaching in universities or colleges fail to function as public intellectuals even within their universities or colleges. I argue only that academic intellectuals seldom become public intellectuals, that this is not accidental, and that it is a serious problem for the American public.

I also recognize that there are those rare occasions when the academic intellectual's professional agenda and the public agenda happen to coincide. This occurs most obviously in new, socially responsive fields like African American Studies, Women's Studies, or Environmental Studies, particularly in the years between their founding and their professionalization (when they become "pure," that is, self-responsive, auto-stimulating disciplines). Nevertheless, these are the exceptions. Typically, the agenda of the academic intellectual and the public agenda differ greatly. They do so because each agenda tends to rise out of association with a group. Academic intellectuals move and breathe within the university as one moves and breathes within a tribe surrounded by an empty wilderness; if religious critics work in the university, they usually go elsewhere for tribal experience. These tribes, or groups, are jealous; they want to claim the emotions and values of their members, so that it is virtually impossible to belong fully to two at once.

When an academic intellectual becomes a public intellectual, the transition is a crisis akin to a religious conversion. Usually it is possible at all only because the academic intellectual belongs to a group independent of the university. Admittedly, there are those intellectuals who can move under their own steam, never having to bundle themselves on the deck of some large vessel as it pulls slowly away from the university. In 1870 William James claimed he abandoned the university's mechanistic scientism because of a change in his own will. He disparaged those who would not dare "to act originally, without carefully waiting for contemplation of the external world to determine all . . . ." He chose instead to "believe in my individual reality and creative power."[5] In the twentieth century, a similar individualistic stance is endorsed, perhaps most poignantly, by existentialists. Typically, however, the conversion occurs when a voluntary, but nonacademic, group attracts the loyalties of an academic intellectual, allowing him or her, even while working in the university, to adopt the styles of that group, whether it be a religious institution, a political movement, a gender-based consciousness raising group, a race-based rights group, an environmental group, an investment group, an artistic community, a sports club, or some other organization. (I am told, for example, that those founders of neoconservatism who were Jewish met regularly in Manhattan in the late 1960s to read the Torah.) Of course, even rebellion against the professional style of the academic intellectual does not necessarily lead to a concern for the public. The rebel may remain uninterested in the public, as some existentialists did. Or those leading breakaway groups in what I have called socially responsive fields may become simply new professionals for the new group. In neither case does the public become any more important than it was for the typical academic intellectual. Nevertheless, those lured away from the university by an alternative group may become public intellectuals as Arthur Schlesinger, Jr., or Jeanne Kirkpatrick, or Daniel Patrick Moynihan, or Michael Novak did when they shifted their primary alliances from the university to political concerns, which are not necessarily the same as first sector concerns.

Most intellectuals, however, are unconverted professionalistic intellectuals and remain so, continuing to ignore the public. They tend to come in two varieties, each corresponding to a historic philosophical orientation and each ignoring the public in a specific way. In the natural sciences and in disciplines appreciative of the sciences, an objectivizing style in the vein of the philosopher John Locke has dominated. Here professionalization has been the effort to focus on realities and structures external to thought. In these disciplines the academic intellectual tends to treat the imagination—as it shapes the arts, political movements, and popular lifestyles—as unimportant. Here, public life is uninteresting when it fails, as it usually does, to attend to the ostensibly static structures ostensibly discovered by science. Conversely, in much of the humanities a subjectivizing style in the vein of the philosopher Immanuel Kant has dominated. Here professionalization has been the effort to focus on human thought. In these disciplines, academic intellectuals tend to insist that reality lies in the subjective imagination, so that the physical and scientific worlds of the public are unimportant. Public life is uninteresting when it does not concern, as it usually does not, issues of high culture or individual rights. Under the guidance of such orientations, the split between the academy and the public has grown, even though it has been denounced. It is spreading even to the private liberal arts college, which may have been the last outpost of higher education congenial to the public intellectual.[6]

Of course, despite the difficulties, some intellectuals have refused to submit to the professionalization of the academy and have insisted that the academy be made once again congenial to the public intellectual, including the religious critic. Sometimes they make the act of teaching a public act, focusing not merely on the advancement of scholarship but on the student's capacity to act publicly. Precedent is on their side, for it is professionalism that is the intruder on campuses, which once typically fostered the development of citizens, even religiously sophisticated citizens. However, it makes better strategic sense to stop seeing the academy as the best place for public intellectuals and to look for a better habitat.

I believe voluntary associations of the third sector offer the public intellectual, particularly the religious critic, a better "psychological home" than does the university. I use the metaphor of "home" in recognition of the fact that anyone's, even an intellectual's, most important awareness is more physical and emotional than cognitive and is largely the effect of the social location of the individual.[7] (The label "political correctness" is just one recent recognition of the power of the academy as a psychological home; that label designates an entire range of nonacademic options, almost a world view that seems to be part of the meaning of the contemporary university.) Accordingly, if a move between psychological homes is made, it is from one thick and value-laden history of social relations, with physical and emotional dimensions, to another; it usually involves a kind of conversion. My point is, intellectuals interested in becoming public intellectuals, particularly those interested in becoming religious critics, would be well advised to adopt some third sector organization as their psychological home.

Let me be clear here. First, I am not suggesting that people whose psychological home is in the nonuniversity third sector are necessarily morally superior but only that they are likely to be more publicly concerned. I recognize that some public views and actions of the third sector are not only morally questionable but socially destructive. But my point is that third sector organizations are more congenial to the development of public awareness and of a sense of the whole. To be associated with the third sector, therefore, is not necessarily to be encouraged to do the right thing, but it is to be encouraged to deliberately and critically entertain the public meaning of one's actions or of how one's actions pertain to some specific vision of the whole. Second, I am not suggesting that academic intellectuals should resign their professorships and seek work in the third sector. I am talking not about place of employment but about a place where certain ideas and attitudes can be openly and critically fostered.

When I say the third sector offers the religious critic a psychological home superior to that offered by the university, I mean only that nonuniversity, third sector organizations better foster what I am calling religious criticism. There is a simple reason for this: the professed norms of the nonuniversity third sector tend to pertain more directly to questions of the public good than do the norms of the university, let alone the norms of the first or second sectors. In the government sector, civil order is the highest norm, and, in the market sector, profit is the highest norm; whereas, in the third sector, some vision of a common good is the highest order. Social concerns are not only legitimate motivators in the third sector, but they are meant to be, however much they fail to be, the overriding motivators. In this respect, I believe the university is no longer a typical third sector organization; it is increasingly dedicated to professional activities that have little to do with the common good.

I recognize that the virtues of the third sector can be easily exaggerated and always should be challenged. Any given voluntary organization can grow oblivious to its original, large social vision and become bogged in the technical milieu of its social action. Further, its paid and voluntary staff workers often begin to treat the organization as an instrument to serve their private ambitions. Further, groups that study the third sector do not typically partake of the philanthropic spirit, if there is one, but act just like any other academic professional society. Independent Sector (IS) and The Association for Research on Nonprofit Organizations and Voluntary Associations (ARNOVA) typically ape fashionable social science methodology, ignoring just those issues of the common good or a sense of the whole that led to the creation of the voluntary associations they study. Finally, third sector organizations have recently been heavily and often rightly criticized, not as flatly inimical to the public good, but as wasteful of public resources. A devastating seven-part series in *The Philadelphia Inquirer* in April 1993 well documents how the entire category of tax-exempt organizations has been opened to organizations that seem to have little or no bearing on the public good, let alone on a sense of the societal whole.[8] Now included among tax-exempt organizations are the National Football League organization (but not the particular teams), highly profitable hospitals (some of which carry only a one-percent charity load), rich universities (some charging as much as $25,000 in comprehensive student fees and devoting most of their budget to commercial and defense research). The same *Inquirer* series describes how salaries of nonprofit executives—particularly hospital, foundation, and university heads—often range from $200,000 to over $1,000,000 per year. It describes how foundations sometimes seem primarily interested in plowing money into the salaries of their own executives, into their own endowment, and into their own plant, all while barely meeting the minimal five-percent rate of contribution required for tax-exempt status. The *Inquirer* series can leave one with the clear impression that, for many nonprofits, the public good seems relatively unimportant.

As Teresa Odendahl's book title *(Charity Begins at Home)* suggests, many "charities" are funded by people far more interested in giving money to their own kind, and many foundations are far more interested in charity for high culture, elite universities, and research hospitals than in charity for the poor, despite clear evidence that for the past quarter century the poor have grown poorer in American society.[9] On the one hand, Waldemar Nielsen in *The Golden Donors* establishes that America is the leader among the developed nations in the number and power of its philanthropies and foundations and that criticism of philanthropy, whether from the political right or left, has often been uninformed. On the other hand, he demonstrates that typical major philanthropists have only vague notions of, or even interests in, how their wealth might be used and that their foundations have often misspent funds.[10] All of the above seems to be stirring another round of government investigation. In June 1993 Representative J. J. "Jake" Pickle as Chair of the Subcommittee on Oversight of the House Committee on Ways and Means began investigations of tax-exempt organizations and promised legislation to tighten requirements for earning tax-exempt status.[11]

These charges are not entirely unanswerable. For example, if foundations pay out much more than five percent of their assets annually, given a four-percent inflation rate and costs of management, they are agreeing to put an end to the good work they seek to accomplish. Also, many nonprofit organizations welcome efforts to tighten regulations on tax exemption, accepting rather than opposing the idea that it is now misused (for example, 24 of the 25 categories for tax-exemption are noncharitable). Also, it can be demonstrated that median annual management costs of foundations are .53 percent of assets, significantly less than management costs of almost all mutual funds.[12] Further, it can be documented that voluntary organizations draw a far higher rate of volunteers than the other two sectors do and that many professionals in the third sector (clergy, foundation workers, arts and social movement workers) willingly take less pay than they could draw in the first or second sectors.[13] This does not prove, but does suggest, that volunteers and paid staff in the nonuniversity third sector are more concerned with serving the common good than their counterparts elsewhere. Further, nonuniversity third sector workers, as I have argued, because they must continue to write or agree to mission statements and applications for tax-exempt status, tend, however hypocritically, to be conscious of their connection with a common good, even of their relation to a sense of the whole society.

The importance of an understanding of the common good in the third sector can be illustrated by reference to organized religion, where a vision of the whole, coupled with a morality growing out of that vision, are central. In the United States, organized religion contributes more total hours of voluntary participation and donates more money than all other parts of the third sector combined. Robert L. Payton and Peter Dobkin Hall have demonstrated the crucial role organized religion plays in the American third sector, at the level of both theory and practice.[14] Citing data generated by Independent Sector, Payton notes that even today people involved in organized religion give virtually twice as much money to the third sector and fifty percent more in volunteer time than people not so involved. Participants in organized religion not only advocate but contribute to global and community causes that, in turn, provide little or no pecuniary benefit for themselves. In religion, unlike first and second sector organizations and unlike higher education, people are encouraged to adopt these causes in a regular and ritualized way. In religion, spiritual and moral norms are overtly advocated, as they cannot be in most university or college classrooms or in most academic research. And in religion, unlike virtually any other third sector organizations, children are included with adults in organizational activities and encouraged to develop something like a sense of the whole; given the enormous and spiritually empty media and advertising competition for the child's attention, this is not insignificant. (Of course, while such accounts of organized religion may demonstrate that its vision of the whole can be effective, they do not demonstrate that those visions of the whole are socially beneficial. Sometimes they have been racist, sexist, xenophobic, and chauvinistic. Sometimes organized religion starts with a sense of the whole but concludes with little more than a self-serving morality hinging on life after death.)

Admittedly, claims for the moral seriousness of voluntary associations—particularly, claims that they offer to the religious critic a superior psychological home—typically will be rejected by academic intellectuals. Educators tend to see themselves as unrivalled in their moral seriousness, despite the fact that they also claim to conduct value-free teaching and research; but this may say more about educators than about the third sector.

II. The Third Sector as Venue

Religious critics and most third sector organizations share a preoccupation with a sense of the whole. Sooner or later they both attempt to unify the self or the society by suggesting a picture of the world in its wholeness. John Dewey argued that "the self is always directed toward something beyond itself and so its own unifications depends upon the idea of the integration of the shifting scenes of the world into that imaginative totality we call the Universe." and he called that directedness and unification "religious."[15] Third sector organizations appear to be more open than universities to what Dewey calls "the religious" and more responsive to that social growth Dewey associates with the term *God*. Accordingly, these third sector organizations offer intellectuals a context congenial to the enunciation of values and world views. By comparison, the university, the research university in particular, seldom raises such "meaning of the whole society" questions and, thus, seldom is open to the kind of debate religious critics must seek. Two aspects of the university's academic professionalism discourage these questions.

First, the *values* of academic professionalism are inimical to questions of the sense of the whole. Service to the discipline seems to the academic professional to be a virtue, compared to which public involvement is a vice. The academic professional honors the discipline and all its paraphernalia (common standards for training, criticism, and certification; professional associations, journals, and canons; and hierarchy and status within the profession). This distracts from, if it does not actively militate against, the serious introduction of larger visions pertaining to the public good.

The standard professional reaction to academic preoccupation with the public good was aptly expressed in the early decades of professionalism by Julien Benda in his 1927 *La Trahison des clercs (The Betrayal of the Intellectuals)*—a book Ernest Gellner calls "the most celebrated sermon concerning the responsibility of intellectuals" ever written.[16] Benda believed that intellectuals should neither serve nor be dependent on public success. Real intellectuals, Benda argued, will say, "My kingdom is not of this world."[17] Truly disinterested, they prize the universal over the particular, the theoretical over the practical, pure reason over custom and experience. Only when armed by such nonhistorical and transcendent standards will intellectuals be able properly to evaluate the historical societies in which they live. But, Benda argued, already in 1927, that intellectuals have betrayed their true mission by allowing themselves and their standards to be too involved in current history. Nevertheless, given the course of developments since 1927, Benda would surely rejoice in the ascendancy of socially disinterested intellectuals today! Now, academics are far more inclined to judge their success by reference to "inherently valuable" professional standards and to be indifferent to the local histories in which they live.[18] We have reached a point today where, as Cornel West says,

> even the critiques of dominant paradigms in the Academy are *academic* ones; that is, they reposition viewpoints and figures within the context of professional politics inside the Academy rather than create linkages between struggles inside and outside of the Academy.[19]

Second, the *style* of professionalism is inimical to questions of the sense of the whole. I refer particularly to the academy's vulnerability to academic fashions. Today, the academy's investment in poststructural trends makes it genuinely difficult to take seriously any view of history in its totality or any public culture. Despite what may have been said by some leaders of poststructuralism (chapter 2), the average poststructuralist thinks "a sense of the whole" is mere chatter, with no meaning in a relativized, pluralized, and historicized world. It seems impossible to speak seriously about a society's "common culture," let alone a sense of the whole—hence, the popularity of multiculturalism.

Most philosophical neopragmatists and deconstructionists have abandoned a serious search for a sense of the whole or a common culture. While some conservative theologians like George Marsden and George Lindbeck might hold with an absolute God, they agree with the poststructuralists that the quest for a common culture should be abandoned.[20] Marsden, Lindbeck, and others at least indirectly sympathetic with poststructural movements, seem to limit their options to two: either abandon talk of a common culture, or pay the cost of the obsolete objectivism and foundationalism that would support such talk. They choose to deny not only objectivism and foundationalism but any explicit cultural vision of history in its totality. They affirm (properly, I believe) relativism, pluralism, and the notion that our language constructs its own world but then confine themselves (improperly, I believe) to a subculture—for example, a religious denomination or a colony of university intellectuals—and deny themselves the right and obligation to argue for a common culture.

Teachers of religion in universities seem, at times, to be honestly divided by modern and poststructural styles. They are increasingly preoccupied by unresolved tensions between, on the one hand, the modern objectivity that gave them a nonthreatening pedagogy and opened public university doors to religious studies and, on the other hand, the poststructural claim that such objectivity is impossible. These unresolved tensions are evident in the conflict between the instructor's professional pretense of neutrality and the new belief that value-free analysis is impossible, the instructor's nonproselytizing detachment and the student's desire to see the personal significance of religious ideas, and the instructor's politically correct demand for the multicultural study of religion and the new belief that neutral, cross-cultural analysis is impossible.

When I propose that efforts to reconcile relativism and pluralism and a realistic view of the whole are better undertaken somewhere other than in the university, I do not object to the secularity of the university. The university must be secular, if that means that its considerations are conducted critically and openly, outside the gates of the sanctuary, free from religious or political controls. Instead, I am arguing that, in their research styles and in their pedagogy, most university and college instructors not only fail to move beyond the poststructural dilemmas but are too preoccupied with "the discipline" to lay the groundwork for a public philosophy. Academic intellectuals seem not to have found a way, first, to accept the new recognition that all analysis is relativistic, particular, local, and communal and, then, to combine that with their own vivid moral and religious sense that there is a real world with horrible problems that should elicit public action. In a word, they see no way beyond Thomas Haskell's paradox in "The Curious Persistence of Rights Talk in an 'Age of Interpretation.'"

The third sector provides a space within which such divisions might be overcome. Third sector organizations are not necessarily opposed to poststructural fashions, but they are, by virtue of their organizational activities, inevitably more involved in public circumstances than universities are. Accordingly, within such associations it is easier for religious critics to acknowledge poststructural lessons and, at the same time, to find their world views and their moral and religious lives referring to a real world beyond themselves.

Add to these rather theoretical reasons the weight of American history, which suggests that third sector organizations have, in fact, typically fostered the freedom for religious and public action. I take one example. In *Free Spaces* Sara Evans and Harry Boyte refer to the case of Denmark Vesey, an instigator of a plan for a multistate slave revolt. As Vesey stood on June 28, 1822, in a Charleston, South Carolina, court for sentencing, his judge said, "It is difficult to imagine what infatuation could have prompted you to attempt an enterprise so wild and visionary. You were a free man; were comparatively wealthy; and enjoyed every comfort compatible with your situation." How, the judge implied, could a free and economically secure black man even entertain the idea of risking everything to liberate poverty-stricken slaves? Evans and Boyte argue that

> Christianity furnished the basic language of freedom for black Americans. . . . They found in the insights, language, and communion of religion a transformative source of self-affirmation. In doing so, they turned questions like those of the incredulous judge back on themselves, and challenged the very values that he equated with contentment and happiness.

Evans's and Boyte's larger question is,

> Where do ordinary people, steeped in lifelong experiences of humiliation, barred from acquisition of basic skills of citizenship . . . gain the courage, the self-confidence, and above all the hope to take action in their own behalf? What are the structures of support, the resources, and the experiences that generate the capacity and the inspiration to challenge 'the way things are' and imagine a different world?[21]

And they answer that voluntary associations of the third sector have provided the historic wellspring of American social initiative.

Admittedly, when the academy replaces its preoccupation with technical competency and status with a concern for coherence between the university and the society, it does offer such a wellspring. But, typically, the university is what Evans and Boyte call a "large-scale institution." Free spaces, they contend, are more often found in "voluntary forms of association with a relatively open and participatory character—many religious organizations, clubs, self-help and mutual aid societies, reform groups, neighborhood, civic, and ethnic groups, and a host of other associations grounded in the fabric of community life." These are places where people "learn a vision of the common good in the course of struggling for change."[22]

Without leaving the university, religious critics might transcend its specialization and indifference to the public by associating themselves also with the sorts of organizations Evans and Boyte name. Through such associations they might better see connections between their intellectual work and the needs of the public.

III. The Third Sector as Vehicle

However, none of this quite explains how third sector organizations do more than foster the freedom and will to address public needs. That is, even if they offer a venue, how do third sector associations avoid ghettoizing the intellectual just as much as the university does? If third sector organizations occupy a separate space, isolated from other social spaces, they may do little to transmit the theories of intellectuals to the full range of the public world. The question is, How can the third sector be understood as a vehicle, an infrastructure, for carrying the religious critic's notion of the public good to the public itself?

This problem is treated indirectly by Susan A. Ostrander and Paul G. Schervish in "Giving and Getting: Philanthropy as a Social Relation."[23] In explaining the sectors, they adopt a form of sociological analysis and reject that geometric analysis that makes sectors into spaces, like separate pieces of a pie. For Ostrander and Schervish, sectors are forms of social relations, and the third sector is about the social relations of giving and getting, rather than the relations peculiar to government and the profit sector (electoral politics and commercial transactions). The relations defined by donors and recipients reach into all areas of society and are not confined to specific social spaces or to particular organizations. When they make sectors forms of relations rather than physical spaces, they account for how the three sectors not only are not mutually exclusive but, on occasion, even coincidental—so that third sector, governmental, and for-profit relations are virtually ubiquitous, often operating in the same institutions in the same spaces and times. A hospital, for example, can be commercially owned and operated and thus be part of the second, for-profit sector, while also carrying charity patients, making it part of the third sector, and receive government support, making it part of the first sector. And such cases are not unusual.

Ostrander and Schervish not only replace the separate spaces sometimes typical of sector analysis with three forms of ubiquitous social relations, they also identify the three forms of social relations with what they call the three media of communication dominant in those forms of social relatedness. The medium for first sector relations is votes; the medium for second sector relations is money. And the medium for third sector relations is appeals—words and images expressing norms, morals, and values. It is votes, money, and appeals to values that accomplish the work of each sector's relations.[24] In particular, it is the third sector's imaginative appeals to value that enables the third sector to be the prime innovator, proving ground, and advocate for a society's evolving moral, aesthetic and spiritual life.

This notion of the third sector as a "form of relations" makes it possible to see how the third sector offers to religious critics not only a psychological home but a vehicle through which their thought can be proliferated. Religious critics examine the society's "appeals to value" as they are found in the society's sense of the whole, particularly its ultimate values, myths, meanings, and rituals. Working out of their own sense of the whole, they use their own appeals to value as a medium to criticize these public appeals to value, calling for their abolition, their enhancement, or their alteration. Their religious criticism is proliferated throughout the society as a third sector form of influence, along with other third sector transactions of "giving and getting."

I amend Ostrander and Schervish only by insisting that, while the essence of the third sector is a distinctive form of relations, these relations are not free floating but emanate from social institutions.[25] Intellectuals, this is to say, would be ill-advised to work the way Stanley Elkin's Transcendentalists work—that is, out of an anti-institutional animus.[26] Appeals to value emanate from a physical center, which is some particular third sector association or voluntary organization, such as a health care center, a rights organization, or a church. Located within such institutions, the religious critic's appeal to value becomes part of the ubiquitous work of those institutions.

The third sector as seen by Ostrander and Schervish can be understood to be in the business of creating public conventions. The third sector's appeals to values are constructs, and when they are adopted by the society they become social conventions extending throughout the society. Ostrander and Schervish subscribe to Anthony Giddens's effort to move beyond what he calls the imperial objectivism of sociological functionalism and the imperial subjectivism of sociological hermeneutics and adopt what Giddens refers to as the structuration of meaning in social institutions. Giddens argues that meaning is constituted in practice and should be understood by reference to practice. Appeals to value, that is, may begin in subjective relativity as imaginative constructs, but, if they are successful, they constitute what Giddens calls structurations, institutionalized social practices that are passed from generation to generation as traditions.[27] For Ostrander and Schervish, social structure is neither the expression of an absolute order, nor subjective experience, but a social practice that "both creates and is created by human action and choice in an interactive process."[28] From another vantage point, Robert Payton, using Edward Shils and Clifford Geertz, in the epigraph to this chapter makes exactly the same point: that the third sector works as a convention-making process.

If the making of conventions is what third sector organizations are understood to do, then the third sector is an ideal psychological home for religious critics who, themselves, seek to criticize and reconstruct the conventions of the spiritual culture. To reiterate, the constructs of the religious critics can be seen in Ostrander and Shervish's terms as appeals to value. When those constructs are accepted in some institution, which, in turn, influences society, then those constructs become social conventions—not in some separate spiritual culture, but in a spiritual culture that permeates the public.

I am proposing that religious critics are more likely to be effective if they work through the convention-making processes of the third sector, rather than through the university. As I noted earlier, intellectuals in the university have been separated from society, not only through professionalization, but through seeing themselves on one side of the two, dualistic styles of thought that divide the academic world. Intellectuals understand themselves to pursue either an objectivitizing, Lockean style of thought that separates them from the imaginative work of the public or to pursue a subjectivizing Kantian style of thought that separates them from the physical work of the public. However, if the third sector is understood to be a ubiquitous form of relation that proliferates appeals to value, and if these appeals to value move from constructs to public conventions, then these dualistic barriers are transcended, just as conventionalism would transcend any form of objectivism or subjectivism (chapter 7). The third sector is a location in which the ideas of religious critics can become public conventions.

In effect, by bringing it all down to social practice, Ostrander and Schervish have made the third sector a vehicle appropriate for the religious critic who seeks to contribute to the creation of conventions about the sense of the whole, about ultimate meaning, about the function of the sacred in public life.

IV. Beyond the Ineffectual Intellectual

My point is that, if the religious critics are not to succumb to the failures typical of academic intellectuals, they must find a way to conceive their vision of the whole concretely and to convey it to the society effectively. If they do not meet that challenge, they will do no better than the socially detached academic intellectuals they would correct. Their understandings of the sacred convention, their efforts to reconceive a myth of America will go begging, lie stillborn. Their theories will remain mere constructs, never to become social conventions that enlarge society with a critical and more viable sense of the religious whole. Their theories will never become, in the pragmatic sense, even candidates for truth. Hence, much rides on the proposal that the third sector offers a venue and a vehicle for the religious critic. Without that answer to the question—or, possibly, a better answer than that answer—the religious critic will be just another socially ineffectual intellectual, contributing no more to the formation of a sense of the whole than professionalized academic intellectuals.

If voluntary organizations of the third sector do not offer the best venue and vehicle for the religious critic, and they may not, then what does? Should more hope be placed in the prospect of a deprofessionalized university? Should greater energy be lodged, after all, in reforming the university, in the effort to make it a viable psychological home and vehicle for the religious critic? Strategically, it may come down to these practical questions, for they concretize, make meaningful, give what James called "cash value," to all other questions about the religious critic.

CHAPTER 10

THE RELIGIOUS CRITIC
AND A MYTH OF AMERICA

In a time such as ours, when inherited myth systems are
in disrepair and no great political leader has yet
emerged, historians, political scientists, and other academics who are paid to educate the young and think
about matters of public importance ought to feel a
special responsibility for proposing alternatives to accepted ideas. Only so can they hope to trigger a successful reorganization of public myths that could com-
mand the support of informed and critical minds. To
leave the field to ignorant and agitated extremists is
dangerous. That, after all, was how Hitler came to
power.

William H. McNeill[1]

I began by recalling how for many generations America
understood itself to be an exception among nations, the unique
recipient of a special blessing from beyond history that sum-
moned the nation to a unique errand within history. This myth
was enlarged, referring not only to the America that was God's
New Israel but to the America that was the home of freedom, the
home of capitalism, the nation on an errand not only into the
wilderness of a continent but into the wilderness of the entire
world. I argued that this myth had once animated the public

173

intellectual so that, when the myth grew implausible, the public activities of intellectuals diminished.

This may not be the end of the matter. As William McNeill has argued, when inherited myths are breaking down, the reorganization of experience by new myths is required if people, including intellectuals, are to contribute to the regeneration of public life. Richard Slotkin adds that mythmaking is accomplished by people: "Myth is not only something *given* but something *made*, a product of human labor, one of the tools with which human beings do the work of making culture and society. ... By our way of remembering, retelling, and re-imagining 'America,' we too engage the myths with history and thus initiate the process by which our culture is steadily revised and transformed."[2]

I add only that myths are conventions, and that the reconstruction and criticism of such conventions is a particular responsibility of religious critics. In myths religious critics find the narrative structure that frames a sense of the whole, which, in turn, gives meaning to the spiritual culture. If the religious critic's responsibility is to be exercised, new thought must be given to the myth of America. What are the conditions for a new myth of America, one that would replace the exceptionalist myth? Within what new contours or boundaries might a plausible myth be set?

Admittedly, myths of the nation are dangerous. After all, the myths that might cure the American condition must be foraged out of the same jungle of metaphors that bred the fanticisms that the myths would seek to eradicate. Even the logical Zbigniew Brzezinski involves himself in this paradox. First he describes the nationalist "metamyth," calling it a "grand transcendental fiction," "an irrational but compelling blend of the religious impulse to seek salvation, of the nationalistic self-identification as being superior to outsiders, and of utopian social doctrines reduced to the level of populist slogans." Metamyths encourage a false escape from harsh truths, galvanize dangerous passions, and gain leverage through terrible instruments of warfare, all making feasible in the twentieth century "the infliction of death on a scale without precedent in human history."[3] And yet Brzezinski calls for a reaffirmation of American spiritual culture, a reaffirmation that would require either a new metamyth or an equivalent narrative structure.

I. Conditions of Mythmaking

Myths function the way Alfred North Whitehead said national symbols function. For Whitehead, symbols are expressions that connect clear and conscious images with inarticulate, largely unconscious, intuitive, emotional, and vague responses to the past. The flag or Lincoln's Gettysburg Address are just such clear images that gain their meaning through association with indistinct and emotional memories of vast, violent contests over ideals and power. National symbols bring pictures of the nation into solidarity with vague physical feelings of the whole national reality. New national symbols, Whitehead claims, arise in times of cultural disruption, when an established picture of the nation no longer connects to an emerging emotional sense of the whole.[4]

The old exceptionalist myth offered just such a combination of clear interpretation and emotional sensibility, coupling the images of "God's chosen people" or "the home of democracy" or "the home of free enterprise" with the vague sense of the struggle to survive in a strange land. But the imagery of chosen people and all its secular descendants no longer resonates to a sense of the American situation. No longer seeing America as an exception among the world's people, as a nation that behaves in exemplary ways and performs a unique service for humankind, Americans (especially, American intellectuals) now acknowledge that moral and spiritual ambiguity are inescapable. America begins not with a "promise," its failings no longer feel like a "declension" of a promise, and its hope no longer feels like a "prophetic" restoration of promise. Rather, the old schema of creation-fall-restoration is replaced by a schema that begins in a typically unspoken recognition of unavoidable ambiguity and searches for a way to keep going despite ambiguity. Although still wanting to improve the nation, Americans now more often recognize that history's ambiguity contaminates all social change. Now change is better seen as the appearance of fireflies in a quagmire than as the arrival of mosquitoes in the Garden of Eden.[5] Any new and viable American myth will begin, as the ancient Hebrew narrative did, in history, amid confusion, in a nomadic form of life[6]; and it will call for new ways to cope with persisting ambiguities of national history. What endures about America is not, then, a grand, exceptional, and transcendent purpose but an imminent process of purpose-making.

Justifiably, many are haunted by the apprehension that the loss of a transcendent purpose can lead to despair and nihilism and then to the demagogic exploitation of a despairing and nihilistic population. But despair, nihilism, and demagogues can be partially countered by an ongoing process of cultural deliberation about the deepest meanings of the whole society. They can be countered through the deliberate development of conventions about American meanings, including religious meanings. It is, in part, to serve this process that American religious critics work.

Any myth that offers a narrative structure for this undertaking will meet elementary conditions. If it is to be intellectually viable, it will not violate the new awareness of the relativity, plurality, and historicity of existence. It will be, in some ways, translatable into action. It will avoid a national understanding so self-critical that it demoralizes the nation from within or so self-righteous that it invites hostility from without. It will see America, not as a supreme episode, but as an episode among many episodes in world history.

This new myth will arise from some empirical sense of the whole of American history. It is likely to claim more than the evidence establishes, even to the point of becoming what McNeill calls a "necessary sort of self-delusion." It will be pragmatically justified; again in McNeill's words, "an appropriately idealized version of the past may also allow a group of human beings to come closer to living up to its noblest ideals."[7] It will frame a sense of the whole from a particular public standpoint. It will offer large visions that provide images in terms of which all else in the society can be understood.

A viable myth of America is unlikely to be "a myth of being," perpetuating structures. It is more likely to be "a myth of becoming," one about process guided by imagination and conventions. At its extreme, it will be about how to live, rather than about what to enshrine, about continually constructing futures, knowing all the while that these futures rest on nothing permanent and soon will be superseded.

Partly because Americans still are grounded in biblical narratives, this myth will take history seriously. But historical myths are being discarded, not created. Robert Bellah has described the demise of the covenant story wherein God and God's people were related in the terms of an agreement with obligations; he and his colleagues are convinced that the myth of the covenant cannot be replaced with stories of individual and material success.[8] Nor will the myth of the frontier work anymore. As Richard Slotkin has argued, no matter how various and enduring, those myths are all damned by their illusory and invidious simplification.[9] These and other existing historical myths offer no viable religious basis for an alternative, positive spiritual culture. Still needed is an historical myth that makes sense in a post-structural era without being skeptical, that abandons the exceptionalist tradition without abandoning a distinctly American and biblical tradition, that is affirmative without being vainglorious, that divines America without divinizing America.

II. Contours of Another Myth of America

While I cannot name that myth and while I cannot specify where and how religious critics might use such a myth to shape the spiritual culture of America, I can offer preliminary speculations about the boundaries within which another myth might flow.

There are clues in two American poets, Wallace Stevens and William Carlos Williams. Stevens describes boundaries for an American myth in "The American Sublime." He asks how Americans are to stand naked before their mockers, stand in a place where the spirit has descended from the sky, into the landscape, and where the landscape is empty, vacant. Here, he says, one must ask whether any sacrament can be appropriate. Can wine be drunk? "What bread does one eat?"[10] Stevens captures, I believe, the absence of any transcendent myth and ritual in America and how this makes it difficult for Americans to understand their identity and their task. He argues that the ground on which any American myth now might be built is empty ground.

William Carlos Williams has many things to say about the meaning of America, but I cite only the way in which he virtually converges with Stevens. In the long poem *Paterson*, that town in New Jersey is Williams's microcosm of America. In this American landscape there is a hollowness; it emits sounds, but sounds too indefinite to be of much use. Here Williams's America is an emptiness surrounded by a surface; it is like "an inverted bell resounding."[11]

Historically, the deepest problem for Americans has not been to deconstruct a permanent ideal inherited from their land of origin. It has been quite the opposite. Except for Africans destined to be slaves, most immigrants who journeyed across the oceans into the natural, social, or cultural wilderness of America were prompted, at least in part, by the failure of an ideal in a land of origin. For them, whether or not to copy the ideal from the land of origin was not the issue.[12]

The problem for Americans was to recognize and respond to the openness of their situation. Fundamental American institutions virtually state the problem as they institutionalize a kind of vacancy. The anti-authoritarian animus of the First Amendment to the Constitution, the unusually open competition of the American marketplace, the endless searchings of America's common law, the anti-elite thrust of its democracy, the unpredictable and often anti-intellectual bias of its religious piety, all ward off the establishment of a strong tradition that would subdue the openness of American space. These American institutions require that their market or political or religious conclusions never be more than temporary and local; they are more about form and process than about substance or continuity.

Americans seem to have specialized in improvisation, and this is manifest in their theater, their jazz, their basketball. America has never embraced the divine right of national leaders, a natural law, a controlled economy, or a hereditary class system—although it has established a monied elite. Longer than any other nation, it has embraced open forms in government, law, economics, and religion.

At the base of American experience, then, is an emptiness, a primordial absence of structures, leaving only contingencies which Americans called real and then embraced. "So much depends," Williams claimed, on local things. One must continually start "out of particulars," one constantly hears "the roar of the present."[13]

When Karl Barth visited the United States in 1962, he called the Americans the most likely authors of a future "theology of freedom."[14] What he may not have appreciated is that, if it were written in an American way, that theology would lack just the sort of foundation that Barth as an idealistic European and as a Calvinistic Christian so naturally presupposed. The freedom that Americans have learned to exercise is a freedom with no permanent criteria. Their communal meaning is a function of the continual reimagination of communal meaning, rather than of given truths. Under these conditions, how can there be an American myth, an American sense of the whole, even a distinct spiritual culture, let alone a theology of freedom?

What is an American religious critic to do?

Look to precedents, perhaps. The Puritans, Daniel J. Boorstin explains, were a people "more interested in institutions that functioned than in generalities that glittered."[15] They lived practically, out of historical contingencies and out of their interpretive responses to historical contingencies, and not out of large, extrahistorical truths.

An explicitly American sense of history has been built gradually by American thinkers. Jonathan Edwards became a post-Lockean empiricist as well as a neo-Platonist.[16] The authors of the American Constitution and the Declaration of Independence were inventors as well as copiers. Emerson was, in part, a particularist and a deconstructionist[17] and Thoreau was, in part, a historical naturalist,[18] and neither of them, finally, was simply a displaced European idealist. James and Dewey became pragmatists, radical empiricists, and constructivists rather than the closet idealists or social determinists they could have been. American poststructuralists are now struggling toward a new, activistic provincialism rather than toward a recrudescent, dualistic, European subjectivism.

Of course American tradition exists, but it seems to exist to be reconsidered. America's blessing is unencumbered revisability; its curse is unrelenting revisability. There may be in this the makings of a myth of America.

The sacred convention that prompts revisions that must be revised may be evil as well as good. There may be in this the makings of an American sense of the sacred.

American religious critics may respond to this strange tradition and this strange God and grope their way, helping to make myths, contributing to conventions, instantiating a sense of the whole and the sacred, seeking thereby to help develop a more viable spiritual culture. It is through this intentional and studious undertaking that the American religious critic may some day fill a unique and public office.

NOTES

Introduction

1. Cornel West, *Race Matters* (Boston: Beacon Press, 1993), p. 5.

2. Zbigniew Brzezinski, *Out of Control: Global Turmoil on the Eve of the Twenty-First Century* (New York: Charles Scribner's Sons, 1993), pp. 115.

3. Linell E. Cady has effectively argued that religion is confined to the margins of public life due both to the indifference of religious thinkers to the public as it is and to the indifference of the public to religion as it is (see *Religion, Theology, and American Public Life* [Albany, NY: State University of New York Press, 1993], especially chapter 1).

4. Garry Wills, *Under God: Religion and American Politics* (New York: Simon and Schuster, 1990); Stephen L. Carter, *The Culture of Disbelief: How American Law and Politics Trivialize Religious Devotion* (New York: Basic Books, 1993).

5. Brzezinski, *Out of Control,* p. 218.

6. See Thomas Bender's account of how, in late-nineteenth-century America, intellectuals left the city and its life, abandoned the public square, and became creatures of the university, "The Erosion of Public Culture" in *Intellect and Public Life: Essays on the Social History of Academic Intellectuals in the United States* (Baltimore: The Johns Hopkins University Press, 1993), pp. 30–46.

7. Russell Jacoby, *The Last Intellectuals: American Culture in the Age of Academe* (New York: Basic Books, Inc., 1987), p. 14. It is true that Jacoby's thesis has been repeatedly challenged; see, e.g., Morris Dickstein, "Literary Critics Stage Comeback as Superstars," *The Times High-*

er Education Supplement (December 4, 1992): p. 17, and *Double Agent: The Critic and Society* (New York: Oxford University Press, 1992).

8. John Dewey, *Human Nature and Conduct,* in *Middle Works,* vol. 14 (Carbondale and Edwardsville: Southern Illinois University Press, 1983), p. 227; John Dewey, *Art as Experience* (New York: Capricorn Books, 1958), p. 194.

9. Daniel Bell, "America's Cultural Wars," *The Wilson Quarterly* (summer 1992): p. 107. See the earlier and similar argument from Robert Bellah, *The Broken Covenant: American Civil Religion in Time of Trial* (New York: The Seabury Press, 1975); Bellah, unlike Bell, bases his criticisms on ostensibly extrahistorical grounds.

10. Max Weber, *The Sociology of Religion,* trans. Ephraim Fischoff (Boston: Beacon Press, 1963), p. 59.

11. Weber, *Sociology of Religion,* chapter 8.

12. Jacoby, *The Last Intellectuals.*

13. Bruce Kuklick, *The Rise of American Philosophy* (New Haven: Yale University Press, 1977); Bruce W. Wilshire, *The Moral Collapse of the University: Professionalism, Purity, and Alienation* (Albany, NY: State University of New York Press, 1990).

14. Martin Anderson, *Impostors in the Temple* (New York: Simon and Schuster, 1992); Dinesh D'Souza, *Illiberal Education: The Politics of Race and Sex on Campus* (New York: Free Press, 1991).

15. Burton Bledstein, *The Culture of Professionalism: The Middle Class and the Development of Higher Education in America* (New York: W. W. Norton & Co., Inc., 1976).

16. This skittishness mars the otherwise fine book by Wilbur Zelinsky, *Nation into State: The Shifting Foundations of American Nationalism* (Chapel Hill: The University of North Carolina Press, 1988).

17. Because it is a narrower term, I will use "poststructuralism" instead of the more popular "postmodernism." Poststructuralist theories are represented most recently by deconstructionists, neopragmatists, and hermeneuticists of several stripes. Little recognized is the fact that, in many respects, they were long preceded by Charles Sanders Peirce, William James, and John Dewey. Most recently, Robert Cummings Neville, in *The Highroad Around Modernism* (Albany, NY: State University of New York Press, 1992) has not only distinguished these classical American thinkers from poststructuralists and postmodernists, but has established how thoroughly the former anticipate the latter. I

have advanced a similar thesis in *History Making History: The New Historicism in American Religious Thought* (Albany, NY: State University of New York Press, 1988), chapters 1–3.

18. Constituting about one fifth of Americans, neatly detached from the other four-fifths of society (Robert Reich, *The Work of Nations* [New York: Alfred A. Knopf, 1991], chapter 21, "Who is 'Us'?").

19. As quoted in Robert B. Westbrook, *John Dewey and American Democracy* (Ithaca, NY: Cornell University Press, 1991), p. 552.

20. Westbrook, *John Dewey*, p. 552.

21. In *Mythistory and Other Essays* (Chicago: The University of Chicago Press, 1986), William McNeill uses "metahistorical synthesis" as well as "mythistory" to refer to the necessary metaphorical superstructure for any sufficient public philosophy.

22. Such invention is the key to Garry Wills's *Inventing America: Jefferson's Declaration of Independence* (Garden City, NY: Doubleday, 1978) and to his *Lincoln at Gettysburg: The Words that Remade America* (New York: Simon & Schuster, 1992).

23. Daniel J. Boorstin, *The Americans: The Colonial Experience* (New York: Vintage Books, 1958), pp. 150–51.

24. John Dewey, *A Common Faith* (New Haven: Yale University Press, 1952), chapter 2.

25. See McNeill, *Mythistory*, chapter 1.

Chapter 1: The Religious Critic and the End of an Era

1. Garry Wills, *Lincoln at Gettysburg: The Words that Remade America* (New York: Simon & Schuster, 1992), p. 38.

2. "Exceptionalism," as I use the term, refers to a claim for uniqueness, rather than to the uniqueness of a claim or to the actual uniqueness of a nation. Thus, just because Americans are not exceptional in their exceptionalism—i.e., other peoples make similar claims about their nations—does not mean they are not exceptionalists. Also, one can be an exceptionalist if one sees one's nation as, in some sense, an exception to the common practice or rule of other nations, even though critical analysis may establish that that nation is not, in fact, such an exception. Historically, many Americans were exceptionalists when they saw America as God's New Israel, even though citizens of other nations may

have made similar claims about their nations. See, e.g., Gerald Robert McDermott's demonstration that at least occasional claims for Christian exceptionalism have been made for fourteenth-century France, sixteenth-century Spain, Russia, and England, and modern South Africa and Poland. Jewish exceptionalism is manifest in contemporary Israel. See, McDermott, *One Holy and Happy Society: The Public Theology of Jonathan Edwards* (University Park, PA: Penn State Press, 1992), Introduction. See also, Donald Harman Akenson, *God's Peoples: Covenant and Land in South Africa, Israel, and Ulster* (Ithaca, NY: Cornell University Press, 1992). Richard Cowardine's "case against American exceptionalism" argues only that the American exceptionalist claim is not unique, not that it is not a claim for uniqueness. Specifically, he argues that nineteenth-century British politics was just as heavily influenced by religion as American politics was. See Cowardine's "Religion and Politics in Nineteenth-Century Britain: The Case Against American Exceptionalism," in *Religion and American Politics: From the Colonial Period to the 1980s,* ed. Mark A. Noll (New York: Oxford University Press, 1990), pp. 225–252.

3. Bellah has distilled the myth of the covenant between God and a people from the exceptionalist myth and has effectively demonstrated that the loss of covenental depths has contributed to national fragmentation, rampant individualism, and the loss of an American public philosophy. Of course, Bellah does not advocate the nationalism or the literalism implicit in the exceptionalist myth. See especially, Robert Bellah, *The Broken Covenant: American Civil Religion in Time of Trial* (Chicago: The University of Chicago Press, 1993).

4. David W. Noble, *The End of American History* (Minneapolis: University of Minnesota Press, 1985), pp. 3–4.

5. David W. Noble, *Historians Against History: The Frontier Thesis and the National Covenant in American Historical Writing since 1830* (Minneapolis: University of Minnesota Press, 1965), chapter 1.

6. Throughout this chapter, I use an old theological narrative of American religious-intellectual development (from the Puritans, to the Enlightenment liberals, to the Romantics, to William James), rather than an alternative theological narrative of American intellectual development (from the Puritans, Edwards particularly, to the several generations of Calvinist scholarship, up to and including the Andover Liberals, to John Dewey) recently presented by Bruce Kuklick in *Churchmen and Philosophers: From Jonathan Edwards to John Dewey* (New Haven: Yale University Press, 1985). While I continue to find the old narrative more useful, my argument here is only slightly affected by this choice, for the

Calvinists (while they did not so distinctly confine their God to history) were exceptionalists and monists, just as much as those emphasized by the older narrative.

7. See Sacvan Bercovitch, *American Jeremiad* (Madison: University of Wisconsin Press, 1978). Bercovitch's claim has been disputed as too simple. For example, Michael Denning in *Mechanic Accents* (London: Verso, 1987) argues that "Bercovitch tends to reduce the concepts of 'hegemony' and 'dominant culture'—which connote in [Antonio] Gramisci and [Raymond] Williams unstable and historically conditioned balances of forces between classes and social groups—to the timeless 'consensus' of American exceptionalism." Denning also argues that Bercovitch tends to "deduce social meaning from formal analysis," that is, that Bercovitch argues improperly from rhetoric to social reality (p. 223).

8. Bercovitch, *American Jeremiad*, pp. 7–8.

9. Noble, *The End of American History*, p. 112.

10. Henry James, *Hawthorne* (New York: Harper, 1979), pp. 42–43.

11. I amplify this interpretation in chapter 10 below.

12. Alexis de Tocqueville, *Democracy in America* (New York: Vintage Books, 1945), vol. 1, p. 30.

13. Conrad Cherry, "Introduction," *God's New Israel: Religious Interpretations of American Destiny* (Englewood Cliffs, NJ: Prentice-Hall Inc., 1971), pp. 22–23.

14. David M. Kennedy, Professor of History and American Studies, Stanford University, speaking before the Commonwealth Club of California in the summer of 1988 on the topic, "How American History Will Judge the Reagan Presidency," said: "As he [Reagan] told his biographer Lou Cannon in 1981, 'What I'd really like to do is to go down in history as the president who made Americans believe in themselves again.' . . . [This statement] is premised on the assumption that Americans did, in fact, disbelieve in themselves before his election, a consideration on which Jimmy Carter dwelled at length in his famous malaise speech in July of 1979."

15. "According to a recent Congressional Research Service study, the United States now has the lowest rate of voter participation of any democracy in the world" (Curtis B. Gans, Director, Committee for the Study of the American Electorate, *New York Times*, July 3, 1988, Section 2, p. 24). According to the same committee, voter participation in

the 1988 presidential election dropped lower than any presidential election rate since 1924, to 50.16 percent (*New York Times,* December 18, 1988, Section 1, p. 18). The 1990 voter turnout was 36 percent, "about equal to" the 1986 midterm turnout, which was the lowest since World War II (*New York Times,* November 11, 1990, Section Y, p. 15). Participation in the 1992 presidential elections rose to 55 percent; that turnout, however, is commonly attributed partly to a hunger for change—that is, to a largely negative motivation, the repudiation of recent politics.

16. Giles Gunn, Preface to *New World Metaphysics: Readings on the Religious Meaning of the American Experience,* ed. Giles Gunn (New York: Oxford University Press, 1981), p. xi (emphasis in original).

17. This is a point suggested repeatedly by Frank Lentricchia in *Criticism and Social Change* (Chicago: University of Chicago Press, 1983), see especially, pp. 38–52.

18. Walter Lippmann, *Essays in the Public Philosophy* (Boston: Little, Brown and Company, 1955), pp. 100–101.

19. See, e.g., Langdon Gilkey, *Society and the Sacred: Toward a Theology of Culture in Decline* (New York: Crossroad, 1981), pp. 22–25.

20. To put it melodramatically, it is as though America came to consciousness in the seventeenth century and grew for three hundred years. In this new land she would build a history so righteous it would instruct the mother country; but the mother country would not listen. Now unexpectedly alone, she had a choice: hold to the sacred ideal in her spiritual life, but recognize that always, in her history, she would be profane; or, unlike almost all other nations, deny that the sacred stands apart, declare her own secular history sacred, and live as though that were so, in the anxious hope that it is so. She accepted the latter option and for practical guidance looked only to the God who spoke in history. She gambled everything, not on an ideal history, but on her history in this world. Then in the twentieth century, after an appalling series of national failures, always followed by the hope that the experiment could be saved, she finally acquiesced to her critics. She acknowledged that the sacred would not be embodied in her story, after all.

21. See chapters 2 and 3.

22. Noble, *End of American History,* p. 67.

23. E.g., Reinhold Niebuhr, *The Irony of American History* (New York: Charles Scribner's Sons, 1952), p. 4.

24. Niebuhr, *The Irony of American History,* p. 155.

25. Niebuhr, *The Irony of American History,* pp. 168–169.

26. Niebuhr, *The Irony of American History,* p. 174. This is the religious prerequisite behind *The Irony of American History,* a book written after, not before, Niebuhr had supposedly abandoned the Barthian God-world dualisms of the 1930s.

27. Their pessimism resembles what Christopher Lasch calls "narcissism." Lasch traces narcissism to a loss of a meaningful American history and contends that this loss had led to spiritual emptiness. See Christopher Lasch, *The Culture of Narcissism: American Life in an Age of Diminishing Expectations* (New York: W. W. Norton & Company, Inc., 1978) and *The Minimal Self: Psychic Survival in Troubled Times* (New York: W. W. Norton & Co., 1984).

28. The technical and now misleading terms for this condition are concupiscence or sensuality. Valerie Saiving, "The Human Situation: A Feminine View," in *Womanspirit Rising: A Feminist Reader in Religion,* ed. Carol P. Christ and Judith Plaskow (New York: Harper & Row, Publishers, 1979), pp. 25–42.

Chapter 2: The Rise of the Professional Intellectual

1. Henry James, *The Portrait of a Lady* (New York: Oxford University of Press, 1981), pp. 77–78 (emphasis in original).

2. Rowland Sherrill argues that it is just such religious sensibilities and subjectivities that are primary in religion, particularly in America. See "Recovering American Religious Sensibility," *Religion and the Life of the Nation: American Recoveries,* ed. by Rowland A. Sherrill (Urbana and Chicago: University of Illinois Press, 1990), pp. 13, 18.

3. The development of professional expertise is chronicled by Christopher Lasch, from his 1965 *New Radicalism in America, 1889–1963* to his 1992 *The True and Only Heaven,* both as it occurred in the past and as it happened in the 60s, 70s, and 80s, both as it unfolded and as it began to stumble.

4. Russell Jacoby, "A New Intellectual History?" *The American Historical Review* 97 (April 1992): p. 416.

5. Russell Jacoby, *The Last Intellectuals: American Culture in the Age of Academe* (New York: Basic Books, Inc., 1987), p. 14.

6. Jacoby suggests that the distinguished intellectuals who do appear in *The New York Times Book Review, Commentary, The New Yorker, The Nation,* and *The New York Review of Books* are old and established, rather than young and making their way through writing for the public (*The Last Intellectuals,* p. 12).

7. Jacoby, *The Last Intellectuals,* pp. 7–8.

8. Peter Novick, *That Noble Dream: The "Objectivity Question" and the American Historical Profession* (New York: Cambridge University Press, 1988), p. 48; see also pp. 22–23. See the general historical argument of Burton J. Bledstein, *The Culture of Professionalism: The Middle Class and the Development of Higher Education in America* (New York: Norton, 1978).

9. Bernard M. Loomer, "Religion and the Mind of the University," in *Liberal Learning and Religion,* ed. by Amos N. Wilder (New York: Harper, 1951), pp. 147–68. For a recent study that elaborates ideas enunciated by Loomer, see Bruce Wilshire, *The Moral Collapse of the University: Professionalism, Purity and Alienation* (Albany, NY: State University of New York Press, 1990).

10. "American Professors and Their Society," *Change* (July/August 1993): p. 26 (emphasis in original).

11. Bruce Kuklick, *The Rise of American Philosophy: Cambridge, Massachusetts 1860–1930* (New Haven: Yale University Press, 1977), p. xxvi.

12. Kuklick, *The Rise of American Philosophy,* p. 572.

13. Harvey does not explain why theology did not remain a humanistic discipline in private universities, where the separation of church and state was not an issue.

14. Van A. Harvey, "On the Intellectual Marginality of American Theology," *Religion and Twentieth-Century American Intellectual Life,* ed. by Michael J. Lacey (New York: Woodrow Wilson International Center for Scholars and Cambridge University Press, 1989), p. 192.

15. Conrad Cherry, unpublished manuscript entitled "Theological and Religious Sciences," p. 4. Cherry cites Claude Welch, *Graduate Education in Religion: A Critical Appraisal* (Missoula, Mont.: University of Montana Press, 1971).

16. Cherry, "Theological and Religious Sciences," p. 52.

17. Cherry, "Theological and Religious Sciences," p. 50. For an

amplification of his perspective on the recent state of the university study of religion, see Conrad Cherry, "Boundaries and Frontiers for the Study of Religion: The Heritage of the Age of the University," *Journal of the American Academy of Religion,* 57 (winter 1989), pp. 807–827.

18. "Throughout their lives they were more concerned to grapple with questions they found personally and socially meaningful than with projects which followed the agendas of the discipline. (One consequence of this was that they directed most of their work to a lay audience.)" Novick, *That Noble Dream,* p. 253.

19. Nelson Goodman, "Notes on the Well-Made World," *Partisan Review* (1984): pp. 277–278. See also Nelson Goodman, *Ways of Worldmaking* (Indianapolis, 1978).

20. Richard Rorty, *Consequences of Pragmatism (Essays: 1972–1980)* (Minneapolis, University of Minnesota Press, 1982), p. 166.

21. Richard Rorty, *Objectivity, Relativism, and Truth* (Philosophical Papers, Volume I) (New York: Cambridge University Press, 1991), p. 66–67.

22. As quoted in Frank Lentricchia, *Criticism and Social Change* (Chicago: University of Chicago Press, 1983), p. 160. He quotes Kenneth Burke, *The Philosophy of Literary Form: Studies in Symbolic Form* (Berkeley and Los Angeles: University of California Press, 1973), p. 110–11.

23. As quoted in Sacvan Bercovitch, *The American Jeremiad* (Madison: University of Wisconsin Press, 1978), p. 190.

24. Bruce Kuklick, "Introduction," William James, *Pragmatism* (Indianapolis: Hackett Publishing Co., 1981), p. xv.

25. Steven C. Rockefeller, *John Dewey: Religious Faith and Democratic Humanism* (New York: Columbia University Press, 1991), p. 315.

26. See, e.g., Cornel West, book review of Richard Rorty, *Philosophy and the Mirror of Nature* in *Union Seminary Quarterly Review,* 37 (fall/winter 1981): p. 194; Frank Lentricchia, *Criticism and Social Change.*

27. It could be argued that neoconservatives remain so oblivious to the historicist methods characteristic of university conversation today that they cannot be called truly contemporary intellectuals, that they sell their intellectual birthright to buy a mess of public credibility. But such a rejoinder may be suspiciously self-serving.

28. Peter Novick, *That Noble Dream*. Future references to Novick's *That Noble Dream* will appear parenthetically, abbreviated as *TND* in the text. The words of the title were uttered by Theodore Clarke Smith in 1934, when he lamented the rise of a new relativism and opined "the final extinction of that noble dream," "of the effort for objective truth," of "the ideal of impartiality" (p. 259 and the epigraph to the book).

29. Leopold von Ranke, the greatest German advocate of *wissenschaftliche Objektivität,* was a philosophical idealist who claimed the historian should "scent the track of the spirit," penetrate to "essences." He saw *wissenschaftliche* history, like philosophy, literature, and theology, as truly *eine Geisteswissenschaft.*

30. Novick, *That Noble Dream,* p. 417. While Halberstam's type of confusion is not unique to our era, it is more aggravated than the confusion in earlier eras; because the most recent relativism is ostensibly deeper running, the inexplicable introduction of a double standard (where relativists get to make absolute judgments after all) is more troubling. See Sheila Greeve Davaney's adroit use of this argument to challenge some prevailing practices of feminists in religious studies— who tend to treat received ideas as relative to masculine bias and to treat their own ideas as innocent of bias and, therefore, authoritative ("Problems with Feminist Theory: Historicity and the Search for Sure Foundations," in *Embodied Love: Sensuality and Relationship as Feminist Values,* ed. by Paula M. Cooey, et al. [San Francisco: Harper & Row, 1987], pp. 79–95).

31. He writes history like a relativist, saying in the second to last paragraph of this 629-page book: "In any case, as I have attempted to show, the evolution of historians' attitudes on the objectivity question has always been closely tied to changing social, political, cultural, and professional contexts" (*TND* p. 628). That is, the framework for his discussion of the career of objectivity is relativistic: you are a relativist or an objectivist, dependent on and relative to your intellectual context. Novick specifies a consistent pattern for the rise of relativism: in periods of "negativity and doubt" relativism arises; in periods of "affirmation and the search for certainty" objectivism rises (*TND* p. 281). Objectivism is likely to flourish in times of optimism and goodwill, and relativism to flourish in times of pessimism (*TND* p. 458, 467). Clearly, thinkers and their thoughts are largely functions of context. Surely, it would follow that Peter Novick and his theory are, then, also creatures of today's chaotic social context and must develop accordingly. But Novick often treats himself, not as a relativist, but as an objectivist, for, he says, the whole point of his book is "to explore the fortunes of the

idea of objectivity among American professional historians over the last century" (*TND* p. 1). This sounds like a set-the-record-straight sort of objectivist claim. And Novick does openly claim just those sorts of personal capacities that would enable him to be objective: "My multi-layered approach," he says, "should protect me against charges of reductionism" (*TND* p. 10). The typical historian's expectations are "so 'accentuate the positive' that what I think of as my attempt at detachment may be read as hostility, on the grounds that the alternative to affirmation must be negativism" (*TND* p. 13). "My greater detachment, if that is what it is, may stem from the fact that I am, by background and training an historian of Europe, writing about an American profession dominated by historians of the United States—a subject hitherto written about exclusively by specialists in American history" (*TND* p. 14).

We are left, then, with a Peter Novick who sounds both relativistic and objectivistic. This, however, may not be problematic, but merely consistent. With all the force of the objective it might be said that Novick, too, is the relativized creature of his own times, and those times are neither dominantly pessimistic (and, thereby, relativistic) nor dominantly optimistic (and, thereby, objective) but chaotic (and thereby confusing), just as Novick is. See Thomas L. Haskell's alternative reading of Novick's inconsistencies in "Objectivity is Not Neutrality: Rhetoric vs. Practice in Peter Novick's *That Noble Dream*," *History and Theory* 29 (May 1990): pp. 129–157, especially pp. 137–144.

32. See chapter 8 for an elaboration of Hollinger's and Haskell's work.

33. See, e.g., Peter Berger, *Rumor of Angels* (Garden City, NY: Doubleday & Company, Inc., 1969). Although Berger discussed intellectual plausibility, his point was not only that intellectual adequacy itself was undermined but that affective, or emotional, credibility was undermined.

34. James T. Kloppenberg, "Objectivity and Historicism: A Century of American Historical Writing," (a review of *That Noble Dream*), in *The American Historical Review* 94 (October 1989): p. 1026.

35. Novick, *That Noble Dream*, p. 263.

36. Nevertheless, Novick professed not to find this condition depressing: "I in no way lament the state of affairs I described; . . . I see it instead as offering rich possibilities" (Peter Novick, "My Correct Views on Everything," *The American Historical Review* 96 [June 1991]: p. 702).

Chapter 3: William James, Public Intellectual

1. George Cotkin, *William James, Public Philosopher* (Baltimore: The Johns Hopkins University Press, 1990), p. 16.

2. William James to Hugo Munsterberg, July 8, 1891, *The Letters of William James,* Vols. I & II, edited by Henry James (Boston: The Atlantic Monthly Press, 1920), p. 313.

3. The complete text reads: "But you shall see no more temper fits from me *(unless you are foolish yourself)* for I have achieved a moral victory over my low spirits and tendency to complain whilst I have been here [Cambridge] these days ... I have actually by steady force of will kept it down and at last got it under for a while and mean to fight it out on that line for the rest of my life, for I see that is my particular mission in the world," William James to Alice James, October 3, 1890, as quoted in Gerald E. Myers, *William James: His Life and Though* (New Haven: Yale University Press, 1986), pp. 38–39 (emphasis in the original).

4. William James to O. W. Holmes, Jr., September 17, 1967, *Letters of James,* I, p. 99.

5. Paternal domination is stressed by Howard M. Feinstein in *Becoming William James* (Ithaca, NY: Cornell University Press, 1984). See Martin Seligman's thesis that depression is the outcome, more than anything else, of a sense of helplessness (Martin Seligman, *Helplessness: On Depression, Development, and Death* [San Francisco: W. H. Freeman, 1975]).

6. Ralph Barton Perry, *The Thought and Character of William James,* 2 vols. (Boston: Little, Brown and Co., 1935), 1: 323 (emphasis in original), p. 7. My earlier denial that issues of "rationalistic idealism or positivistic empiricism" could ever drive James to depression was too uncomplicated (see William Dean, "Empiricial Theology: A Revisable Tradition," *Process Studies* 19 [summer 1990]: p. 88).

7. William James to Tom Ward, March [?] 1869, *Letters of James,* I, pp. 152–53 (emphasis in original).

8. William James, "The Dilemma of Determinism," *The Will to Believe and Other Essays in Popular Philosophy* (Cambridge, MA: Harvard University Press, 1979), p. 117.

9. Cotkin, *William James,* p. 57.

10. William James, *The Varieties of Religious Experience* (Cambridge, MA: Harvard University Press, 1985), p. 134. William Clebsch, among

others, calls this passage autobiographical (William A. Clebsch, *American Religious Thought: A History* [Chicago: The University of Chicago Press, 1973], p. 140).

11. William James to Henry James, Jr., April 13, 1986, in Ralph Barton Perry, *The Thought and Character of William James*, briefer version (New York: George Braziller, 1954), p. 105 (emphasis in original).

12. William James to Henry James, Sr., September 5, 1867, *Letters of James*, I, p. 96.

13. William James to O. W. Holmes, Jr., January 3, 1968, *Letters of James*, I, p. 127.

14. William James to Thomas W. Ward, Jan. ___, 1968, *Letters of James*, I, p. 129 (emphasis in original).

15. William James to Thomas W. Ward, Jan. ___, 1886, *Letters of James*, I, p. 129 (emphasis in original).

16. Notebooks of William James, *Letters of James*, I, p. 148 (emphasis in original).

17. To put such stress on these early years is not unusual. Cotkin says, "Although interpretations differ over the exact genesis of James's difficulties and their resolution, all scholars essentially respect the important nexus between youthful problems and mature philosophical doctrines" (Cotkin, *William James*, p. 6).

18. Frank Lentricchia, *Ariel and the Police: Michel Foucault, William James, Wallace Stevens* (Madison: University of Wisconsin Press, 1988), p. 106.

19. Today such a commentary on the centrality of decision, interest, and speculation is not exceptional but commonplace in science or in the philosophy of science. This is evident not only in the fashionable sociological philosophies of science, such as Paul Feyerabend, *Against Method: Outline of an Anarchistic Theory of Knowledge* (London: Verso, 1978) and Thomas S. Kuhn, *The Structure of Scientific Revolutions* (Chicago: University of Chicago Press, 1970), but in new histories of scientific method and practice. Graham Rees argues that empirical method itself literally began in speculation, for Francis Bacon devised his inductive method in order to validate the speculative system he had already developed ("Francis Bacon's Biological Ideas: A New Manuscript Source," in *Occult and Scientific Mentalities in the Renaissance*, ed. by Brian Vickers [New York: Cambridge University Press, 1984], pp. 279–314). Stephen Jay Gould argues that James Hutton's eighteenth-

century hypothesis about a continuously recycling earth began as a piece of a speculative puzzle. This is ironic, for Hutton's theory—"the greatest reconstruction of geology," Gould says—is the centerpiece in geology's nineteenth-century antispeculative attack on theology's speculations. Yet, Hutton's theory began in his question: if erosion creates life-giving soil, and carries it to the oceans, why does any soil remain? Because, speculates Hutton, God created a cycle whereby sediments not only sink and consolidate in the oceans but later are uplifted by the Earth's interior heat. Hutton had a practical "puzzle arising from his own experience as a farmer," and he speculated that God, as final cause, created a cyclical process of regeneration. Only later did Hutton make field observations that lent empirical credibility to his speculation (Stephen Jay Gould, "Hutton's Purpose," *Hen's Teeth and Horse's Toes* [New York: W. W. Norton & Company, 1983], pp, 83, 90).

20. James's diary in 1873, *Letters of James,* I, p. 171.

21. William James, *Pragmatism* (Cambridge: Harvard University Press, 1979), p. 140.

22. The phrase "discourse of heroism" is Cotkin's in *William James.*

23. William James to William Dean Howells, November 16, 1900, Howells Papers, Houghton Library, Harvard University (as quoted in Cotkin, *William James,* p. 124).

24. See Myers, *William James,* footnote 109, p. 597.

25. Myers, *William James,* p. 430.

26. James might have felt personally responsible for the excesses of bigness, for his own published efforts to overcome public malaise might have encouraged an inappropriate activism, even the heroics implicit in Theodore Roosevelt's prosecution of the Spanish-American war. After all, Roosevelt appeared to be a perfect embodiment of just the strenuous, heroic life James himself had advocated. So James the philosopher may have felt particularly called upon to address this war and its consequences.

27. As quoted in Myers, *William James,* pp. 438–40 (emphasis in original).

28. James, *Pragmatism,* pp. 17–18.

29. Lentricchia, *Ariel,* p. 111 (emphasis in original).

30. Lentricchia, *Ariel,* pp. 119–120.

Chapter 4: Religious Narrative and the Avoidance of Nature

1. John Updike, *Hugging the Shore: Essays and Criticisms* (New York: Vintage Books, 1983), p. xvii.

2. Gary Snyder, *The Practice of the Wild* (San Francisco: North Point Press, 1990), p. 19.

3. See George A. Lindbeck, *The Nature of Doctrine: Religion and Theology in a Post-liberal Age* (Philadelphia: Westminster Press, 1984), pp. 57–63.

4. George A. Lindbeck, "The Church's Mission to a Postmodern Culture," in Frederic B. Burnham, *Postmodern Theology: Christian Faith in a Pluralistic World* (New York: Harper & Row, Publishers, 1989), p. 51.

5. Paul Feyerabend, *Against Method: Outline of an Anarchistic Theory of Knowledge* (London: Verso, 1984), chapter 1.

6. "It is now fashionable to assert that science is just another cultural activity, successful merely on its own terms. This is nonsense." Paul Davies (professor of mathematical physics at the University of Adelaide in Australia and author of *God and the New Physics*), in "The Holy Grail of Physics," *The New York Times Book Review* (March 7, 1993): p. 12.

7. In a revised but unpublished manuscript of a very important lecture delivered in Chicago on November 7, 1988, entitled, "Hans W. Frei and the Future of Theology in America."

8. Jeffrey Stout, *The Flight from Authority: Religion, Morality, and the Quest for Autonomy* (Notre Dame: University of Notre Dame Press, 1981), p. 97.

9. Jeffrey Stout, *Ethics after Babel: The Languages of Morals and Their Discontents* (Boston: Beacon Press, 1988), p. 186.

10. Hans W. Frei, *The Eclipse of Biblical Narrative: A Study in Eighteenth and Nineteenth Century Hermeneutics* (New Haven: Yale University Press, 1974), p. 280.

11. Frei, *Eclipse*, p. 218.

12. Lindbeck, *Doctrine*, p. 62.

13. Lindbeck, *Doctrine*, p. 114 (emphasis added).

14. Lindbeck, *Doctrine*, p. 84.

15. One might ask, is not the second order language also a product of narrow communities? Does the narrative truly escape the group sub-

jectivity of first order language? Are not grammar and formal rules always already loaded with specific, local views of the world and, thus, implicit claims to truth? Is not Lindbeck inflating a relative narrative into an ostensibly irrelative metalanguage, even though the metalanguage is a function of a particular language after all?

Within three pages of *The Nature of Doctrine*, Lindbeck speaks of Scripture's "own domain of meaning," of "the text" which absorbs the world, and of Scripture functioning as "the lens." These all are accounts of ostensibly second order functions (Lindbeck, *Doctrine*, pp. 117–119). It must be remembered, however, that access to Scripture's "own" meaning or to "the" text or to "the" lens comes only through particular historical circumstances. This would appear to reduce Scripture's "own meaning" to merely "our" meaning or make "the" text and "the" lens merely "our" text and lens. (For an important statement of this and similar criticisms, see Terrence W. Tilley, "Incommensurability, Intratextuality, and Fideism," *Modern Theology* 5 [January 1989]: pp. 87–111.)

The truth-empty character of second order language can be challenged by noting that its purportedly formal grammar of faith is, after all, a claim born of a particular twentieth-century, academic, and neo-neo-orthodox faith. The second order language can be seen, then, as the product of a particular historic community's commonsensical view of the world. To the extent that the view is specific and uninformed by positions beyond the group's interests, it omits unintentionally and unnecessarily just those interests that do not accord with its own, such as particular scientific interpretations of nature. Accordingly, in the claim to being truth empty, the most dangerous of blindnesses may be allowed, the unrecognized blindness.

16. Thomas S. Kuhn, *The Structure of Scientific Revolutions* (Second Edition, Enlarged) (Chicago: The University of Chicago Press, 1974), p. 4.

17. Admittedly, nature cannot be accessed except through human frames of interpretation, so that it never is known in its rawness. However, Ian Barbour, more than anyone else, has shown how this acknowledgment of the power of interpretation does not nullify the capacity of the sciences to comment on "reality." For Barbour's best rendering of this point, see Ian G. Barbour, *Religion in an Age of Science: The Gifford Lectures 1989–1991, Volume 1* (San Francisco: Harper & Row, Publishers, 1990).

18. Kuhn, *Structure*, pp. 115, 117.

19. Lindbeck, *Doctrine,* p. 62.

20. Lindbeck, *Doctrine,* p. 62–63.

21. See the discussion of John Wheeler and Charles Darwin in chapter 7 below.

22. Gerhard von Rad, *The Theology of Israel's Historical Traditions,* Vol. 1: *Old Testament Theology,* translated by D. M. G. Stalker, 2 vols. (New York: Harper & Brothers, 1962), I, pp. 138–139.

23. von Rad, *Old Testament Theology,* I, p. 140.

24. Gerhard von Rad, *Wisdom in Israel* (Nashville and New York: Abingdon Press, 1977), p. 161.

25. von Rad, *Wisdom in Israel,* p. 159.

26. H. Paul Santmire, *The Travail of Nature: The Ambiguous Ecological Promise of Christian Theology* (Philadelphia: Fortress Press, 1985), p. 192.

27. In *The Travail of Nature* Santmire convincingly argues from works by Walter Brueggemann and Clauss Westermann. See also "Toward a New Theology of Nature," *Dialog* 25 (winter 1986): pp. 43–50.

Chapter 5: Religious Naturalism and the Avoidance of Ambiguity

1. William James, *Pragmatism* (Cambridge: Harvard University Press, 1978), pp. 64–65.

2. I recognize that Emerson's idealism is often treated—improperly, I believe—as nothing more than Emerson's way of talking about history, rather than of referring beyond history to an extrahistorical order of things. See, John Dewey, referring to Emerson: "His ideas are not fixed upon any Reality that is beyond or behind or in any way apart, and hence they do not have to be bent. They are versions of the Here and Now, and flow freely" (*Characters and Events* [New York: Henry Holt and Co., 1929], I, p. 75). See also, David L. Smith, "Emerson and Deconstruction: The Ends of Scholarship," *Soundings* 67 (winter 1984): pp. 379–398; Stanley Cavell, "Emerson, Coleridge, Kant," in *Post-Analytic Philosophy,* ed. by John Rajchman and Cornel West (New York: Columbia University Press, 1985), pp. 84–107.

3. Ralph Waldo Emerson, "Nature" (the 1836 version), *The Complete Essays and Other Writings of Ralph Waldo Emerson*, ed. by Brooks Atkinson (New York: The Modern Library, 1940, 1950), p. 3.

4. Emerson, "Nature," p. 13.

5. See, e.g., Catherine Albanese, *Nature Religion in America: From the Algonkian Indians to the New Age* (Chicago: The University of Chicago Press, 1990).

6. Sidney Hook notwithstanding; see Sidney Hook, "Pragmatism and the Tragic Sense of Life," *Contemporary American Philosophy,* Second Series, edited by John E. Smith (New York: Humanities Press, Inc., 1970), pp. 170–193.

7. Reinhold Niebuhr argues that agape "has its primary justification in an 'essential reality' which transcends the realities of history, namely, the character of God" (*The Nature and Destiny of Man: A Christian Interpretation,* vol. 2 [New York: Charles Scribner's Sons, 1949], p. 96).

8. Richard Nixon, "Dealing with Gorbachev," *The New York Times Magazine* (March 13, 1988): p. 79.

9. Sacvan Bercovitch, *The Rites of Assent: Transformations in the Symbolic Construction of America* (New York: Routledge, 1993), especially pp. 18–25.

10. Sidney Hook, *Out of Step: An Unquiet Life in the Twentieth Century* (New York: Harper & Row, 1987).

11. My own attempts to describe the roots of empirical theology can be found in *American Religious Empiricism* (Albany, NY: State University of New York Press, 1986), chapter 1; and *History Making History: The New Historicism in American Religious Thought* (Albany, NY: State University of New York Press, 1988), chapters 2 and 5.

12. I have argued in greater detail for the presence of this tension within James's thought in "From Piecemeal Supernaturalism to Piecemeal Jamesism," *The American Journal of Theology and Philosophy* 15 (January 1994).

13. I have argued for the presence of this tension within the thought of the empirical theologians in "Empiricism and God," in *Empirical Theology: A Handbook,* edited by Randolph C. Miller (Birmingham, AL: Religious Education Press, 1992).

14. See Wilfrid Sellars on "The Myth of the Given" in "Empiricism and the Philosophy of Mind," in Herbert Feigl and Michael Scriven, eds.

Minnesota Studies in the Philosophy of Science, vol. 1 (Minneapolis: University of Minnesota Press, 1956), pp. 253–329.

15. James, *Pragmatism,* p. 140.

16. James may have described Bergson's impact on his world view better in a letter to Bergson than he did in his chapter on Bergson in *a Pluralistic Universe:* "But whereas I have hitherto found no better way of defending Tychism [chance-ridden development] than by affirming the spontaneous addition of *discrete* elements of being (or their subtraction) thereby playing the game with intellectualist weapons, you set things straight at a single stroke, by your fundamental conception of the continuously creative nature of reality." In a letter to Bergson dated June 13, 1907, in *The Letters of William James,* Vols I & II, edited by Henry James (Boston: The Atlantic Monthly Press, 1920), II, p. 292.

17. William James, *A Pluralistic Universe* (Cambridge, MA: Harvard University Press, 1977), p. 149.

18. James, *Universe,* p. 144.

19. James, *Universe,* p. 55.

20. James, *Universe,* p. 27 (emphasis in original).

21. Benjamin Paul Blood, with whom James had corresponded since at least 1896, had propounded a theory of pluralistic mysticism, in place of the usual monistic mysticism. James found Blood's combination of radical empiricism and pluralism appealing and said as much in his last writing, "A Pluralistic Mystic," in William James, *Essays in Philosophy* (Cambridge, MA: Harvard University Press, 1978), pp. 172–190), and in a letter to Blood dated June 25, 1910 (*The Letters of William James* II, pp. 347–348).

22. James, *Universe,* pp. 16, 23.

23. James, *Universe,* pp. 54 (emphasis in original).

24. James, *Universe,* pp. 28, 144 (emphasis in original).

25. James, *Universe,* p. 17.

26. To simplify the narrative, I emphasize James; similar work by George Burman Foster was published at roughly the same time and was more theologically developed. See Foster's *The Finality of the Christian Religion* (Chicago: The University of Chicago Press, 1906), *The Function of Religion in Man's Struggle for Existence* (Chicago: The University of Chicago Press, 1909), and "Pragmatism and Knowledge," *The American Journal of Theology* 11 (October 1907).

Chapter 6: The Religious Thinker and the Acceptance of History

1. John Dewey, *Art as Experience* (New York: Capricorn Books, 1958), p. 195.

2. William James, *A Pluralistic Universe* (Cambridge, MA: Harvard University Press, 1977), p. 27 (emphasis in original).

3. William James, "A Pluralistic Mystic," *Essays in Philosophy* (Cambridge, MA: Harvard University Press, 1978), pp. 172–190; Nancy Frankenberry, "Classical Theism, Panentheism, and Pantheism: On the Relation between God Construction and Gender Construction," *Zygon* 28 (March 1993): pp. 29–46.

4. See especially: George Burman Foster, *The Finality of the Christian Religion* (Chicago: The University of Chicago Press, 1906), *The Function of Religion in Man's Struggle for Existence* (Chicago: The University of Chicago Press, 1909), and "Pragmatism and Knowledge," *The American Journal of Theology* 11 (October 1967); Gerald Birney Smith, *Social Idealism and the Changing Theology* (New York: The Macmillan Co., 1912); Shailer Mathews, *The Atonement and the Social Process* (New York: The Macmillan Co., 1930); Shirley Jackson Case, *The Christian Philosophy of History* (Chicago: The University of Chicago Press, 1943); and Edward Scribner Ames, *Religion* (Chicago: John O. Pyle, 1949; first published in 1929).

5. Richard J. Bernstein says of West, "He is trying to do for our time what Dewey did for his" (in Robert S. Boyton, "Princeton's Public Intellectual," *The New York Times Magazine* [September 15, 1991]: p. 43).

6. Cornel West, *The American Evasion of Philosophy: A Genealogy of Pragmatism* (Madison: The University of Wisconsin Press, 1989), p. 106.

7. "Long after Dewey had rejected the Hegelian notion of a cosmic organic unity, he continued to believe in organic unity as a social ideal and to search for a unifying moral faith" (Steven Rockefeller, *John Dewey: Religious Faith and Democratic Humanism* [New York: Columbia University Press, 1991], p. 81).

8. Cornel West, "Why Haven't They Matched the Success of Others?" *Los Angeles Times* (September 8, 1991): Section M, p. 1.

9. John Dewey, "Religion and Our Schools," in *John Dewey: The Middle Works, 1899–1924,* ed. Jo Ann Boydston (Carbondale, IL: Southern Illinois University Press, 1977), Vol. 4, p. 169.

10. Cornel West, *Prophetic Fragments* (Grand Rapids, MI: William B. Eerdmans Publishing Company, 1988, and Trenton, NJ: Africa World Press, Inc., 1988), p. 195.

11. For example, West is critical of the transcendental, neo-Kantian anthropology of Juan Luis Segundo largely because it is not "organically linked with the prophetic churches and progressive movements" that surround him (*Prophetic Fragments,* p. 202).

12. Cornel West, *Prophetic Fragments,* p. 271.

13. Cornel West, *The Ethical Dimensions of Marxist Thought* (New York: Monthly Review Press, 1991), p. xvii (emphasis in original).

14. Cornel West, "Nietzsche's Prefiguration of Postmodern American Philosophy," *Boundary 2* IX (spring/fall 1981): p. 242.

15. West, "Nietzsche's Prefiguration": p. 242.

16. Cornel West, "Nihilism in Black America," *Dissent* 38 (spring 1991): pp. 221–222.

17. West, "Nihilism": pp. 223–24.

18. West, *Evasion,* p. 233 (emphasis in original).

19. "Interview with Cornel West" conducted by Anders Stephanson in *Universal Abandon?: The Politics of Postmodernism,* ed. by Andrew Ross (Minneapolis: University of Minnesota Press, 1988), p. 277 (emphasis in original).

20. West, *Evasion,* p. 233.

21. West, *Evasion,* p. 234.

22. Cornel West, "The Historicist Turn in Philosophy of Religion," in *Knowing Religiously,* ed. by Leroy S. Rouner (Notre Dame, IN: University of Notre Dame Press, 1985), p. 44.

23. West, "The Historicist Turn," p. 44.

24. See Richard J. Bernstein, *Beyond Objectivism and Relativism: Science, Hermeneutics, and Praxis* (Philadelphia: University of Pennsylvania Press, 1983); Frank Lentricchia, *Ariel and the Police: Michel Foucault, William James, Wallace Stevens* (Madison: University of Wisconsin Press, 1988), and "En Route to Retreat: Making it to Mepkin

Abbey," *Harper's Magazine* (January 1992): pp. 68–78; Jeffrey Stout, *The Flight from Authority: Religion, Morality, and the Quest for Autonomy* (Notre Dame, IN: University of Notre Dame Press, 1981).

25. Gordon D. Kaufman, *Relativism, Knowledge, and Faith* (Chicago: The University of Chicago Press, 1960).

26. These shifts are first registered in Gordon Kaufman, "God as Symbol" in *God the Problem* (Cambridge, MA: Harvard University Press, 1972).

27. Gordon D. Kaufman, *The Theological Imagination: Constructing the Concept of God* (Philadelphia: The Westminster Press, 1981), pp. 11, 21.

28. Gordon D. Kaufman, *Theology for a Nuclear Age* (Philadelphia: Westminster Press, 1985), p. 22.

29. Gordon D. Kaufman, *Theological Imagination*, pp. 50–51.

30. Gordon D. Kaufman, *Theological for a Nuclear Age*, p. 41.

31. Gordon D. Kaufman, *In Face of Mystery: A Constructive Theology* (Cambridge, MA: Harvard University Press, 1993).

32. See, e.g., William C. Placher, *Unapologetic Theology: A Christian Voice in a Pluralistic Conversation* (Louisville, KY: Westminster/John Knox Press, 1989), pp. 11–15.

33. John Locke, *An Essay Concerning Human Understanding*, edited by A. D. Woozley (New York: New American Library, 1974), p. 65. See also Woozley's claim that "the whole *Essay* was devoted to the aim of distinguishing knowledge from belief" (ibid., p. 15).

34. Locke, *An Essay*, ed. Woozley, p. 322 (emphasis in original).

35. John Locke, *An Essay Concerning Human Understanding*, ed. by Peter H. Nidditch (Oxford: Clarendon Press, 1975), Book 3, chapter 9, paragraph 14, p. 483.

36. Alfred North Whitehead, *Process and Reality: Corrected Edition*, ed. by David Ray Griffin and Donald W. Sherburne (New York: The Free Press, 1978), p. 147.

37. Locke, *An Essay*, ed. Woozley, p. 242.

38. Kaufman has said, "It is the content of the notion of God, not the manner in which that notion is created and shaped in human consciousness, that determines whether God is a proper object of worship and devotion" (*God the Problem*, p. 11). He separates the question of how

ideas are reached from the question of their validity. And Kaufman's answer in *God the Problem* and in every book thereafter is that the validity of imagined theological truths must be tested pragmatically. Thus, a theological truth should be judged, not in terms of how we came to it, but "in terms of the adequacy with which it is fulfilling the objectives we humans set for it" (*Theology for a Nuclear Age*, p. 19; see also, Kaufman, *Theological Imagination*, pp. 46–51, 255–60).

39. Of course, to quote Gordon Kaufman, "where it is the *world-itself* . . . the whole within which everything else falls—including not only all facts but also all our symbols and concepts—there is nothing outside our conception against which we can place it to see whether it corresponds.'" Hence, Kaufman is skeptical of epistemological approaches to theological knowledge. In metaphysics and theology, he says, "the ordinary truth-criterion of correspondence simply cannot be directly applied" (Kaufman, *Theological Imagination*, pp. 254–55). Kaufman is surely correct in arguing that the *ordinary* truth-criterion cannot be directly applied in matters of religious knowledge. As we will see, however, radical empiricism is an epistemology that is most important in just those cases where the ordinary truth-criterion cannot be directly applied.

40. Richard Rorty, *Consequences of Pragmatism (Essays: 1972–1980)* (Minneapolis: University of Minnesota Press, 1982), p. 193.

41. Steven Jay Gould, *Wonderful Life: The Burgess Shale and the Nature of History* (New York: W. W. Norton & Company, 1989), p. 51. Gould seems in this to stand apart from the "throw of the dice" or "wheel of fortune" analogies that characterize so much of his work; see, e.g., "The Wheel of Fortune and the Wedge of Progress," *Natural History* (March 1989): pp. 14–21.

42. William James, *Pragmatism* (Cambridge, MA: Harvard University Press, 1978), p. 118. "A sensation," James says, "is rather like a client who has given his case to a lawyer and then has passively to listen in the courtroom to whatever account of his affairs, pleasant or unpleasant, the lawyer finds it most expedient to give" (*Pragmatism*, pp. 118–119).

43. Dewey, *Art as Experience,* pp. 193–194 (I have inserted the comma).

44. Dewey, *Art as Experience,* pp. 191–195.

45. As John Dewey noted, Stevenson's imagined locomotive became a real locomotive and changed forever the environment it entered (John

Dewey, *A Common Faith* [New Haven: Yale University Press, 1958], p. 49).

46. Walter Lippmann, *A Preface to Morals* (New York: The Macmillan Company, 1929), p. 318.

47. In the words of Ecclesiastes 3:3, 3:5, and 3:7, there is

a time to break down, and a time to build up . . .
a time to cast away stones, and a time to gather stones together . . .
a time to keep silence, and a time to speak.

If this was Ecclesiastes time to speak, it may bear some resemblance to the time in which today's American intellectuals live. Harvey H. Guthrie, Jr., has said, "Then, when the national fall of 586 B.C. had shut off ongoing communal history as the locus of God's revelation of himself, theological interest moved more toward nature and individual morality, and wisdom became increasingly important. . . . All this led to a rather rigid orthodoxy, characterized by extreme confidence in its own grasp of the meaning of life and the purposes of God and by a rather narrow, prudential moralism. Against the imposition of such doctrine on the reality of existence Job and Ecclesiastes are, in different ways, protests" ("The Book of Ecclesiastes," *The Interpreter's One-Volume Commentary on the Bible,* ed. by Charles M. Laymon [Nashville: Abingdon Press, 1971], p. 320).

Chapter 7: The Reality of Conventions

1. *Pragmatism* (Cambridge, MA: Harvard University Press, 1975), p. 108.

2. "Human Rights: The West Gets Some Tough Questions," *The New York Times* (June 20, 1993): section E, p. 5.

3. Thomas L. Haskell, "The Curious Persistence of Rights Talk in the 'Age of Interpretation,'" *The Journal of American History* 74 (December 1987): p. 991.

4. Alisdair Macintyre may have offered the best recent defense of a kind of absolutism, that implicit in the universal validity of formal Aristotelian virtues. However, Macintyre purchases this Aristotelianism by making it the only alternative to subjectivistic emotivism, committing what appears to be the fallacy of the excluded middle. In the process he

too quickly reduces American pragmatism to emotivism, thus dismissing what the pragmatists saw as a third option between absolutism and emotivism. See *After Virtue: A Study in Moral Theory* (Notre Dame, IN: University of Notre Dame Press, 1981), p. 63.

5. Haskell, "The Curious Persistence": p. 1002.

6. Further, Nietzsche's very relativism (that situations make theories, not the other way around) would seem to undermine those of his postmodern disciples who absolutize Nietzsche's theories. Haskell correctly observes in a footnote that, if relativists with whom we talk exempt their own views from the situation dependency they criticize in others, then "we would be fools to continue the conversation" with them (Haskell, "The Curious Persistence": p. 1003).

7. Haskell, "The Curious Persistence": pp. 1001, 1004–5, 1008–9.

8. Peter L. Berger and Thomas Luckmann, *The Social Construction of Reality: A Treatise in the Sociology of Knowledge* (Garden City, NY: Doubleday & Company, 1966), p. 55.

9. Giddens's effort to move beyond what he calls the imperial objectivism of sociological functionalism and the imperial subjectivism of sociological hermeneutics leads him to discuss the "structuration of social systems." The parallels between social structure and conventions are significant. See Anthony Giddens, *The Constitution of Society: Outline of the Theory of Structuration* [Berkeley, CA: University of California Press, 1984], chapter 1; also "Action, Subjectivity, and the Constitution of Meaning," *Social Research* 53 (autumn 1986): pp. 529–541.

10. Berger and Luckmann, *Social Construction,* p. 57.

11. Ludwig Wittgenstein, *On Certainty,* edited by G. E. M. Anscombe and G. H. von Wright, trans. by Denis Paul and G. E. M. Anscombe (New York: Harper & Row, Publishers, 1969), p. 15e, pars. 94.

12. Wittgenstein, *On Certainty,* p. 21, pars. 140–144.

13. Wittgenstein, *On Certainty,* p. 15, pars. 95–100.

14. Wittgenstein, *On Certainty,* p. 81. He goes on to advance the following puzzling line of inquiry in paragraphs 617 and 618: "Indeed, doesn't it seem obvious that the possibility of a language-game is conditioned by certain facts? In that case it would seem as if the language-game must '*show*' the facts that make it possible. (But that's not how it is.) Then can one say that only a certain regularity in occurrences makes induction possible? The 'possible' would of course have to be '*logically possible*'" (p. 82, emphasis in original). See also Wittgenstein's acknowl-

edgment that world conditions can alter how language is used in *Philosophical Investigations,* translated by G. E. M. Anscombe (New York: The Macmillan Company, 1965), p. 56e, par. 142.

15. Edmund Runggaldier, *Carnap's Early Conventionalism: An Inquiry into the Historical Background of the Vienna Circle* (Amsterdam: Editions Rodopi B. V., 1984), p. 121.

16. Runggaldier, *Carnap's Conventionalism,* p. 122. Carnap was to break with conventionalism five years into his career, in 1936 (see Hilary Putnam, "Convention: A Theme in Philosophy," *Realism and Reason* (Cambridge, Eng.: Cambridge University Press, 1983), p. 172.

17. Runggaldier, *Carnap's Conventionalism,* p. 30.

18. Rudolf Carnap, "Autobiography," *The Philosophy of Rudolf Carnap,* edited by Paul Arthur Schilpp (LaSalle, IL: Open Court, 1953), p. 15.

19. H. Poincaré, *Science and Hypothesis* (New York: Dover Publications, 1952), p. 50.

20. Poincaré, *Science and Hypothesis,* p. xxiii. See Peter Alexander, "Conventionalism," *The Encyclopedia of Philosophy,* vols. 1–8, ed. by Paul Edwards (New York: Macmillan Publishing Co., Inc. & The Free Press, 1967), 2, p. 216, and Alexander, "Poincaré," *Encyclopedia of Philosophy,* 6, pp. 360–363.

21. Henri Poincaré, *The Value of Science,* trans. by George Bruce Halsted (New York: Dover Publications, Inc., 1958), pp. 14, 114.

22. Poincaré, *Science and Hypothesis,* p. xxiii.

23. Arthur Eddington, *The Philosophy of Physical Science* (New York: The Macmillan Company, 1939), chapter 2.

24. A. S. Eddington, *The Nature of the Physical World* (New York: The Macmillan Co., 1929), pp. 238, 239.

25. Eddington, *Philosophy of Physical Science,* p. 27.

26. Kuhn and Goodman share their epistemological conventionalism with their Harvard colleague, Hilary Putnam, who in this chapter is an admitted conventionalist arguing against a subjective historicism (see *Realism and Reason,* chapters 9 and 10; *Reason, Truth and History* [Cambridge, Eng.: Cambridge University Press, 1982], esp. chapters 5–7).

27. See David A. Hollinger, *In the American Province: Studies in the*

History and Historiography of Ideas (Bloomington, IN: Indiana University Press, 1985), pp. 109–111.

28. Nelson Goodman, *Ways of Worldmaking* (Indianapolis, IN: Hackett Publishing Company, 1978), pp. 138–139, see also p. 132.

29. Goodman, *Ways of Worldmaking,* p. 118.

30. Unlike Kuhn and Goodman, Paul Feyerabend prizes the maverick thinker, stressing not consensus but dissensus, not tradition but anarchy. Nevertheless, like Kuhn and Goodman, Feyerabend prizes maverick thinkers because they enlarge the conventions of science though the introduction of disparate ideas. "A scientist who is interested in maximal empirical content . . . will accordingly adopt a pluralistic methodology, . . . and he will try to improve rather than discard the views that appear to lose in competition" (Paul Feyerabend, *Against Method: Outline of an Anarchistic Theory of Knowledge* [London: Verso, 1984], p. 47).

31. Alfred North Whitehead, *Modes of Thought* (New York: The Free Press, 1966), pp. 92, 143.

32. Whitehead, *Modes,* p. 144.

33. Alfred North Whitehead, *Process and Reality: An Essay in Cosmology,* edited by David Ray Griffin and Donald W. Sherburne (New York: The Free Press, 1979), p. 92.

34. Although Hans Vaihinger, with his "useful fictions," might seem to be an epistemological conventionalist, I would argue that he is not. For Vaihinger, truth is found in correspondence. It follows, then, that Vaihinger would say his "fictions" were not true but false, whereas for the American pragmatists, for example, a fiction that is useful becomes in some sense true. Vaihinger says his "fictionalism does not admit the principle of Pragmatism which runs: 'An idea which is found to be useful in practice proves thereby that it is also true in theory, and the fruitful is thus always true.'" Hans Vaihinger, *The Philosophy of "As if",* translated by C. K. Ogden (New York: Harcourt, Brace & Company, Inc., 1924), p. viii.

35. I presuppose here a matter-spirit monism or interactionism (in opposition to those forms of dualism that permit the mind to proceed on a track of its own, quite independently of the body in which the mind is located, or the body to proceed independently of the mind).

36. Jeremy Bernstein, in his sixty-page vignette on Wheeler, worries that Wheeler's ideas are improperly confused with Eastern mysticism (see "John Wheeler: Retarded Learner," *Quantum Profiles* [Princeton,

NJ: Princeton University Press, 1991], especially, pp. 130–132). For other commentaries on Wheeler's personal outlook and his general ideas, see John Horgan, "Profile: Physicist John A. Wheeler: Questioning the 'It from Bit,'" *Scientific American* (June 1991): pp. 36–38; John Gliedman, "Quantum Universe," *Science Digest* (October 1984): pp. 36–39, 96–97; J. A. Wheeler, "The Universe as Home for Man," *The Nature of Scientific Discovery,* edited by Owen Gingerich (Washington, DC: Smithsonian Institution Press, 1975); John Archibald Wheeler, "Man's View of the Cosmos in America, 1776–1976," *A Time to Hear and Answer: Essays for the Bicentennial Season,* edited by Taylor Littlejohn (Tuscaloosa, AL: University of Alabama Press, 1977).

37. John Archibald Wheeler, "Beyond the Black Hole," *Some Strangeness in the Proportion: A Centennial Symposium to Celebrate the Achievements of Albert Einstein,* edited by Harry Woolf (Reading, MA: Addison-Wesley Publishing Co., 1980), pp. 354, 356.

38. John Archibald Wheeler, "Genesis and Observership," *Foundational Problems in the Special Sciences,* edited by Robert E. Butts and Jaakko Hentikka (Boston: D. Reidel Publishing Co., 1977), p. 7.

39. Wheeler, "Beyond the Black Hole," p. 356.

40. Wheeler, "Beyond the Black Hole," pp. 356–369; J. A. Wheeler, "The 'Past' and the 'Delayed-Choice' Double-Slit Experiment," *Mathematical Foundations of Quantum Theory,* edited by A. N. Marlow (New York, NY: Academic Press, 1978).

41. J. S. Bell, *Physics* 1, (1964): p. 195; for accounts of Bell's importance see N. David Mermin, *Boojums All the Way Through: Communicating Science in a Prosaic Age* (New York: Cambridge University Press, 1990), pp. 177–185, and Heinz R. Pagels, *The Cosmic Code,* (New York: Simon & Schuster, 1982), pp. 166–176.

42. A. Einstein, B. Podolsky, N. Rosen, "Can Quantum Mechanical Description of Physical Reality be Considered Complete?" *Physical Review* 47 (1935): p. 777.

43. N. David Mermin, "Is the Moon There When Nobody Looks: Reality and the Quantum Theory," *Physics Today* (April 1985): p. 38.

44. See John Gribbin, *In Search of Schrödinger's Cat: Quantum Physics and Reality* (New York: Bantam Books, 1984), pp. 224–227.

45. See A. Aspect, J. Dalibard, and G. Roger, *Physical Review Letters,* 39 (December 1982): p. 1804; Arthur L. Robinson, "Demonstrating Single Photon Interference," *Science* (February 1986): pp. 671–672; P.

C. W. Davies, *The Ghost in the Atom: A Discussion of the Mysteries of Quantum Physics* (New York: Cambridge University Press, 1986), pp. 17, 19; Menas Kafatos and Robert Nadeau, *The Conscious Universe: Part and Whole in Modern Physical Theory* (New York: Springer-Verlag New York Inc., 1990).

46. Wheeler, "Beyond the Black Hole," p. 352.

47. Wheeler, "Beyond the Black Hole," p. 363.

48. This is not to deny that Wheeler makes statements that are disconcerting to someone arguing that he is neither a subjectivist nor a subjective idealist—nor, on the other hand, a critical realist. For example, he says, "I confess that sometimes I do take 100 percent seriously the idea that the world is a figment of the imagination and, other time [sic], that the world does exist out there independent of us" (Bernstein, "John Wheeler: Retarded Learner," p. 132).

49. Wheeler, "Beyond the Black Hole," p. 354; also John Archibald Wheeler, "Bohr, Einstein, and the Strange Lesson of the Quantum," *Mind in Nature*, ed. by Richard Elvee (San Francisco: Harper & Row, Publishers, 1982), pp. 19–20.

50. William James, "Remarks on Spencer's Definition of Mind as Correspondence," *Essays in Philosophy* (Cambridge, MA: Harvard University Press, 1978); and "Great Men and Their Environment," *The Will to Believe and other Essays in Popular Philosophy* (Cambridge, MA: Harvard University Press, 1979). See my account of how James emphasized variation to criticize Spencer's selectivist and deterministic rendition of evolutionary theory in *History Making History: The New Historicism in American Religious Thought* (Albany, NY: State University of New York Press, 1988), pp. 101–104.

51. Richard Dawkins, *The Blind Watchmaker* (New York: W. W. Norton & Company, 1986); Edward Osborn Wilson, *On Human Nature* (Cambridge, MA: Harvard University Press, 1978). The Gaia theory seeks, finally, to locate biological phenomena within feedback mechanisms once confined to chemistry and physics, making the biosphere "a self-regulating entity" capable of giving the Earth, once like Mars, a moderate environment. But Gaia's two principal proponents, James Lovelock and Lynn Margulis, still see the self-regulation and the interaction between organisms and environment in deterministic ways, so that the plant or microbe community has no choice but to interact the way they do. Further, Lovelock and Margulis are careful to deny all teleology or anything analogous to decision, leaving the field to efficient causation. Lovelock's "Parable of Daisyworld," while it illustrates how

a world with dark and light daisies can maintain a desirable atmospheric temperature, nevertheless argues that the daisyworld process works as part of a (larger than expected) mechanism. Thus, revolutionary as the Gaia theory is, it still makes the biosphere a machine. See, James Lovelock, *The Ages of Gaia: A Biography of Our Living Earth* (New York: W. W. Norton & Company, 1988). See also Lynn Margulis, "Early Life: The Microbes Have Priority," in *Gaia: A Way of Knowing*, ed. by William Irwin Thompson (Great Barrington, MA: Lindisfarne Press, 1987), pp. 98–109; and James E. Lovelock, *Gaia: A New Look at Life on Earth* (New York: Oxford University Press, 1979, 1987).

52. Sahotra Sarkar uses the term "neo-Lamarckians" to characterize the proponents of directed mutation in "Lamarck *Contre* Darwin" in *Organism and the Origins of Self,* edited by Alfred I. Tauber (Boston: Kluwer Academic Publishers, 1991), p. 240; so also does Patricia L. Foster, "Directed Mutation in *Escherichia Coli:* Theory and Mechanisms," in *Organisms and the Origins of Self,* pp. 222–25.

53. John Cairns, Julie Overbaugh, and Stephen Miller, "The Origin of Mutants," *Nature* 335 (September 8, 1988): 145.

54. Cairns, et al., "The Origin of Mutants": pp. 145, 142. Commenting on this article, Roger Lewin argues, "Because the randomness of mutation has been so fundamental to evolutionary biology since the 1940s, few researchers have cared to test the notion directly" ("A Heresy in Evolutionary Biology," *Science* [September 16, 1988]: p. 1431). It should be added that proponents of directed mutation may not necessarily refute Luria and Delbrück's specific notions but only add to their work a special case that they did not investigate (see Sahotra Sarkar in "Lamarck *Contre* Darwin").

55. See particularly the reviews of the literature in the chapters by Sahotra Sarkar and Patricia L. Foster in *Organism and the Origins of Self.* See also the critical commentaries by J. E. Miller and R. E. Lenski, *Nature* 344 (1990): pp. 173–175; and the subsequent exchange between John Cairns and Mittler and Lenski in "Causes of Mutation and Mu Excision," *Nature* 345 (May 1990): p. 213. See also the review of research sparked by Cairns's work in Billy Goodman, "Heredity Made to Order," *Mosaic* 23/1 (spring 1992): pp. 24–33. Barry G. Hall argues "that mutation rates are not biological constants, and that probabilities of mutation are modulated by normally encountered environmental factors" in "Adaptive Evolution that Requires Multiple Spontaneous Mutations. I. Mutations Involving Insertion Sequence," *Genetics* 120 (December 1988): pp. 887–897.

56. See, especially, Donald MacPhee, "Directed Evolution Reconsidered," *American Scientist* 81 (November-December 1993): pp. 554–561. MacPhee argues that glucose normally suppresses mutations, but that Cairns's experiments were undertaken in a glucose-free environment, thus allowing mutations to proceed at a nonsuppressed rate, which only appeared to be extraordinary. MacPhee contends that his argument preserves neo-Darwinian mutations, which are undirected and random.

57. Kenneth Cmiel, "After Objectivity: What Comes Next in History?" *American Literary History* 2 (spring 1990): p. 173.

58. Cmiel, "After Objectivity," pp. 179–180.

59. Haskell, "Convention and Hegemonic Interest in the Debate over Antislavery: A Reply to Davis and Ashworthy," *American Historical Review* 29 (October 1987): p. 837.

60. Haskell, "Objectivity is not Neutrality," *History and Theory* 29 (May 1990): p. 133 (emphasis in original).

61. Haskell, "Objectivity is not Neutrality": p. 132.

62. Charles Taylor, *Multiculturalism and "The Politics of Recognition,"* ed. Amy Gutmann (Princeton, NJ: Princeton University Press, 1992), pp. 72–73.

63. Kloppenberg, "Objectivity and Historicism: A Century of American Historical Writing," *The American Historical Review* 94 (October 1989): p. 1016.

64. See especially, James T. Kloppenberg, "Deconstruction and Hermeneutics as Strategies for Intellectual History: The Recent Work of Dominick LaCapra and David Hollinger," *Intellectual History Newsletter* 9 (1987): pp. 3–22.

65. Ludwig Wittgenstein, *Letters to Russell, Keynes, and Moore,* ed. G. Von Wright (Ithaca, NY: Cornell University Press, 1974), p. 10. James asks, "Does the river make its banks, or do the banks make the river?" in William James, *Pragmatism* (Cambridge, MA: Harvard University Press, 1975), p. 120. These connections were pointed out by Everett Tarbox, "Wittgenstein, James and a Bridge to Radical Empiricism," *The American Journal of Theology and Philosophy* 13 (May 1992): pp. 89–103; and "James and Wittgenstein: Toward a Linguistic Pragmatism," *The American Journal of Theology and Philosophy* 15 (January 1994).

66. H. J. Folse, *The Philosophy of Niels Bohr* (Amsterdam: North Holland, 1985), pp. 49–51, 180–181; C. F. von Wiezsächer, "The Birth and

Growth of Quantum Mechanics," *Niels Bohr: A Centenary Volume,* ed. by A. P. French and P. J. Kennedy (Cambridge: Harvard University Press, 1985), p. 186; R. V. Jones, "Complementarity as a Way of Life," *Niels Bohr: A Centenary Volume,* p. 320; Gerald Holton, *The Thematic Origins of Scientific Thought* (Cambridge: Harvard University Press, 1973), pp. 136–141.

67. In "Discussion on 'Universe as Home,'" *The Nature of Scientific Discovery,* ed. by Owen Gingerich (Washington, DC: Smithsonian Institution Press, 1975), p. 579.

68. Cmiel, "After Objectivity": p. 174.

69. David Hollinger, *In the American Province: Studies in the History and Historiography of Ideas* (Bloomington, IN: Indiana University Press, 1985), p. 21.

70. Let me stress that I cover only conventionalists who are historians, philosophers, or natural scientists. Obviously, the list could be greatly extended not only in those areas but in other areas as well. For example, James M. Buchanan and F. A. Hayek are conventionalists as they contend that economic orders arise from the free choices of people and thus are, in principle, unpredictable. See James M. Buchanan, "Order Defined in the Process of Its Emergence," *Liberty, Market and State: Political Economy in the 1980s* (New Washington Square, NY: New York University Press, 1985), pp. 73–74; F. A. Hayek, *The Fatal Conceit: The Errors of Socialism* in *The Collected Works of F. A. Hayek,* ed. by W. W. Bartley III (Chicago: The University of Chicago Press, 1989), pp. 8–10.

For guidance to physics and biology literature, as well as for attendant insights, I am deeply indebted to my colleagues Richard Fuller and Richard Elvee.

Chapter 8: The Reality of the Sacred Convention

1. *Moby Dick or The White Whale* (New York: Harper & Brothers Publishers, 1950), p. 13.

2. Friederich Schleiermacher, *The Christian Faith,* trans. by H. R. Mackintosh and J. S. Stewart (Edinburgh: T. & T. Clark, 1960); Paul Tillich, *Systematic Theology,* vol. 1 (Chicago: The University of Chicago Press, 1951); George Lindbeck, *The Nature of Doctrine: Religion and Theology in a Postliberal Age* (Philadelphia: The Westminster Press,

1984); Gordon D. Kaufman, *In Face of Mystery: A Constructive Theology* (Cambridge: Harvard University Press, 1993); Charles Birch and John B. Cobb, Jr., *The Liberation of Life: From the Cell to the Community* (New York: Cambridge University Press, 1981). I am treating the expression attributed to Cobb as Cobb's own, not only because each author is in substantial agreement with the entire book, but because Cobb appears to have been primarily responsible for the theological sections, in one of which that expression is used (see Birch and Cobb, *Liberation,* pp. 8 and 195).

3. Kaufman, *In Face of Mystery.*

4. William James, "Remarks on Spencer's Definition of Mind as Correspondence," in *Essays in Philosophy* (Cambridge, MA: Harvard University Press, 1978), p. 21 (emphasis in original).

5. William James, "Is Life Worth Living," *The Will to Believe and Other Essays in Popular Philosophy* (Cambridge, MA: Harvard University Press, 1979), p. 55; James, *The Varieties of Religious Experience: A Study in Human Nature* (Cambridge, MA: Harvard University Press, 1985), p. 407.

6. This is implicit in tradition history criticism. See, e.g., Martin Noth, "The Laws in the Pentateuch: Their Assumptions and Meaning" in *The Laws in the Pentateuch and Other Studies,* trans. by D. R. Ap-Thomas (London: SCM Press, Ltd., 1984); Gerhard von Rad, *The Problem of the Hexateuch and Other Essays* (New York: McGraw-Hill Book Co., 1955) and *Tradition and Theology in the Old Testament,* ed. Douglas A. Knight (Philadelphia: Fortress Press, 1977); Norman Gottwald, *The Tribes of Israel: A Sociology of the Religion of Liberated Israel, 1250–1050* (Maryknoll, NY: Orbis Books, 1979) and "Introduction: The Bible and Liberation: Deeper Roots and Wider Horizons," *The Bible and Liberation: Political and Social Hermeneutics,* ed. by Norman K. Gottwald, rev. ed. (Maryknoll, NY: Orbis Books, 1983). It is implicit also in recent deconstructionist biblical analysis. See, e.g., Susan A. Handelman, *The Slayers of Moses: The Emergence of Rabbinic Interpretation in Modern Literary Theory* (Albany, NY: State University of New York Press, 1982) and José Faur, *Golden Doves with Silver Dots: Semiotics and Textuality in Rabbinic Tradition* (Bloomington, IN: Indiana University Press, 1986). See also my discussion in *History Making History: The New Historicism in American Religious Thought* (Albany, NY: State University of New York Press, 1988), pp. 36–38.

7. Robin Scroggs, "Sociological Introduction of the New Testament: The Present State of Research" in Gottwald, ed., *The Bible and Libera-*

tion; John G. Gager, *Kingdom and Community: An Anthropological Approach to Civilization* (Englewood Cliffs, NJ: Prentice-Hall, 1975); and Wayne Meeks *The First Urban Christians: The Social World of the Apostle Paul* (New Haven: Yale University Press, 1983).

8. See, e.g., Shailer Mathews, *The Atonement and the Social Process* (New York: The Macmillan Co., 1930) and *The Growth of the Idea of God* (New York: Macmillan, 1931); and Shirley Jackson Case, *Jesus: A New Biography* (New York: Greenwood Press, 1968), *The Social Origins of Christianity* (New York: Cooper Square Publishers, Inc., 1975), *The Origins of Christian Supernaturalism* (Chicago: The University of Chicago Press, 1946), and *The Christian Philosophy of History* (Chicago: The University of Chicago Press, 1943).

9. John Dewey, *A Common Faith* (New Haven: Yale University Press, 1952), p. 49.

10. Peter Berger, *A Rumor of Angels: Modern Society and the Rediscovery of the Supernatural* (Garden City, NY: Doubleday & Co., 1969), p. 2.

11. Berger, *A Rumor of Angels,* pp. 66–67.

12. Elie Wiesel, *Night,* trans. by Stella Rodway (New York, NY: Avon, 1960), p. 43.

13. See especially, William H. Bernhardt, *Operational Theism* in *The Cognitive Quest for God and Operational Theism* (Denver, CO: The Criterion Press, Inc.), pp. 203–205; Bernard Loomer, *The Size of God: The Theology of Bernard Loomer in Context,* edited by William Dean and Larry Axel (Macon, GA: Mercer University Press, 1987); Elie Wiesel, *The Trial of God,* trans. Marion Wiesel (New York: Random House, 1979); Frederick Sontag, *The God of Evil* (New York: Harper & Row, 1970); and John K. Roth, "A Theodicy of Protest," in *Encountering Evil: Live Options in Theodicy,* Stephen T. Davis, editor (Atlanta, GA: John Knox Press, 1981), pp. 7–22. See also Carl Jung, *Answer to Job,* for the classic non-American exposition of this understanding.

14. Jerome A. Stone, *The Minimalist Vision of Transcendence: A Naturalist Philosophy of Religion* (Albany, NY: State University of New York Press, 1992), p. 15.

15. Dewey, *A Common Faith,* p. 42.

16. Bourne argued that "there was always that unhappy ambiguity in his [Dewey's] doctrine as to just how values were created, and it became easier and easier to assume that just any growth was justified and almost

any activity valuable so long as it achieved ends" (Randolph Bourne, "The Twilight of the Idols," *Untimely Papers,* ed. by James Oppenheim [New York: W. W. Heubsch, 1919], p. 130).

17. See especially, John Dewey, *Human Nature and Conduct,* in *The Middle Works, 1899–1924,* vol. 12 (Carbondale and Edwardsville: Southern Illinois University Press, 1983), pp. 227, 180–81. I follow Steven C. Rockefeller's emphasis of Dewey's mysticism as that is set forth in his *John Dewey: Religious Faith and Democratic Humanism* (New York: Columbia University Press, 1991), pp. 501–12.

18. Dewey, *A Common Faith,* pp. 16, 85, 23. Certainly, at other points Dewey is skittish of any talk about divine causation, saying "the actual religious quality in the experience described is the *effect* produced . . . not the manner and cause of its production" (Dewey, *A Common Faith,* p. 14; [emphasis in original]).

19. Contrary to what I have said here, Dewey once uncharacteristically identified "the experience of oneness" with the experience of "God if you please" (a letter from John Dewey to Scudder Klyce in Rockefeller, *John Dewey,* p. 507).

20. Dewey, *A Common Faith,* pp. 43, 87, 13. As Dewey said, these "ends to which we attach our faith are not shadowy and wavering"; they "are not of ourselves" (Dewey, *A Common Faith,* p. 87).

21. Dewey, *A Common Faith,* p. 53.

22. Dewey sometimes refers to *our* estimate of those ideals that prompt us. Thus, he argues that whatever is "good" is good because we call it good. He will say: "the 'divine' is thus a term of human choice and aspiration." "The idealizing imagination seizes upon the most precious things found in climacteric moments of experience and projects them. We need no external criterion and guarantee for their goodness" (Dewey, *A Common Faith,* pp. 54, 48. This is a point overlooked by Henry Nelson Wieman and Bernard Meland, who unselfconsciously see such harmony as an objective and universal reality, rather than a relative or even a human good. For an account of Dewey's disagreement here with Meland and Wieman, see Rockefeller, *John Dewey,* pp. 511, 525.)

Thus, it is not as though there were any criterion outside history that determines that God conforms to "the good" in history; for Dewey, as a consistent historicist, has no ideals working outside history. In short, a particular harmony is good because *we* determine, here and now, that it is good; there is no higher court of appeals. Nevertheless, for Dewey the term "God" "selects those factors in existence that generate and support our ideal of good as an end to be striven for" (Dewey, *A Common Faith,* p. 53). (The possibility of judgment without criteria has been honored by the neopragmatists in the last few years and is the reason for their seriousness about "conversation." Admittedly, to use the language of Jeffrey Stout, it is all a sort of bricolage, for the conversational judgments are always only ad hoc, stumbled on, hit or miss, piecemeal, made up as you go, never tied to any universal or eternal grounds. See Jeffrey Stout, *Ethics After Babel: The Languages of Morals and Their Discontents* [Boston: Beacon Press, 1988], pp. 74–75, and especially, chapters 11 and 12.)

23. Dewey harshly and sweepingly criticizes organized religion, reducing it to that practice that takes old reconciliations and applies them to new situations—typically invoking a God that is absolute and supernatural. As little more than a museum for obsolete religious conventions, organized religion deprives people of their true religious responsibility, which is continually to reinterpret, to adjust harmoniously and mutually, new ideals and new environments in order to foster new social development. Organized religion undermines that natural responsibility for convincing people that the adjustment already has been accomplished for them by God and an earlier community in close contact with God.

24. James L. Crenshaw, *A Whirlpool of Torment: Israelite Traditions of God as an Oppressive Presence* (Philadelphia: Fortress Press, 1984), p. 114.

25. Crenshaw, *Whirlpool,* pp. 112, 113, 114.

26. Crenshaw, *Whirlpool,* pp. 109, 118.

27. Judith Plaskow, "Facing the Ambiguity of God," *Tikkun: A Bimonthly Jewish Critique of Politics, Culture, and Society* 6 (September-October 1991): p. 70. Plaskow cites Catherine Madsen and a number of respondents in the spring 1989 issue of the *Journal of Feminist Studies in Religion.*

28. Plaskow, "Facing the Ambiguity": p. 96.

29. Paul Tillich, *The Dynamics of Faith* (New York: Harper & Row, Publishers, 1957), p. 15; see also, Paul Tillich, *Systematic Theology,* Vols. I–III (Chicago: The University of Chicago Press, 1951), I, p. 217.

30. See Morris Peckham, *Man's Rage for Chaos: Biology, Behavior and the Arts* (New York: Schocken Books, 1965). Peckham's addition to Dewey is not only extensively to relate Dewey's thesis to the history of

the arts but to emphasize, unlike Dewey, the importance of disorder as a means to more adequate orders, or harmonies.

31. Unlike Dewey, who makes God a part of the whole, Loomer vacillates about whether God is equated to the whole of the world or to a part of the world. At places he argues that "God is to be identified with the totality of the world"; at other places God is a part of the world: the "organic restlessness," "the symbol of ultimate values and meanings," "the creative advance," a "restlessness or a tropism" to live better (see Loomer, *The Size of God,* pp. 23, 41, 42).

32. Loomer, *The Size of God,* see especially pp. 41.

33. There is the counterargument, best set forth by David Griffin, that if God has only finite power, then history's ambiguity does not establish God's moral ambiguity, for God may be perfect but incapable of overcoming history's moral ambiguity. This argument relies, Bernard Loomer has suggested, on empirically unwarranted abstractions about God. See David R. Griffin, *God, Power, and Evil: A Process Theodicy* (Philadelphia: Westminster Press, 1976) and Bernard M. Loomer, "Response to David R. Griffin," *Encounter* 36 (1975): pp. 361–69.

34. See Tyron Inbody's valuable commentary on these issues in "Religious Empiricism and the Problem of Evil," *The American Journal of Theology and Philosophy* 12 (January 1991): p. 47.

35. Especially, Wiesel, *Night;* John K. Roth, "On Losing Trust in the World," Richard L. Rubenstein, "The Dean and the Chosen People," and Irving Greenberg, "Cloud of Smoke, Pillar of Fire" all in *Holocaust: Religious and Philosophical Implications,* edited by John K. Roth and Michael Berenbaum (New York: Paragon House, 1989).

36. She claims not to be primarily interested in the metaphorical significance of boxing, but the book in which that disclaimer is printed in primarily about the metaphorical significance of boxing: *On Boxing* (Garden City, NY: Dolphin/Doubleday, 1987), see p. 4.

37. Joyce Carol Oates, "The Cruelest Sport," *The New York Review of Books* 34 (February 3, 1992): p. 3. See Oates's description of a savage professional fight in *You Must Remember This* (New York: E. P. Dutton, 1987), pp. 246–52.

38. Oates, *On Boxing,* p. 4.

39. Oates, *On Boxing,* p. 69. No Manichean, Oates refuses to locate evil in nature alone, arguing that pornography is about spirit, not nature: "That the taboo is spiritual rather than physical, or sexual—that our

most valuable human experience, love, is being desecrated, parodied, mocked—is surely at the core of our culture's fascination with pornography" (p. 106).

40. Oates, "The Cruelest Sport": p. 6.

41. Oates, *On Boxing,* p. 116.

42. Oates, "The Cruelest Sport": p. 3.

43. See my brief defense of this strand of thought in *American Religious Empiricism* (Albany, NY: State University of New York Press, 1986), chaps. 1 and 4.

44. For a defense of the importance of the tropism toward complexity in nature, see M. Mitchell Waldrop, *Complexity: The Emerging Science at the Edge of Order and Chaos* (New York: Simon & Schuster, 1992). Murray Gell-Mann's Sante Fe Institute examines questions of complexity in nature. Other scientists, such as Jacob Bronowski or Stephen Jay Gould, deny the theory that there is a grand tropism toward greater complexity operating in nature, attack nonmechanistic (vitalistic or supernatural) causes of complexification, and then proceed to introduce their mechanistic cause for complexification. They tend to substitute one extrahistorical and objectivistic account for another. Further, Bronowski and Gould treat vitalistic and supernaturalistic accounts as if they were the only possible alternatives to their accounts, so that they have only to establish the insufficiency of the vitalistic and supernaturalistic accounts, without having to establish the sufficiency of their own mechanistic account. They never, to my knowledge, entertain the possibility that increasing complexity can be explained historically. That is, they do not my knowledge entertain the idea that a tropism toward complexity might arise in history as an accidental convention of natural history, nor suggest that this tropism might, like all traditions, be temporary and reversible. See J. Bronowski, "New Concepts in the Evolution of Complexity: Stratified Stability and Unbounded Plans," *Zygon* 5 (March 1970): pp. 18–35; Stephen Jay Gould, "The Wheel of Fortune and the Wedge of Progress," *Natural History* (March 1989): pp. 14–21; and "Tires to Sandals," *Natural History* (April 1989): pp. 8–15.

Bronowski posits fourth and fifth "principles of evolution," which together describe nature's evolutionary ratchet—a mechanism that selects for and then preserves greater variability. Bronowski treats these ratchets as simply given in the mechanics of the system, thus explaining away teleology. By not explaining the origin of these amazing rachets, he appears only to beg his causal line of inquiry. Any theological defender of the cosmological argument for the existence of God could warn Bronowski of the dangers of that tactic.

Gould becomes so exercised over the chanciness of mass extinctions and their "different rules" for survival, that he writes as though, amid such a "crap shoot," it is virtually impossible for progress to occur, thus sounding like Marxists who on doctrinal grounds are so certain that capitalism must collapse that they fail empirically to notice that, year after year, it has not collapsed. Finally, Gould uses the now-popular double standard according to which it is acceptable to relativize your opponents' and unselfconsciously absolutize your own theories. For example, in commenting about the so-called development of the species, he patiently explains that the natural theologians' view of developmental grandeur is a product of a bygone era's theological biases, and that Darwin's view of developmental grandeur is a product of the progressivistic era, but that his own understanding of development grandeur is simply a reading of nature's "own ways" and its "intrinsic value" (Steven Jay Gould, "Modified Grandeur," *Natural History* [March 1993]: p. 20).

45. Stephen Jay Gould, *Wonderful Life: The Burgess Shale and the Nature of History* (New York: W. W. Norton & Company, 1989), p. 208. He demonstrates that the range of "stereotyped designs" has been greatly, arbitrarily, and repeatedly diminished by mass extinctions. But then he makes an inconspicuous but enormously important admission that, among the survivors of each extinction during the last 500 million years, there has been a regular tendency to proliferate the range of their species—that is, to increase their complexity. Thus, while nonliving events (the landing of asteroids that cause the mass extinctions) may decrease the diversity of designs, within the life of surviving species, the constant tendency between mass extinctions has been to increase in complexity.

Chapter 9: The Religious Critic in the Third Sector

1. Robert L. Payton, *Philanthropy: Voluntary Action for the Common Good* (New York: Macmillan Publishing Co., 1988), p. 40.

2. Stanley M. Elkins, *Slavery: A Problem in American Institutional and Intellectual Life* (Chicago: The University of Chicago Press, 1976), p. 143.

3. James Douglas, *Why Charity? The Case for a Third Sector* (Beverly Hills, CA: Sage Publications, 1983), p. 11. Douglas refers to "the absence of any adequate theoretical framework" for the third sector and acknowledges that a structure and rationale for the third sector has

"never been worked out and that there was no comprehensive body of theory about the place of charity in a free society" (pp. 13, 17).

4. Whether or not the university is part of the third sector, I refer to the third sector without the university. I acknowledge that the third sector status of the university is an open question. With the growth both of government- and business-sponsored research, of public funding even of private education, and of the public university's direct accountability to government, it might be said that higher education no longer belongs to the third sector but to the first or second sector, or to both. On the other hand, this may overlook the significant nongovernment, non-marketplace status of the university. In any case, it is true that in the twentieth century higher education is more influenced by government and business than it is by the third sector religious institutions—as it was prior to the twentieth century. The last point is made by George M. Marsden, "Introduction," *The Secularization of the Academy,* eds. George M. Marsden and Bradley J. Longfield (New York: Oxford University Press, 1992), p. 20. Marsden mashalls the support of Thorstein Veblen, *The Higher Learning in America: A Memorandum on the Conduct of Universities by Business Men* (New York: B. W. Jeubsch, 1918) and Page Smith, *Killing the Spirit: Higher Education in America* (New York: Viking, 1990), esp. pp. 10–12.

5. *The Letters of William James, Vol. I, ed. Henry James* (Boston: The Atlantic Monthly Press, 1920), p. 148.

6. See, e.g., Roger Bowen, "A College That No Longer Puts Teaching First Pays a High Price for Its Exalted Reputation," *The Chronicle of Higher Education* 38 (June 10, 1992): pp. B3–B4.

7. Peter Berger and Thomas Luckmann, *The Social Construction of Reality: A Treatise in the Sociology of Knowledge* (Garden City, NY: Doubleday, 1966). Also see Berger, *A Rumor of Angels: Modern Society and the Rediscovery of the Supernatural* (Garden City, NY: Doubleday and Company, Inc., 1969), pp. 1–60, and *The Sacred Canopy: Elements of a Sociological Theory of Religion* (Garden City, NY: Doubleday & Company, Inc., 1967) for discussions of how social construction is a function of religious location.

8. Gilbert M. Gaul and Neill A. Borowski, "Warehouses of Wealth: The Tax-free Economy," *The Philadelphia Inquirer* (a daily series running from April 18 through April 24, 1993).

9. Teresa Odendahl, *Charity Begins at Home: Generosity and Self-Interest Among the Philanthropic Elite* (New York: Basic Books, 1990).

10. Waldemar Nielsen, *The Golden Donors: A New Anatomy of the Great Foundations* (New York: E. P. Dutton, 1985).

11. Bill McAllister, "Charities Scored on Hill for CEO Pay, Perks," *Washington Post,* June 16, 1993: p. A4. See also the opening statement of Chairman Pickle at the hearings on June 15, 1993.

12. See "Myths about Private Foundations," John Edie, principal author, The Council on Foundations, May 18, 1993.

13. See Philip H. Mirvis, "The Quality of Employment in the Nonprofit Sector: An Update on Employee Attitudes in Nonprofits versus Business and Government," *Nonprofit Management and Leadership* 3 (fall 1992): p. 2337; Anne Preston, "Compensation Patterns in the Sector," *Careers for Dreamers and Doers: A Guide to Management Careers in the Nonprofit Sector,* eds. Lilly Cohen and Dennis R. Young (New York: The Foundation Center, 1989), pp. 25–39.

14. Robert L. Payton, "God and Money," in *The Responsibilities of Wealth,* edited by Dwight F. Burlingame (Bloomington, IN: Indiana University Press, 1992). Peter Dobkin Hall, *Inventing the Nonprofit Sector and other Essays on Philanthropy, Voluntarism, and Nonprofit Organizations* (Baltimore: The Johns Hopkins University Press, 1992), especially chapter 3. Hall notes the gross neglect of religion's role in the third sector in research on the third sector.

15. John Dewey, *A Common Faith* (New Haven: Yale University Press, 1952), p. 19.

16. Ernest Gellner, "La trahison de la trahison des clercs," *The Political Responsibility of Intellectuals,* ed. by Ian Maclean, Alan Montefiore, and Peter Winch (Cambridge, Eng.: Cambridge University Press, 1990), p. 17.

17. Julien Benda, *The Betrayal of the Intellectuals,* trans. Richard Aldington (Boston: The Beacon Press, 1959), p. 30.

18. Ernest Gellner, supporting the public intellectual, contends that it is Benda's chosen intellectuals who commit the real betrayal ("La trahison," pp. 19, 26). For Gellner, the public intellectual will not look beyond history but will be embedded in the particularities and relativities of history. It is through such historical involvement that intellectuals can most adequately address public issues. Gellner's reasoning would support the idea that third sector associations would foster the theoretical work of religious critics. Third sector affairs are so closely tied to specific social activities that they offer a local vantage point on history in its totality.

19. Cornel West, _Race Matters_ (Boston: The Beacon Press, 1993), p. 41.

20. See especially, Marsden, "Introduction," p. 39.

21. Sara M. Evans and Harry C. Boyte, _Free Spaces: The Sources of Democratic Change in America_ (New York: Harper & Row, Publishers, 1986), pp. 1–2. Their specific references to the role of Christianity in the slave culture are taken from Vincent Harding, _There is a River: The Black Freedom Struggle in America_ (New York: Harcourt, 1981).

22. Evans and Boyte, _Free Spaces,_ pp. 17–18.

23. Susan Ostrander and Paul G. Schervish, "Giving and Getting: Philanthropy as a Social Relation," _Critical Issues in Philanthropy: Strengthening Theory and Practice,_ edited by Jon Van Til (San Francisco: Jossey-Bass Publishers, 1990), pp. 67–97.

24. I should note that for Ostrander and Schervish "philanthropy" extends far beyond charity, particularly in that philanthropy's largest component is "consumption philanthropy," which includes churches, schools, cultural institutions, and professional organizations, all of which make participants recipients as well as donors of philanthropic gifts.

25. Ostrander and Schervish seem not only to de-spatialize but to de-institutionalize philanthropy, thus making it, I believe, a trojan horse for a dispositional love ethic with no particular social embodiment. Schervish has explicitly separated philanthropy from institutions. Referring to his own definition of philanthropy, he says, "One implication of the foregoing considerations is a noninstitutional conception of the realm of philanthropy" ("Philanthropy as a Moral Identity," _Taking Giving Seriously,_ ed. by Patricia Dean [Indianapolis: Indiana University Center on Philanthropy, 1993], p. 91). By contrast, I argue that social relations and their media need to be based in institutions—for example, money needs banks and investment institutions, as nations of the former Soviet Union are learning. Equally, any appeal to values needs an institutional base, and most third sector organizations provide such a base.

26. Alfred North Whitehead would agree with Ostrander and Schervish's refusal to isolate the third sector (see Whitehead's discussion of field theory, and "the fallacy of simple location" in _Science and the Modern World_ [New York: The Free Press, 1953], p. 58). However, Whitehead would argue, that the third sector necessarily must be grounded in something concrete, in this case, an organization. Denying the reality of disembodied relations, Whitehead introduced the common

sense empirical notion that they must be grounded in a spatial-temporal actuality and called this the "ontological principle" (Alfred North Whitehead, *Process and Reality: An Essay in Cosmology* [New York: The Free Press, 1978], p. 13 and elsewhere).

27. Anthony Giddens, "Action, Subjectivity, and the Constitution of Meaning," *Social Research* 53 (autumn 1986): pp. 529–541. Giddens credits Ludwig Wittgenstein as the source for this practical notion of meaning, even though this puts him in the awkward position of repeatedly having to deny that social practice can be reduced to linguistic practice—an awkwardness that would have been avoided if Giddens had looked to the American pragmatists, who were not inclined to reduce social practice to linguistic practice. See also, Anthony Giddens, *The Constitution of Society: Outline of the Theory of Structuration* (Berkeley: The University of California Press, 1984).

28. Ostrander and Schervish, "Giving and Getting," p. 70. Citing Anthony Giddens, they go on to say: "Once created, social structure defines the terms and boundaries of choice, presenting both obstacles and possibilities." See Giddens, *The Constitution of Society,* chapter 1.

Chapter 10: The Religious Critic and a Myth of America

1. William H. McNeill, *Mythistory and Other Essays* (Chicago: The University of Chicago Press, 1986), p. 32.

2. Richard J. Slotkin, *Gunfighter Nation* (New York: Atheneum, 1992), pp. 659–660.

3. Zbigniew Brzezinski, *Out of Control: Global Turmoil on the Eve of the Twenty-First Century* (New York: Charles Scribner's Sons, 1993), pp. 19–20.

4. Alfred North Whitehead, *Symbolism: Its Meaning and Effect* (New York: Capricorn Books, 1959), p. 74. Chapter 3 of this book is Whitehead's highly suggestive discussion of the role of symbols in creating social identity. For further discussion of Whitehead's notion of symbolism see *Process and Reality: Corrected Edition,* ed. David Ray Griffin and Donald W. Sherburne (New York: The Free Press, 1978), chapter 8. Sacvan Bercovitch uses a similar scheme to analyze national myths. His cultural symbology, which he calls "ideological mimesis," is an interplay between imaginative text and historical context, between clear concepts and the messy history to which they refer, both of which change with the society (Sacvan Bercovitch, *The Rites of Assent: Trans-*

formations in the Symbolic Construction of America [New York: Rout-ledge, 1993], p. 15).

5. See my "Fireflies in a Quagmire," *Journal of Religion* 48 (October 1968): pp. 376–395.

6. See Jacques Derrida, "Edmond Jabés and the Question of the Book," trans. by Alan Bass, *Writing and Difference* (Chicago: The University of Chicago Press, 1978), p. 64. Derrida is, himself, a Jewish immigrant from Morocco to France.

7. McNeill, *Mythistory,* p. 14.

8. See Robert N. Bellah, *The Broken Covenant: American Civil Religion in Time of Trial* (New York: Seabury Press, 1975); Robert N. Bellah, Richard Madsen, William M. Sullivan, Ann Swidler, and Steven M. Tipton, *Habits of the Heart: Individualism and Commitment in American Life* (New York: Harper & Row, Publishers, 1985) and *The Good Society* (New York: Alfred A. Knopf, 1991).

9. See Slotkin, *Gunfighter Nation; Regeneration Through Violence: The Mythology of the American Frontier 1600–1860* (Middletown, CT: Wesleyan University Press, 1973); *The Fatal Environment: The Myth of the Frontier in the Age of Industrialization, 1800–1890* (New York: Antheneum, 1985).

10. *The Collected Poems of Wallace Stevens* (New York: Vintage Books, 1982), p. 130.

11. William Carlos Williams, *Paterson* (New York: New Directions, 1963), p. 123.

12. In fact, academic intellectuals may be the only large American group still intimidated by mandates from a land of origin (Western Europe), the only group that still, with a kind of late-adolescent insistence, has to keep telling itself that it really should treat the old structures of Reason, Fact, and Divine Law like a parent's unsolicited advice and set them aside.

13. See "The Red Wheelbarrow," *The Collected Earlier Poems of William Carlos Williams* (Norfolk, CT: New Directions Books, 1951), p. 277; *Paterson,* pp. 3, 144.

14. Karl Barth, *Evangelical Theology: An Introduction* (New York: Holt, Rinehart and Winston, 1963), p. xii.

15. Daniel J. Boorstin, *The Americans: The Colonial Experience* (New York: Vintage Books, 1958), p. 16.

16. Compare empiricist interpretations of Perry Miller, "Jonathan Edwards on the Sense of the Heart," *Harvard Theological Review* 41 (April 1948) and David Laurence, "Jonathan Edwards, John Locke, and the Canon of Experience," *Early American Literature* 15 (1980), which I prefer, to the Platonist response of Normal Fiering, *Jonathan Edwards's Moral Thought and Its British Context* (Chapel Hill: The University of North Carolina Press, 1981).

17. See Stanley Cavell, "Emerson, Coleridge, and Kant," *Post-Analytic Philosophy*, ed. by John Rajchman and Cornel West (New York: Columbia University Press, 1985); and David L. Smith, "Emerson and Deconstructionism," *Soundings* 67 (winter 1984), pp. 379–398.

18. See Joel Porte, *Emerson and Thoreau: Transcendentalists in Conflict* (Middletown, CT: Wesleyan University Press, 1965), chapters 5 and 6; Donald Worster, *Nature's Economy: A History of Ecological Ideas* (Cambridge, Eng.: Cambridge University Press, 1977), chapters 3–5.

BIBLIOGRAPHY

I list here the most important writings used in the making of this book, as well as many of the most important American books and articles pertaining to: the role of the public intellectual; the myth of America; the historical, philosophical, and theological resources for analyzing and reconceiving the role of the religious critic; and the scientific, philosophical, and historical resources for theories of conventionalism and of the third sector.

Books and Selections from Books

Akernson, Donald Harman. *God's Peoples: Covenant and Land in South Africa, Israel, and Ulster.* Ithaca, NY: Cornell University Press, 1992.

Albanese, Catherine. *Nature Religion in America: From the Algonkian Indians to the New Age.* Chicago: The University of Chicago Press, 1990.

Alexander, Peter. "Conventionalism." In *The Encyclopedia of Philosophy,* edited by Paul Edwards. New York: Macmillan Publishing Co., Inc., & The Free Press, 1967.

Ames, Edward Scribner. *Religion.* Chicago: John O. Pyle, 1949; first published in 1929.

Anderson, Martin. *Impostors in the Temple.* New York: Simon and Schuster, 1992.

Barbour, Ian G. *Religion in an Age of Science: The Gifford Lectures 1989–1991,* Volume 1. San Francisco: Harper & Row, Publishers, 1990.

Barth, Karl. *Evangelical Theology: An Introduction.* New York: Holt, Rinehart and Winston, 1963.

Bellah, Robert N. *The Broken Covenant: American Civil Religion in Time of Trial,* New York: Seabury Press, 1975.

————, Richard Madsen, William M. Sullivan, Ann Swidler, and Steven M. Tipton. *The Good Society.* New York: Alfred A. Knopf, 1991.

————, Richard Madsen, William M. Sullivan, Ann Swidler, Steven M. Tipton. *Habits of the Heart: Individualism and Commitment in American Life.* New York: Harper & Row, Publishers, 1985.

Benda, Julien. *The Betrayal of the Intellectuals.* Translated by Richard Aldington. Boston: The Beacon Press, 1959.

Bender, Thomas. *Intellect and Public Life: Essays on the Social History of Academic Intellectuals in the United States.* Baltimore: The Johns Hopkins University Press, 1993.

Bercovitch, Sacvan. *The American Jeremiad.* Madison, WI: University of Wisconsin Press, 1978.

————. *The Rites of Assent: Transformations in the Symbolic Construction of America.* New York: Routledge, 1993.

Berger, Peter. *A Rumor of Angels: Modern Society and the Rediscovery of the Supernatural.* Garden City, NY: Doubleday and Company, Inc., 1969.

————. *The Sacred Canopy: Elements of a Sociological Theory of Religion.* Garden City, NY: Doubleday & Company, Inc., 1967.

————, and Thomas Luckmann. *The Social Construction of Reality: A Treatise in the Sociology of Knowledge.* Garden City, NY: Doubleday & Company, 1966.

Bernstein, Jeremy. "John Wheeler: Retarded Learner." In *Quantum Profiles.* Princeton, NJ: Princeton University Press, 1991.

Bernstein, Richard J. *Beyond Objectivism and Relativism: Science, Hermeneutics, and Praxis.* Philadelphia: University of Pennsylvania Press, 1983.

Bledstein, Burton. *The Culture of Professionalism: The Middle Class and the Development of Higher Education in America.* New York: W. W. Norton & Co., Inc., 1976.

Blood, Benjamin Paul. "A Pluralistic Mystic." In Williams James, Essays in Philosophy. Cambridge, MA: Harvard University Press, 1978.

Boorstin, Daniel J. The Americans: The Colonial Experience. New York: Vintage Books, 1958.

Bourne, Randolph. "The Twilight of the Idols." In Untimely Papers, edited by James Oppenheim. New York: W. W. Heubsch, 1919.

Brzezinski, Zbigniew. Out of Control: Global Turmoil on the Eve of the Twenty-First Century. New York: Charles Scribner's Sons, 1993.

Buchanan, James M. "Order Defined in the Process of Its Emergence." In Liberty, Market and State: Political Economy in the 1980s. Washington Square, NY: New York University Press, 1985.

Burke, Kenneth. The Philosophy of Literary Form: Studies in Symbolic Form. Berkeley and Los Angeles: University of California Press, 1973.

Cady, Linell E. Religion, Theology, and American Public Life. Albany, NY: State University of New York Press, 1993.

Carnap, Rudolf. "Autobiography." In The Philosophy of Rudolf Carnap, edited by Paul Arthur Schilpp. LaSalle, IL: Open Court, 1953.

Carter, Stephen L. The Culture of Disbelief: How American Law and Politics Trivialize Religious Devotion. New York: Basic Books, 1993.

Case, Shirley Jackson. The Origins of Christian Supernaturalism. Chicago: The University of Chicago Press, 1946.

———. Jesus: A New Biography. New York: Greenwood Press, 1968.

———. The Christian Philosophy of History. Chicago: The University of Chicago Press, 1943.

———. The Social Origins of Christianity. New York: Cooper Square Publishers, Inc., 1975.

Cavell, Stanley. "Emerson, Coleridge, and Kant." In Post-Analytic Philosophy, edited by John Rajchman and Cornel West. New York: Columbia University Press, 1985.

Cherry, Conrad, editor. God's New Israel: Religious Interpretations of American Destiny. Englewood Cliffs, NJ: Prentice-Hall, Inc., 1971.

Clebsch, William A. *American Religious Thought: A History*. Chicago: The University of Chicago Press, 1973.

Cooey, Paula M., Sharon A. Farmer, and Mary Ellen Ross, editors. *Embodied Love: Sensuality and Relationship as Feminist Values*. San Francisco: Harper & Row, 1987.

Cotkin, George. *William James, Public Philosopher*. Baltimore: The Johns Hopkins University Press, 1990.

Cowardine, Richard. "Religion and Politics in Nineteenth-Century Britain: The Case Against American Exceptionalism." In *Religion and American Politics: From the Colonial Period to the 1980s*, edited by Mark A. Noll. New York: Oxford University Press, 1990.

Crenshaw, James L. *A Whirlpool of Torment: Israelite Traditions of God as an Oppressive Presence*. Philadelphia: Fortress Press, 1984.

Davies, P. C. W. *The Ghost in the Atom: A Discussion of the Mysteries of Quantum Physics*. New York: Cambridge University Press, 1986.

Davis, Stephen T., editor. *Encountering Evil: Live Options in Theodicy*. Atlanta: John Knox Press, 1981.

Dawkins, Richard. *The Blind Watchmaker*. New York: W. W. Norton & Company, 1986.

Dean, Patricia, editor. *Taking Giving Seriously*. Indianapolis: Indiana University Center on Philanthropy, 1993.

Dean, William. *American Religious Empiricism*. Albany, NY: State University of New York Press, 1986.

———, "Empiricism and God." In *Empirical Theology: A Handbook*, edited by Randolph C. Miller. Birmingham, AL: Religious Education Press, 1992.

———. *History Making History: The New Historicism in American Religious Thought*. Albany, NY: State University of New York Press, 1988.

———, "Humanistic Historicism and Naturalistic Historicism." In *Theology at the End of Modernity*, edited by Sheila Davaney. Philadelphia: Trinity Press International, 1992.

———, "Pluralism and the Problem of God: A Sketch of an American Predicament." In *God, Values, and Empiricism*, edited by Creighton Peden. Macon: Mercer University Press, 1990.

————, "The Persistence of Experience: A Commentary on Gordon Kaufman's Theology." In *New Essays in Religious Naturalism*, edited by Larry Axel and Creighton Peden. Macon: Mercer University Press, 1994.

————, and Larry Axel, editors. *The Size of God: The Theology of Bernard Loomer in Context*. Macon: Mercer University Press, 1987.

Denning, Michael. *Mechanic Accents*. London: Verso, 1987.

Derrida, Jacques. "Edmond Jabès and the Question of the Book." In *Writing and Difference*, translated by Alan Bass. Chicago: The University of Chicago Press, 1978.

Dewey, John. *A Common Faith*. New Haven: Yale University Press, 1952.

————. *Art as Experience*. New York: Capricorn Books, 1958.

————. *Characters and Events: Popular Essays in Social and Political Philosophy*, edited by Joseph Ratner. New York: Henry Holt and Co., 1929.

————. *Human Nature and Conduct*. Vol. 14 of *John Dewey: Middle Works, 1899–1924*, edited by Jo Ann Boydston. Carbondale and Edwardsville: Southern Illinois University Press, 1983.

————. *The Public and Its Problems*. Denver: Swallow, 1927.

Dickstein, Morris. *Double Agent: The Critic and Society*. New York: Oxford University Press, 1992.

Douglas, James. *Why Charity? The Case for a Third Sector*. Beverly Hills, CA: Sage Publications, 1983.

D'Souza, Dinesh. *Illiberal Education: The Politics of Race and Sex on Campus*. New York: Free Press, 1991.

Eddington, A. S. *The Nature of the Physical World*. New York: The Macmillan Co., 1929.

————. *The Philosophy of Physical Science*. New York: The Macmillan Company, 1939.

Elkins, Stanley M. *Slavery: A Problem in American Institutional and Intellectual Life*. Chicago: The University of Chicago Press, 1976.

Emerson, Ralph Waldo. "Nature" (the 1836 version). In *The Complete Essays and Other Writings of Ralph Waldo Emerson,* edited by Brooks Atkinson. New York: The Modern Library, 1940, 1950.

Evans, Sara M., and Harry C. Boyte. *Free Spaces: The Sources of Democratic Change in America.* New York: Harper & Row, Publishers, 1986.

Faur, José, *Golden Doves with Silver Dots: Semiotics and Textuality in Rabbinic Tradition.* Bloomington: Indiana University Press, 1986.

Feinstein, Howard M. *Becoming William James.* Ithaca, NY: Cornell University Press, 1984.

Feyerabend, Paul. *Against Method: Outline of an Anarchistic Theory of Knowledge.* London: Verso, 1984.

Fiering, Norman. *Jonathan Edwards's Moral Thought and Its British Context.* Chapel Hill: The University of North Carolina Press, 1981.

Folse, H. J. *The Philosophy of Niels Bohr.* Amsterdam: North Holland, 1985.

Foster, George Burman. *The Finality of the Christian Religion.* Chicago: The University of Chicago Press, 1906.

———. *The Function of Religion in Man's Struggle for Existence.* Chicago: The University of Chicago Press, 1909.

Foster, Patricia L. "Directed Mutation in *Escherichia Coli:* Theory and Mechanisms." In *Organism and the Origins of Self,* edited by Alfred I. Tauber. Boston: Kluwer Academic Publishers, 1991.

Frankenberry, Nancy. *Religion and Radical Empiricism.* Albany, NY: State University of New York Press, 1987.

Frei, Hans W. *The Eclipse of Biblical Narrative: A Study in Eighteenth and Nineteenth Century Hermeneutics.* New Haven: Yale University Press, 1974.

Gager, John G. *Kingdom and Community: An Anthropological Approach to Civilization.* Englewood Cliffs, NJ: Prentice-Hall, 1975.

Gellner, Ernest. "La trahison de la trahison des clercs." In *The Political Responsibility of Intellectuals,* edited by Ian Maclean, Alan

Montefiore, and Peter Winch. Cambridge, Eng.: Cambridge University Press, 1990.

Giddens, Anthony. *The Constitution of Society: Outline of the Theory of Structuration.* Berkeley: University of California Press, 1984.

Gilkey, Langdon. *Society and the Sacred: Toward a Theology of Culture in Decline.* New York: Crossroad, 1981.

Goodman, Nelson. *Ways of Worldmaking.* Indianapolis, IN: Hackett Publishing Company, 1978.

Gottwald, Norman. "Introduction: The Bible and Liberation: Deeper Roots and Wider Horizons." In *The Bible and Liberation: Political and Social Hermeneutics,* edited by Norman K. Gottwald, rev. ed. Maryknoll, NY: Orbis Books, 1983.

————. *The Tribes of Israel: A Sociology of the Religion of Liberated Israel, 1250–1050.* Maryknoll, NY: Orbis Books, 1979.

Gould, Stephen Jay. "Hutton's Purpose." In *Hen's Teeth and Horse's Toes.* New York: W. W. Norton & Company, 1983.

————. *Wonderful Life: The Burgess Shale and the Nature of History.* New York: W. W. Norton & Company, 1989.

Gribbin, John. *In Search of Schrödinger's Cat: Quantum Physics and Reality.* New York: Bantam Books, 1984.

Griffin, David R. *God, Power, and Evil: A Process Theodicy.* Philadelphia: Westminster Press 1976.

Gunn, Giles, editor. *New World Metaphysics: Readings on the Religious Meaning of the American Experience.* New York: Oxford University Press, 1981.

Hall, Peter Dobkin. *Inventing the Nonprofit Sector and other Essays on Philanthropy, Voluntarism, and Nonprofit Organizations.* Baltimore: The Johns Hopkins University Press, 1992.

Handelman, Susan A. *The Slayers of Moses: The Emergence of Rabbinic Interpretation in Modern Literary Theory.* Albany, NY: State University of New York Press, 1982.

Harding, Vincent. *There is a River: The Black Freedom Struggle in America.* New York: Harcourt, 1981.

Harvey, Van A. "On the Intellectual Marginality of American Theology." In *Religion and Twentieth-Century American Intellectual Life,* edited by Michael J. Lacey. New York: Woodrow Wilson

International Center for Scholars and Cambridge University Press, 1989.

Hayek, F. A. *The Fatal Conceit: The Errors of Socialism.* Vol. 12 of *The Collected Works of F. A. Hayek,* edited by W. W. Bartley III. Chicago: The University of Chicago Press, 1988.

Hollinger, David A. *In the American Province: Studies in the History and Historiography of Ideas.* Bloomington: Indiana University Press, 1985.

Holton, Gerald. *The Thematic Origins of Scientific Thought.* Cambridge, MA: Harvard University Press, 1973.

Hook, Sidney. "Pragmatism and the Tragic Sense of Life." In *Contemporary American Philosophy*, Second Series, edited by John E. Smith. New York: Humanities Press, Inc., 1970.

———. *Out of Step: An Unquiet Life in the Twentieth Century.* New York: Harper & Row, 1987.

Jacoby, Russell. *The Last Intellectuals: American Culture in the Age of Academe.* New York: Basic Books, Inc., 1987.

James, William. "A Pluralistic Mystic," "Remarks on Spencer's Definition of Mind as Correspondence." In *Essays in Philosophy.* Cambridge, MA: Harvard University Press, 1978.

———. *A Pluralistic Universe.* Cambridge, MA: Harvard University Press, 1977.

———, "Great Men and Their Environment." In *The Will to Believe and Other Essays in Popular Philosophy.* Cambridge, MA: Harvard University Press, 1979.

———, "Is Life Worth Living?" "The Dilemma of Determinism." In *The Will to Believe and Other Essays in Popular Philosophy.* Cambridge, MA: Harvard University Press, 1979.

———. *Pragmatism.* Cambridge, MA: Harvard University Press, 1978.

———. *The Letters of William James,* Vols. 1–2, edited by Henry James. Boston: The Atlantic Monthly Press, 1920.

———. *The Varieties of Religious Experience: A Study in Human Nature.* Cambridge, MA: Harvard University Press, 1985.

Jung, Carl G. *Answer to Job,* translated by R. F. C. Hull. London: Routledge and Paul, 1954.

Kaufman, Gordon D. *Relativism, Knowledge, and Faith*. Chicago: The University of Chicago Press, 1960.

———. *God the Problem*. Cambridge, MA: Harvard University Press, 1972.

———. *In Face of Mystery: A Constructive Theology*. Cambridge, MA: Harvard University Press, 1993.

———. *The Theological Imagination: Constructing the Concept of God*. Philadelphia: The Westminster Press, 1981.

———. *Theology for a Nuclear Age*. Philadelphia: Westminster Press, 1985.

Knight, Douglas A., editor. *Tradition and Theology in the Old Testament*. Philadelphia: Fortress Press, 1977.

Kuhn, Thomas S. *The Structure of Scientific Revolutions* (Second Edition, Enlarged). Chicago: The University of Chicago Press, 1974.

Kuklick, Bruce. *Churchmen and Philosophers: From Jonathan Edwards to John Dewey*. New Haven: Yale University Press, 1985.

———, "Introduction." In William James, *Pragmatism*. Indianapolis: Hackett Publishing Co., 1981.

———. *The Rise of American Philosophy: Cambridge, Massachusetts 1860–1930*. New Haven: Yale University Press, 1977.

Lasch, Christopher. *The Culture of Narcissism: American Life in an Age of Diminishing Expectations*. New York: W. W. Norton & Company, Inc., 1978.

Lentricchia, Frank. *Ariel and the Police: Michel Foucault, William James, Wallace Stevens*. Madison: University of Wisconsin Press, 1988.

———. *Criticism and Social Change*. Chicago: University of Chicago Press, 1983.

Lindbeck, George A. "The Church's Mission to a Postmodern Culture." In *Postmodern Theology: Christian Faith in a Pluralistic World*, edited by Frederic B. Burnham. San Francisco: Harper & Row, Publishers, 1989.

———. *The Nature of Doctrine: Religion and Theology in a Post-liberal Age*. Philadelphia: Westminster Press, 1984.

Lippmann, Walter. *A Preface to Morals.* New York: The Macmillan Company, 1929.

———. *Essays in the Public Philosophy.* Boston: Little, Brown and Company, 1955.

Locke, John. *An Essay Concerning Human Understanding,* edited by A. D. Woozley. New York: New American Library, 1974.

Loomer, Bernard M. "Religion and the Mind of the University." In *Liberal Learning and Religion,* edited by Amos N. Wilder. New York: Harper, 1951.

Lovelock, James E. *Gaia: A New Look at Life on Earth.* New York: Oxford University Press, 1979, 1987.

———. *The Ages of Gaia: A Biography of Our Living Earth.* New York: W. W. Norton & Company, 1988.

Macintyre, Alisdair. *After Virtue: A Study in Moral Theory.* Notre Dame, IN: University of Notre Dame Press, 1981.

Margulis, Lynn. "Early Life: The Microbes Have Priority." In *Gaia: A Way of Knowing,* edited by William Irwin Thompson. Great Barrington, MA: Lindisfarne Press, 1987.

Marsden, George M. "Introduction." *The Secularization of the Academy,* edited by George M. Marsden and Bradley J. Longfield. New York: Oxford University Press, 1992.

———. *The Soul of the American University.* New York: Oxford University Press, 1994.

Mathews, Shailer. *The Atonement and the Social Process.* New York: The Macmillan Co., 1930.

———. *The Growth of the Idea of God.* New York: Macmillan, 1931.

McDermott, Gerald Robert. *One Holy and Happy Society: The Public Theology of Jonathan Edwards.* University Park, PA: Penn State Press, 1992.

McNeill, William H. *Mythistory and Other Essays.* Chicago: The University of Chicago Press, 1986.

Meeks, Wayne. *The First Urban Christians: The Social World of the Apostle Paul.* New Haven: Yale University Press, 1983.

Mermin, N. David. *Boojums All the Way Through: Communicating*

Science in a Prosaic Age. New York: Cambridge University Press, 1990.

Myers, Gerald E. *William James: His Life and Thought.* New Haven: Yale University Press, 1986.

Neville, Robert Cummings. *The Highroad Around Modernism.* Albany, NY: State University of New York Press, 1992.

Niebuhr, Reinhold. *The Irony of American History.* New York: Charles Scribner's Sons, 1952.

———. *The Nature and Destiny of Man: A Christian Interpretation.* 2 vols. New York: Charles Scribner's Sons, 1949.

Nielsen, Waldemar. *The Golden Donors: A New Anatomy of the Great Foundations.* New York: E. P. Dutton, 1985.

Noble, David W. *Historians Against History: The Frontier Thesis and the National Covenant in American Historical Writing since 1830.* Minneapolis: University of Minnesota Press, 1965.

———. *The End of American History.* Minneapolis: University of Minnesota Press, 1985.

Novick, Peter. *That Noble Dream: The "Objectivity Question" and the American Historical Profession.* New York: Cambridge University Press, 1988.

Oates, Joyce Carol. *On Boxing.* Garden City, NY: Dolphin/Doubleday, 1987.

Odendahl, Teresa. *Charity Begins at Home: Generosity and Self-Interest Among the Philanthropic Elite.* New York: Basic Books, 1990.

Ostrander, Susan, and Paul G. Schervish, "Giving and Getting: Philanthropy as a Social Relation." In *Critical Issues in Philanthropy: Strengthening Theory and Practice,* edited by Jon Van Til. San Francisco: Jossey-Bass Publishers, 1990.

Pagels, Heinz R. *The Cosmic Code.* New York: Simon & Schuster, 1982.

Payton, Robert L. "God and Money." In *The Responsibilities of Wealth,* edited by Dwight F. Burlingame. Bloomington: Indiana University Press, 1992.

———. *Philanthropy: Voluntary Action for the Common Good.* New York: Macmillan Publishing Co., 1988.

Peckham, Morris. *Man's Rage for Chaos: Biology, Behavior and the Arts.* New York: Schocken Books, 1965.

Perry, Ralph Barton. *The Thought and Character of William James.* 2 vols. Boston: Little, Brown and Co., 1935.

Placher, William C. *Unapologetic Theology: A Christian Voice in a Pluralistic Conversation.* Louisville, KY: Westminster/John Knox Press, 1989.

Poincaré, Henri. *Science and Hypothesis.* New York: Dover Publications, 1952.

———. *The Value of Science,* translated by George Bruce Halsted. New York: Dover Publications, 1958.

Porte, Joel. *Emerson and Thoreau: Transcendentalists in Conflict.* Middletown, CT: Wesleyan University Press, 1965.

Preston, Anne. "Compensation Patterns in the Sector." In *Careers for Dreamers and Doers: A Guide to Management Careers in the Nonprofit Sector,* edited by Lilly Cohen and Dennis R. Young. New York: The Foundation Center, 1989.

Putnam, Hilary. "Convention: A Theme in Philosophy." In *Realism and Reason.* Cambridge, Eng.: Cambridge University Press, 1983.

———. *Reason, Truth and History.* Cambridge, Eng.: Cambridge University Press, 1982.

Ramsey, Bennet. *Submitting to Freedom: The Religious Vision of William James.* New York: Oxford University Press, 1993.

Rees, Graham. "Francis Bacon's Biological Ideas: A New Manuscript Source." In *Occult and Scientific Mentalities in the Renaissance,* edited by Brian Vickers. New York: Cambridge University Press, 1984.

Reich, Robert. *The Work of Nations.* New York: Alfred A. Knopf, 1991.

Rockefeller, Steven C. *John Dewey: Religious Faith and Democratic Humanism.* New York: Columbia University Press, 1991.

Rorty, Richard. *Consequences of Pragmatism Essays: 1972–1980.* Minneapolis: University of Minnesota Press, 1982.

———. *Objectivity, Relativism, and Truth* (Philosophical Papers, Volume I). New York: Cambridge University Press, 1991.

Roth, John K., and Michael Berenbaum, editors. *Holocaust: Religious and Philosophical Implications*. New York: Paragon House, 1989.

Runggaldier, Edmund. *Carnap's Early Conventionalism: An Inquiry into the Historical Background of the Vienna Circle*. Amsterdam: Editions Rodopi B. V., 1984.

Saiving, Valerie. "The Human Situation: A Feminine View." In *Womanspirit Rising: A Feminist Reader in Religion*, edited by Carol P. Christ and Judith Plaskow. New York: Harper & Row, Publishers, 1979.

Santmire, H. Paul. *The Travail of Nature: The Ambiguous Ecological Promise of Christian Theology*. Philadelphia: Fortress Press, 1985.

Sarkar, Sahotra, "Lamarck *Contre* Darwin." In *Organism and the Origins of Self*, edited by Alfred I. Tauber. Boston: Kluwer Academic Publishers, 1991.

Schervish, Paul. "Philanthropy as a Moral Identity." In *Taking Giving Seriously*, edited by Patricia Dean. Indianapolis: Indiana University Center on Philanthropy, 1993.

Scroggs, Robin. "Sociological Introduction of the New Testament: The Present State of Research." In *The Bible and Liberation: Political and Social Hermeneutics*, edited by Norman K. Gottwald, revised edition. Maryknoll, NY: Orbis Books, 1983.

Seligman, Martin. *Helplessness: On Depression, Development, and Death*. San Francisco: W. H. Freeman, 1975.

Sellars, Wilfrid. "Empiricism and the Philosophy of Mind." In *Minnesota Studies in the Philosophy of Science*, Vol. 1, edited by Herbert Feigl and Michael Scriven. Minneapolis: University of Minnesota Press, 1956.

Sherrill, Rowland A. "Recovering American Religious Sensibility." In *Religion and the Life of the Nation: American Recoveries*, edited by Rowland A. Sherrill. Urbana and Chicago: University of Illinois Press, 1990.

Slotkin, Richard J. *Gunfighter Nation*. New York: Atheneum, 1992.

———. *Regeneration Through Violence: The Mythology of the American Frontier, 1600–1860*. Middletown, CT: Wesleyan University Press, 1973.

————. *The Fatal Environment: The Myth of the Frontier in the Age of Industrialization, 1800–1890.* New York: Atheneum, 1985.

Smith, Page. *Killing the Spirit: Higher Education in America.* New York: Viking, 1990.

Smith, Gerald Birney. *Social Idealism and the Changing Theology.* New York: The Macmillan Co., 1912.

Snyder, Gary. *The Practice of the Wild.* San Francisco: North Point Press, 1990.

Sontag, Frederich. *The God of Evil.* New York: Harper & Row, 1970.

Stone, Jerome A. *The Minimalist Vision of Transcendence: A Naturalist Philosophy of Religion.* Albany, NY: State University of New York Press, 1992.

Stout, Jeffrey. *Ethics After Babel: The Languages of Morals and Their Discontents.* Boston: Beacon Press, 1988.

————. *The Flight from Authority: Religion, Morality, and the Quest for Autonomy.* Notre Dame, IN: University of Notre Dame Press, 1981.

Taylor, Charles. "The Politics of Recognition." In *Multiculturalism and "The Politics of Recognition",* edited by Amy Gutmann. Princeton, NJ: Princeton University Press, 1992.

Tillich, Paul. *Systematic Theology,* 3 vols. Chicago: The University of Chicago Press, 1951.

————. *The Dynamics of Faith.* New York: Harper & Row, Publishers, 1957.

Tocqueville, Alexis de. *Democracy in America.* New York: Vintage Books, 1945.

Updike, John. *Hugging the Shore: Essays and Criticisms.* New York: Vintage Books, 1983.

Vaihinger, Hans *The Philosophy of "As if",* translated by C. K. Ogden. New York: Harcourt, Brace & Company, Inc., 1924.

Veblen, Thorstein. *The Higher Learning in America: A Memorandum on the Conduct of Universities by Business Men.* New York: B. W. Jeubsch, 1918.

von Rad, Gerhard. *Old Testament Theology.* 2 vols., translated by D. M. G. Stalker. New York: Harper & Row, 1962, 1965.

————. *The Problem of the Hexateuch and Other Essays.* New York: McGraw-Hill Book Co., 1955.

————. *Wisdom in Israel.* Nashville and New York: Abingdon Press, 1977.

von Wiezsächer, C. F., "The Birth and Growth of Quantum Mechanics." In *Niels Bohr: A Centenary Volume,* edited by A. P. French and P. J. Kennedy. Cambridge, MA: Harvard University Press, 1985.

Waldrop, M. Mitchell. *Complexity: The Emerging Science at the Edge of Order and Chaos.* New York: Simon & Schuster, 1992.

Weber, Max. *The Sociology of Religion.* Translated by Ephraim Fischoff. Boston: Beacon Press, 1963.

Welch, Claude. *Graduate Education in Religion: A Critical Appraisal.* Missoula, Mont.: University of Montana Press, 1971.

West, Cornel. "Interview with Cornel West." *Universal Abandon?: The Politics of Postmodernism,* edited by Andrew Ross. Minneapolis: University of Minnesota Press, 1988.

————. *Prophetic Fragments.* Grand Rapids, MI: William B. Eerdmans Publishing Company, 1988, and Trenton, NJ: Africa World Press, Inc., 1988.

————. *Race Matters.* Boston: Beacon Press, 1993.

————. *The American Evasion of Philosophy: A Genealogy of Pragmatism.* Madison, WI: The University of Wisconsin Press, 1989.

————. *The Ethical Dimensions of Marxist Thought.* New York: Monthly Review Press, 1991.

————, "The Historicist Turn in Philosophy of Religion." In *Knowing Religiously,* edited by Leroy S. Rouner. Notre Dame, IN: University of Notre Dame Press, 1985.

Westbrook, Robert B. *John Dewey and American Democracy.* Ithaca: Cornell University Press, 1991.

Wheeler, John Archibald. "Beyond the Black Hole." In *Some Strangeness in the Proportion: A Centennial Symposium to Celebrate the Achievements of Albert Einstein,* edited by Harry Woolf. Reading, MA: Addison-Wesley Publishing Co., 1980.

————, "Bohr, Einstein, and the Strange Lesson of the Quantum." In

Mind in Nature, edited by Richard Elvee. San Francisco: Harper & Row, Publishers, 1982.

————, "Discussion of 'Universe as Home.'" In *The Nature of Scientific Discovery,* edited by Owen Gingerich. Washington, DC: Smithsonian Institution Press, 1975.

————, "Genesis and Observership." In *Foundational Problems in the Special Sciences,* edited by Robert E. Butts and Jaakko Hentikka. Boston: D. Reidel Publishing Co., 1977.

————, "Man's View of the Cosmos in America, 1776–1976." In *A Time to Hear and Answer: Essays for the Bicentennial Season,* edited by Taylor Littlejohn. Tuscaloosa, AL: University of Alabama Press, 1977.

————, "The 'Past' and the 'Delayed-Choice' Double-Slit Experiment." In *Mathematical Foundations of Quantum Theory,* edited by A. N. Marlow. New York: Academic, 1978.

————, "The Universe as Home for Man." In *The Nature of Scientific Discovery,* edited by Owen Gingerich. Washington, DC: Smithsonian Institution Press, 1975.

Whitehead, Alfred North. *Modes of Thought.* New York: The Free Press, 1963.

————. *Process and Reality: An Essay in Cosmology,* edited by David Ray Griffin and Donald W. Sherburne. New York: The Free Press, 1979.

————. *Science and the Modern World.* New York: The Free Press, 1953.

————. *Symbolism: Its Meaning and Effect.* New York: Capricorn Books, 1959.

Wills, Garry. *Inventing America: Jefferson's Declaration of Independence.* Garden City, NY: Doubleday, 1978.

————. *Lincoln at Gettysburg: The Words that Remade America.* New York: Simon and Schuster, 1992.

————. *Under God: Religion and American Politics.* New York: Simon and Schuster, 1990.

Wilshire, Bruce W. *The Moral Collapse of the University: Professionalism, Purity, and Alienation.* Albany, NY: State University of New York Press, 1990.

Wilson, Edward Osborn. *On Human Nature*. Cambridge, MA: Harvard University Press, 1978.

Wittgenstein, Ludwig. *Letters to Russell, Keynes, and Moore,* edited by G. von Wright. Ithaca: Cornell University Press, 1974.

———. *On Certainty,* edited by G. E. M. Anscombe and G. H. von Wright, translated by Denis Paul and G. E. M. Anscombe. New York: Harper & Row, Publishers, 1969.

———. *Philosophical Investigations,* translated by G. E. Anscombe. New York: The Macmillan Company, 1965.

Worster, Donald. *Nature's Economy: A History of Ecological Ideas.* Cambridge, Eng.: Cambridge University Press, 1977.

Zelinsky, Wilbur. *Nation into State: The Shifting Foundations of American Nationalism.* Chapel Hill: The University of North Carolina Press, 1988.

Articles in Periodicals

Bell, Daniel. "America's Cultural Wars." *The Wilson Quarterly* (summer 1992).

Bowen, Roger. "A College That No Longer Puts Teaching First Pays a High Price for Its Exalted Reputation." *The Chronicle of Higher Education* 38 (June 10, 1992).

Boyton, Robert S. "Princeton's Public Intellectual." *The New York Times Magazine* (September 15, 1991).

Bronowski, J. "New Concepts in the Evolution of Complexity: Stratified Stability and Unbounded Plans." *Zygon* 5 (March 1970).

Cairns, John, J. E. Mittler, and R. E. Lenski. "Causes of Mutation and Mu Excision." *Nature* 345 (May 1990).

Cairns, John, Julie Overbaugh, and Stephan Miller. "The Origin of Mutants." *Nature* 335 (September 8, 1988).

Cherry, Conrad. "Boundaries and Frontiers for the Study of Religion: The Heritage of the Age of the University." *Journal of the American Academy of Religion* 57 (winter 1989).

Cmiel, Kenneth, "After Objectivity: What Comes Next in History?" *American Literary History* 2 (spring 1990).

Davies, Paul. "The Holy Grail of Physics." *The New York Times Book Review* (March 7, 1993).

Dean, William. "A Present Prospect for American Religious Thought." *Journal of the American Academy of Religion* 60 (winter 1992).

———, "Empirical Theology: A Revisable Tradition." *Process Studies* 19 (summer 1990).

———, "Fireflies in a Quagmire." *Journal of Religion* 48 (October 1968).

———, "From Piecemeal Supernaturalism to Piecemeal Jamesism." *The American Journal of Theology and Philosophy* 15 (January 1994).

———, "Religion and American Public Philosophy." *Religion and American Culture: A Journal of Interpretation* 1 (winter 1991).

Dickstein, Morris. "Literary Critics Stage Comeback as Superstars." *The Times Higher Education Supplement* (December 4, 1992).

Edie, John, principal author. "Myths about Private Foundations," The Council on Foundations (May 18, 1993).

Foster, George Burman. "Pragmatism and Knowledge." *The American Journal of Theology* 11 (October 1907).

Frankenberry, Nancy. "Classical Theism, Panentheism, and Pantheism: On the Relation between God Construction and Gender Construction." *Zygon* 28 (March 1993).

Gaul, Gilbert M., and Neill A. Borowski. "Warehouses of Wealth: The Tax-free Economy." *The Philadelphia Inquirer* (April 18–24, 1993).

Giddens, Anthony. "Action, Subjectivity, and the Constitution of Meaning." *Social Research* 53 (autumn 1986).

Gliedman, John. "Quantum Universe." *Science Digest* (October 1984).

Goodman, Billie. "Heredity Made to Order." *Mosaic* 23 (spring 1992).

Goodman, Nelson, "Notes on the Well-Made World." *Partisan Review* (1984).

Gould, Stephen Jay. "Modified Grandeur." *Natural History* (March 1993).

———, "The Wheel of Fortune and the Wedge of Progress." *Natural History* (March 1989).

———, "Tires to Sandals." *Natural History* (April 1989).

Hall, Barry G. "Adaptive Evolution that Requires Multiple Spontaneous Mutations. I. Mutations Involving Insertion Sequence." *Genetics* 120 (December 1988).

Haskell, Thomas L. "Objectivity is not Neutrality." *History and Theory* 29 (May 1990).

———, "The Curious Persistence of Rights Talk in the 'Age of Interpretation.'" *The Journal of American History* 74 (December 1987).

———, "Convention and Hegemonic Interest in the Debate over Antislavery: A Reply to Davis and Ashworthy." *American Historical Review* 29 (October 1987).

Horgan, John. "Profile: Physicist John A. Wheeler: Questioning the 'It from Bit.'" *Scientific American* (June 1991).

Inbody, Tyron. "Religious Empiricism and the Problem of Evil." *The American Journal of Theology and Philosophy* 12 (January 1991).

Jacoby, Russell. "A New Intellectual History?" *The American Historical Review* 97 (April 1992).

Kloppenberg, James T. "Deconstruction and Hermeneutics as Strategies for Intellectual History: The Recent Work of Dominick LaCapra and David Hollinger." *Intellectual History Newsletter* 9 (1987).

———, "Objectivity and Historicism: A Century of American Historical Writing." *The American Historical Review* 94 (October 1989).

Laurence, David. "Jonathan Edwards, John Locke, and the Canon Experience." *Early American Literature* 15 (1980).

Lentricchia, Frank. "En Route to Retreat: Making it to Mepkin Abbey." *Harper's Magazine* (January 1992).

Lewin, Roger. "A Heresy in Evolutionary Biology." *Science* (September 16, 1988).

Loomer, Bernard M. "Response to David R. Griffin." *Encounter* 36 (1975).

Lovett, Clara M. "American Professors and Their Society." *Change* (July/August 1993).

McAllister, Bill. "Charities Scored on Hill for CEO Pay, Perks." *Washington Post* (June 16, 1993).

Mermin, N. David. "Is the Moon There When Nobody Looks: Reality and the Quantum Theory." *Physics Today* (April 1985).

Miller, Perry. "Jonathan Edwards on the Sense of the Heart." *Harvard Theological Review* 41 (April 1948).

Mirvis, Philip H. "The Quality of Employment in the Nonprofit Sector: An Update on Employee Attitudes in Nonprofits versus Business and Government." *Nonprofit Management and Leadership* 3 (fall 1992).

Nixon, Richard. "Dealing with Gorbachev." *The New York Times Magazine* (March 13, 1988).

Novick, Peter. "My Correct Views on Everything." *The American Historical Review* 96 (June 1991).

Oates, Joyce Carol. "The Cruelest Sport." *The New York Review of Books* 34 (February 3, 1992).

Plaskow, Judith. "Facing the Ambiguity of God." *Tikkun: A Bimonthly Jewish Critique of Politics, Culture, and Society* 6 (September-October 1991).

Robinson, Arthur L. "Demonstrating Single Photon Interference." *Science* (February 1986).

Santmire, H. Paul. "Toward a New Theology of Nature." *Dialog* 25 (winter 1986).

Smith, David L. "Emerson and Deconstruction: The Ends of Scholarship." *Soundings* 67 (winter 1984).

Tarbox, Everett, "James and Wittgenstein: Toward a Linguistic Pragmatism." *The American Journal of Theology and Philosophy* 15 (January 1994).

———, "Wittgenstein, James and a Bridge to Radical Empiricism." *The American Journal of Theology and Philosophy* 13 (May 1992).

Tilley, Terrence W. "Incommensurability, Intratextuality, and Fideism." *Modern Theology* 5 (January 1989).

West, Cornel. "Nietzsche's Prefiguration of Postmodern American Philosophy." *Boundary 2* 9 (spring/fall 1981).

———, "Nihilism in Black America." *Dissent* 38 (spring 1991).

———, Review of *Philosophy and the Mirror of Nature. Union Seminary Quarterly Review* 37 (fall/winter 1981).

———, "Why Haven't They Matched the Success of Others?" *Los Angeles Times* (September 8, 1991, Section M).

INDEX

249